Polestar of the Ancients

*The Aristotelian Tradition in Classical
and English Literary Criticism*

Polestar of the Ancients

*The Aristotelian Tradition in Classical
and English Literary Criticism*

John O. Hayden

Newark: University of Delaware Press
London: Associated University Presses

© 1979 by John O. Hayden

Associated University Presses, Inc.
Cranbury, New Jersey 08512

Associated University Presses
Magdalen House
136-148 Tooley Street
London SE1 2TT, England

Library of Congress Cataloging in Publication Data

Hayden, John O.
    Polestar of the ancients.
    Bibliography: p.
    Includes index.
    1. Criticism—History. 2. Literature—Philosophy—
History. I. Title.
PN86.H36   801   77-74411
ISBN 0-87413-125-1

This book is for
GEORGE DEKKER

Contents

Acknowledgments

Scholars, both past and present, have greatly assisted me in writing this book. And yet rather than represent particular instances of direct use of scholarship in a clutter of numbers and notes, I have preferred to include bibliographies of the sources I found useful, saving the notes for instances of direct quotation. Some scholars, however, provided such substantial influence as to deserve more immediate recognition. Walter Jackson Bate's *Criticism: The Major Texts* and *From Classic to Romantic* gave me some of my basic ideas about the history of criticism and especially the phenomenon known as Romanticism. George Watson's *Literary Critics* suggested the breakdown of the term *criticism*. M. H. Abram's *Mirror and the Lamp* helped in a negative way by presenting a case that all the evidence seemed to me to prove incorrect.

Several scholars have given me help in more immediate ways. George Dekker of Stanford University read the manuscript in all stages and offered advice for its improvement. The study in fact grew out of conversations between us a number of years back. Arthur Amos, a colleague at Davis, kindly read and criticized the chapter on Sidney. Vernon Hall of the University of Wisconsin was very generous in copying and sending to me his bibliography, *Literary Criticism: Plato Through Johnson*, while it was still in typescript. Students in a number of graduate and undergraduate seminars have doubtless suggested many of the ideas in this study, and to them I am also indebted.

The Regents of the University of California made this study possible by granting me a Humanities Institute Award, which allowed me a summer off to begin my work. The National Endowment for the Humanities awarded me a fellowship to complete it. I am deeply obligated to both organizations.

The Interlibrary Loan Department of the Library of the University of California at Davis have as usual been most friendly and efficient in serving my scholarly wants; I would especially like to thank Vera Loomis, Susan Moger, and Cynthia Cheney. My typist, Elaine Bukhari, deserves her own citation for efficiency, vigilance, and patience.

I would also like to thank my wife, who showed great patience and understanding during the writing of this study.

I wish also to thank the following publishers for having given me permission to quote from published works:

The Bobbs-Merrill Company, Inc., for permission to quote from Longinus: *On Great Writing*, translated by G.M.A. Grube, copyright© 1957, by the Liberal Arts Press, reprinted by permission of the Bobbs-Merrill Company, Inc.

Oxford University Press, for permission to quote from John Dryden, *Essays of John Dryden*, edited by W. P. Ker, 1900; *Horace for English Readers*, translated by E. C. Wickham, 1903; Samuel Johnson, *Lives of the English Poets*, 1905; *Aristotle on the Art of Poetry*, translated by Ingram Bywater, 1909; G.G. Smith, ed., *Elizabethan Critical Essays*, 1937; Samuel Taylor Coleridge, *Biographia Literaria*, edited by John Shawcross, 1965; and William Wordsworth, *The Prose Works of William Wordsworth*, edited by W.J.B. Owen and J.W. Smyser, 1974.

Yale University Press, for permission to quote from Samuel Johnson, *The Works of Samuel Johnson*, Yale ed., 1958-71.

Polestar of the Ancients

*The Aristotelian Tradition in Classical
and English Literary Criticism*

When I was myself, in the rudiments of my poetry, without name or reputation in the world, having rather the ambition of a writer than the skill; when I was drawing the outlines of an art without any living master to instruct me in it; . . . when thus, as I may say, before the use of the loadstone, or knowledge of the compass, I was sailing in a vast ocean, without other help than the pole-star of the Ancients. . .

John Dryden, "A Discourse Concerning the Origin and Progress of Satire"

1

Introduction

Long calculations or complex diagrams affright the timorous and unexperienced from a second view; but if we have skill sufficient to analise them into simple principles, it will be discovered that our fear was groundless. "Divide and conquer," is a principle equally just in science as in policy. Complication is a species of confederacy, which, while it continues united, bids defiance to the most active and vigorous intellect; but of which every member is separately weak, and which may therefore be quickly subdued if it can once be broken.

Samuel Johnson, Rambler *137*

i

The major problem plaguing histories and discussions of literary criticism is the meaning of the term *criticism*. Like Samuel Taylor Coleridge, I am aware that an overweening demand for definition is a good way of "barricadoing the road to truth"; yet at times in certain disciplines the road becomes washed out and requires rebuilding.

Since at least the late seventeenth century, *criticism* has become a catch-all term denoting any discussion of literature. The problem has not gone unnoticed. George Saintsbury, in the first history of literary criticism, begins by quarreling with the term *criticism*, which, he points out, etymologically denotes judgment, and then promises to limit his history to such evaluative criticism.[1] About halfway through the second of three volumes, however, Saintsbury notes that there is practically no literary judgment as such until Dryden, and then in the final volume he enthusiastically supports what can only be described as Romantic appreciation, all but devoid of judgment.

Some scholars have quietly made distinctions in various meanings of the term *criticism*, but confusion inevitably results from such silence. Others have attempted to define categories of meaning within the term. For instance, George Watson makes a tripartite division by adding a modifier.[2] Thus, legislative criticism refers to Renaissance manuals, mainly rhetorics, that prescribe how to produce literary works. Theoretical criticism denotes all theory that concerns literature in any way, including aesthetics and creative theory. The final category, descriptive criticism, refers to the analysis of literary works, both that which does and that which does not contain evaluation. None of these categories (except the first, which is practically useless) appears to me sufficiently delineated to be helpful.

But an awareness of the problem involved in terminology is better than nothing. In the first chapter of M. H. Abrams's *Mirror and the Lamp*, an attempt is made to establish critical categories, but the indeterminate use of the term *criticism* throughout makes the discussion ultimately unintelligible, at least in my experience.[3] Supposedly dividing along four "coordinates of art criticism" (universe, audience, artist, and work), Abrams separates *criticism* into mimetic theories, pragmatic theories, expressive theories, and objective theories, respectively. The trouble is that Abrams, very likely because of confusion over the term *criticism*, cuts the cake the wrong way; his tidy categories do not do what categories are supposed to do, that is, distinguish one item from another. The mimetic and pragmatic theories are not mutually exclusive; for example, Horace and Sidney ascribe to both theories.[4] If one follows Abrams's scheme, moreover, he will arrive with Abrams at a fragmented view of the history of literary theory and will conclude that a decisive break in literary theory occurred in the early nineteenth century.

Alternative divisions and categories, however, exist. I would, first of all, divide *criticism* into three main categories: evaluation, literary theory, and creative theory.

Like George Watson, I would insist that literary theory should be distinguished from the close scrutiny of specific literary works. But Watson's "descriptive criticism" is too broad a category and leads one away from the etymology of the word *criticism*—judgment. Analysis and interpretation are not excluded by Watson, and, although they are both essential steps leading to evaluation, neither of these per se is actually a "critical" endeavor in any but the most vague sense. I prefer *evaluation* as a much more practicable category—either judgment has taken place or it has not. My meaning comes closest to what is usually meant today by "practical criticism"; the need for the modifier, by the way, shows the extent of the problem, the almost total loss of the original meaning of *criticism.*

Other forms of literary discussion that are often confused with my first category, evaluation, I intend to exclude from consideration. One is *literary impressionism,* by which Pater, for example, attempts to create a new work of art by artistically expressing his feelings about a literary work; another is *literary appreciation,* by which one describes one's own liking for a particular work and thus creates enthusiasm for it. Even impressionism and appreciation presuppose evaluation, however; otherwise why treat this work rather than another?

My second category is *literary theory,* which indeed is much more important than evaluation since theory serves as the basis of judgments. Literary theory is perhaps the easiest of the categories to understand; it attempts to answer the question, What is literature and how does it work?

The third and last category is what I call *creative theory.* It is psychologistic by nature and usually involves a discussion of the imagination. It attempts to answer the question, How is literature created by the mind? A phenomenon that arose for the first time in a large way in eighteenth-century England, probably under the influence of Locke's subjective epistemology, it became a major source of interest to Wordsworth and Coleridge, perhaps the most famous names in creative theory. Coleridge, it is also worth mentioning, is the only critic who managed to mix creative theory with another category of "criticism." Whether a work was derived from the fancy or the imagination made a qualitative difference, and thus creative theory became a form of evaluation.

There are several other categories I wish also to distinguish. Aesthetics, a branch of philosophy, can loosely be described as the study of beauty. At best, the distinction between aesthetics and literary theory is vague and confusing; but it is probably best to view aesthetics as having a wider scope than literary theory inasmuch as aesthetics concerns all the fine arts. Most often aesthetics becomes entangled in comparisons or parallels between the arts; and the comparisons are, at least in my opinion, of dubious use and validity and can lead to problems that would not otherwise have arisen. In the eighteenth century, the English were very much engaged in what could be called aesthetic interests, studies of the sublime and the beautiful. In any case, I will not be dealing with the subject as described above except insofar as literary concerns are thought to be in the most general sense "aesthetic."

Finally, there are literary studies that perform none of the functions described above under the various categories and yet are often lumped under the term *criticism:* studies in the history of ideas and in literary history that attempt to be purely descriptive. To call these endeavors *criticism* can only mislead.

When I am specifically referring to any one of the three categories of *criticism,* I intend always to call them by their proper names: evaluation, literary theory, and creative theory. I am not, however, zealous to set the world straight on terminology otherwise. Following current usage, I have no qualms in calling Aristotle a "critic."

Until very nearly the eighteenth century, only two of my three categories were practiced—literary theory and evaluation —and very little evaluation from before that time has survived. That creative theory was probably just then evolving perhaps explains why the term *criticism* began to take on multiple meanings in the late seventeenth century; it happened to be a convenient catch-all term.

ii

In the study that follows I intend to concentrate on the second category, literary theory. And the literary theorists I distinguish as belonging to three main traditions: the Aristotelian, the Neoclassical Rationalist, and the Romantic. Of these I intend to concentrate on the Aristotelian, but the others will receive attention as necessary.

The Aristotelian tradition, which could just as well be called the Humanist or the Classical tradition, had its origins, as the name I have selected indicates, in Aristotle's *Poetics*. The fundamental principles of Aristotle were taken over and in some cases refined and modified by Horace and Longinus before being passed on to the English branch of the tradition— Sidney, Dryden, Dr. Johnson, Coleridge, Wordsworth, and Arnold—to mention only the highest points and to go no furthur in time.

The characteristics of the tradition can be reduced to five, all of them found in each of the theorists in one form or another. First of all, literature is viewed by these critics as mimetic or imitative. By this is meant that literature represents life, that there is a special close relationship between them.

In literature mimesis is primarily involved with the whole ess of human action, especially psychology and motivation. Aristotle, who originated the concept as we know it, was undoubtedly affected by his emphasis on tragedy and epic when he claimed that the imitation of literature was of human action, and yet human action, including thought and feeling, is nevertheless the crux of mimesis.

Mimesis, to put it another way, also functions in lyric poetry. Any acceptable view of expressionism (that is, one does not propose a frivolous subjectivism) would view the lyric merely as a shift in what is being imitated—from human characters in action (in the narrative and dramatic genres) to the inner world of the narrator (in the lyric).

Mimesis, in any case, is not something merely "historical,"

a quaint concept held by the Greeks, revived in the Renaissance, and extinguished in the late eighteenth century. It is probably the most important single concept in literary theory and is certainly the basis of the most important judgments made about particular works of literature. That the characterization in a work is not lifelike, is unbelievable, has traditionally been, and remains, one of the most serious objections that can be made against that work.

Historically, the mimetic concept has been of considerable consequence. Renaissance Italian theorists tended to misunderstand the concept and made it the basis of their demand for overall realism. Mimesis was converted into a stricter concept of verisimilitude, which led to such absurdities as the three Unities. This misunderstanding was perhaps owing to the reintroduction by the Renaissance Neoplatonists of Plato's illusionist view of mimesis, which we will have to examine. Still later through a fairly elaborate syllogism, imitation was taken to mean imitation of models, and this interpretation has serious repercussions on literature produced at the time.

But total verisimilitude is not really required by the concept of mimesis. There is nothing objectionable per se about the fantasy in science fiction or romance or fairy tale. On the contrary, the tendency in such works that leads them away from a credible representation of human nature is what relegates them to the lower categories of literary endeavor or dismisses them as mere entertainment. In an early review of a gothic novel, Samuel Taylor Coleridge remarked:

> The romance-writer possesses an unlimited power over situations; but he must scrupulously make his characters act in congruity with them. Let him work *physical* wonders only, and we will be content to *dream* with him for a while; but the first *moral* miracle which he attempts, he disgusts and awakens us.[5]

While the events in a work are only open to objections on the score of improbability depending on the "givens" or assumptions of the work (e.g., if realistic), a "moral miracle" or serious defect in characterization is never acceptable in any serious piece of literature worthy of the name.

As far as I am aware, mimesis has not often been put in this way—as the crucial close relationship of literature and life—but such a concept (under various guises) *has* often been used as a key criterion to determine value in literature, even though it is usually not explicit in the evaluation. I believe, moreover, that this concept is what was intended by Aristotle and by those critics who worked in the tradition he initiated. In other words, such a concept exists; it seems to me equivalent to the concept emphasized by the Aristotelian tradition, and so I call the concept mimesis. Like a lifeline, the mimetic concept nourishes literary theory and literature itself. Once it is cut, literature grows sickly; then sentimentality, sensationalism, and a whole host of literary diseases begin to spread their infection.

iii

Mimesis, the close tie between literature and life, does not, however, stand alone. It has been taken by itself and interpreted as necessitating a kind of historical accuracy or photographic realism. But hand in glove, or rather in an organic union, the concept of universality is interfused with that of mimesis. That is to say, the representation of life involved in mimesis is not direct, but reality is tranformed by the artist to point up its universal, permanent qualities.

To elaborate: literature does indeed represent reality through the use of particulars, but the particulars always tend ultimately to generals, to the normal. The concept is very like Aristotle's metaphysic, in which ideal forms are seen as working through concretes. The abnormal, or the untypical, has little value in this view. Walter Bagehot, explaining the success of Scott's strange character Meg Merrilies in *Guy Mannering*, perhaps helps make the traditional position clear by analyzing an exception. Bagehot explains that Scott built up the character of Meg slowly, and then observes:

> This is the only way in which the fundamental objection to making eccentricity the subject of artistic treatment can be obviated. Monstrosity ceases to be such when we discern the laws of nature which evolve it: when a real science explains its phenomena, we find that it is in strict accordance with what we call the natural type, but that some rare adjunct or uncommon casualty has interfered and distorted a nature, which is really the same, into a phenomenon which is altogether different. Just so with eccentricity in human character; it becomes a topic of literary art only when its identity with the ordinary principles of human nature is exhibited in the midst of, and as it were, by means of, the superficial unlikeness. Such a skill, however, requires an easy careless familiarity with usual human life and common human conduct.[6]

Such a view of the universality of literature depends for its validity on a belief that human nature, especially human emotions, do not change fundamentally despite a minor fluctuation of sensibility from age to age. Basic motivations, such as hatred, desire, envy, are considered more or less constant, even while the particular objects or sources or expression of such emotions vacillate. Homer's characters are still intelligible to us; the accidental never obliterates the permanent.

On the other hand, the particularity or concreteness of things and people are not depreciated by the Aristotelian theorists: all objects and people are not alike, even within types. But by the same token, particularity by and of itself is not worth representing. Dickensian eccentrics are perhaps as good an example of misplaced particularity as can be found.

iv

In a recent study of literary theory, a connection between the nature and the function of literature is proposed: "The use of poetry follows from its nature: every object or class of objects is most efficiently and rationally used for what it is, or is centrally."[7] In terms of what has already been said regarding the mimetic and universal nature of literature, the double concept of mimesis/universality seems not to exist for its own sake, but rather to point to some purpose behind literature.

The Aristotelian theorists do believe that literature has a function or purpose. Perhaps the most concise definition of that purpose was afforded by Horace in his *Ars Poetica:* literature both teaches and pleases. This "Horation formula" sets forth the two functions that are alternatively emphasized by those in the tradition.

Pleasure is sometimes stressed. It is, however, even more often taken for granted, for how can literature perform any other purpose if it does not please well enough to attract readers? When pleasure, therefore, is directly discussed, it is usually considered a sine qua non.

Attitudes in the tradition toward the teaching function are not so simple to describe. Beyond agreeing basically on some sort of moral function, the tradition in fact is inconsistent and divides into two differing positions. One set of theorists sees the moral function of literature as indirect. Literature provides the reader with stories or descriptions of human experience, along with an implicit interpretation on the part of the author. The reader learns about people, motivations, and values from literature and thereby becomes a more enlightened moral agent. This, I believe, was the view originally proposed by Aristotle but lost to the tradition until revived in the early nineteenth century.

The other set of theorists, from Horace to Dr. Johnson, held a much narrower view of the morality of literature—what might be called the didactic view. Literature works directly, by providing precepts and examples, to strengthen the moral fiber of the reader. At the extreme, such theorists demand poetic justice in every serious work of literature—vice must be punished and virtue rewarded. When art is said to be moral, this didactic position is what most people summon to mind.

The first three characteristics—mimesis, universality, and morality—concern the nature and function of literature. The last two characteristics of the Aristotelian tradition concern the approach that the theorists take toward literature.

The first of these is the empirical approach. Theorists working in the tradition make the basis of their theory the actual experience of reading, working up from that experience to the formation of principles through the use of reason and imagination. Rules, moreover, are considered valid only insofar as they conform to experience. The basic approach is never reversed; never is literature required to conform to rules arrived at deductively. Human thought, of course, moves dialectically through both deduction and induction, but Aristotelian theorists avoid the kind of principles that are formed without regard to the nature of actual literary works. The most famous instance of the empirical approach in the tradition was Dr. Johnson's dismissal of the Unities on the grounds that in actual fact the human mind did not demand the kind of unimaginative conventions their proponents claimed.

With such an empirical approach sustaining them, the theorists in the tradition have by and large maintained a flexible approach in their theory. While they do work with principles, they are seldom, if ever, dogmatic. Only infrequently is one asked to take a point on faith. Usually examples are given and analyzed so that the reader will arrive at the same conclusions on his own.

Now it is possible that I have proposed too many characteristics. Surely the last two, empiricalness and flexibility, are so closedly related as to comprise one characteristic; for it is not likely that a theorist will be flexible if he is not empirical. Similarly, the first three characteristics—mimesis, universality, and purposeiveness—are closely bound together. Mimesis and universality, as we have seen, are inseparable, and together they point toward function. In the wider view of moral function, in fact, they provide the basis—human experience represented in its universal aspects—for moral learning to take place.

W. K. Wimsatt, Jr., has remarked that there exist ultimately two "so-far irreducible critical experiences": "the double difficulty, of poetry in relation to the world, and of criticism in relation to value."[8] Literary theory does indeed finally come down to dealing with two problems, literature and life, literature and value. But to describe the Aristotelian tradition I have found it expedient to use five characteristics, which are finally reducible to two—literature and life and the methods used. Literature and value is so important a matter that I will discuss it later by itself.

vi

The characteristic approaches of the Aristotelian tradition—empirical and flexible—are necessary as criteria to distinguish it from the Neoclassical Rationalist tradition. This tradition, if indeed it can be called such, was comparatively short-lived; it arose in the sixteenth century and expired in the eighteenth.[9] It was a European phenomenon that began in Italy, where commentators on Aristotle's *Poetics* started a process of codification. The movement toward hard-and-fast rules began to be imported into France and England by the end of the sixteenth century.

In essence, Neoclassical Rationalism consists of a travesty of the Aristotelian tradition. The principles of the latter tradition were excerpted and transformed into inflexible rules. Even some principles erroneously ascribed to the Aristotelian tradition, such as the Unities of time and place, were subjected to the process of codification.

The principal differences between the two traditions, then, were not concerned with views of the nature of literature. On these they were more or less agreed. It was in their approaches to the formation of theory that they are to be distinguished.

Where the Aristotelian theorists were empirical, the Neoclassical Rationalists relied heavily on a priori logic and on what they saw as classical authority. Where the Aristotelians were flexible in arriving at and in applying principles, the Neoclassical Rationalists were rigid.

Their theories as to the nature of literature were of course affected by their approaches, but in ways that are not immediately obvious; and in fact, Neoclassical Rationalist versions are often taken as representing the views of the Aristotelian tradition. Mimesis was no longer the principle of the close relationship of literature and life; it became the basis of an unimaginative verisimilitude, which generated such ridiculous rules as the Unities. Universality, no longer functioning to keep theory from a narrow realism, was used as the basis for demanding a stultifying typicality of characterization. And the morality of literature became strict poetic justice.

In France the new tradition took root and flowered in the theories of such seventeenth-century figures as Corneille and Boileau. In England, which, as Walter Jackson Bate has argued, already had a great native literature founded on less rigid principles and which in any event usually tended to be more empirical than France, the tradition did not thrive. In Sidney's theory there are signs of the influence of the new trends, which became accelerated after the Restoration, but even then they dominated only minor figures such as Thomas Rymer. Neoclassical Rationalism in the eighteenth century is often mistaken for the parent Aristotelian tradition, especially in the case of Dr. Johnson, but lately scholars have been emphasizing the flexibility that obtained in Johnson's critical works. Neoclassical Rationalism was a short-lived aberration and should not be confused with Neoclassicism, a term that should denote only the renewal of classicism.

vii

Romantic has long been a term in disrepute, but no one has ever been able either to eliminate it or to find a fitting substitute. A. O. Lovejoy, in an article written in 1924, pointed out some of the difficulties inherent in the term, especially its multiple interpretations. [10] Lovejoy himself did not finally recommend that the term be exorcised from literary histories; and yet, following the extraordinary logic that if a term has received a number of contradictory definitions, none of them is valid, he did suggest the plural form, romanticisms.

Lovejoy and the other disenchanted notwithstanding, I intend to use the word *Romanticism* in the singular to refer to a historical phenomenon that began in eighteenth-century Europe and is still with us. Although I am concerned almost wholly with the literary theory that derived from what I call Romanticism, I believe that there is an entire world view that is Romantic, complete with metaphysic, epistemology, ethic, and aesthetic. For more information I must refer the reader to Walter Jackson Bate's study *From Classic to Romantic*, which details and documents the general premises of Romanticism. [11] It must suffice to say here that the basis of the world view is feeling, and that emphasis is placed on the subjective and the particular.

In terms of literary theory, the Romantic tradition differs from the Aristotelian in its view of the nature and function of literature. Literature, according to Romantic theory, is not mimetic; it is not connected to life and, as a result, is purified— *la poésie pure.* Since the ties with life were severed, literature often turned inward and expressed the actual feelings of the writer, although expressionism is not essential to Romantic theory. With the new emphasis on the particular, the concept of the universal, of course, no longer had any place. And since the knowledge derived from a universal view of life is no longer possible, literature is not considered purposive beyond giving pleasure, usually of a uniquely aesthetic kind. This non-purposive view is called *art for art's sake.*

In summing up this tradition, just as in the case of the Neoclassical Rationalist, I have had to resort to considerable simplification, and yet I believe that these principles as stated do underlie Romantic literary theory. There are other Romantic manifestations in literature and literary theory that derive either directly from more basic Romantic literary theory or from the Romantic world view. Such would be primitivism and exoticism, but these are secondary characteristics and are symptomatic rather than fundamental.

With this distinction in mind, it is possible to place the flowering of the Romantic tradition much later than is customary. Rather than flourishing during the early years of the nineteenth century, during the so-called Romantic Revolution, Romanticism came into its own later in the century with such theorists as Edgar Allan Poe, Théophile Gautier, and Walter Pater. William Wordsworth's preface to the *Lyrical Ballads* and Samuel Taylor Coleridge's *Biographia Literaria*, usually taken as Romantic manifestoes, are in fact highly reactionary documents that even speak out against signs of incipient Romanticism. In spite of some secondary Romantic characteristics, they are, moreover, both squarely within the Aristotelian tradition of literary theory.

One of the principal reasons for the view of a monumental break in the history of literary criticism around 1800 derives from the failure to make the tripartite distinction of the term *criticism* (into evaluation, literary theory, and creative theory). As far as literary theory went, the Aristotelian tradition, with its mimesis, universality, and purposiveness, continued. But along with such literary theory, there was in the eighteenth century an increasing interest in creative theory, and both Wordsworth and Coleridge shared this interest in how literature comes into being in the mind of the poet. When M. H. Abrams in *The Mirror and the Lamp* claims that mimesis (the mirror) gave way to expressive theories (the lamp), he is in error, unless he is referring only to distinctly minor theorists; for mimesis held its own, while, in addition, there was a new emphasis on creative theory.

During the seventeenth and eighteenth centuries, the central Aristotelian tradition held firm, even though certain disintegrative processes were at work. With Neoclassical Rationalism, the central tradition began to harden; with Romanticism it began to dissolve. Today, only two of the three traditions have survived: the Aristotelian and the Romantic. Although its professed adherents are few, the Aristotelian tradition of literary theory is probably the stronger of the two. But it is now showing signs of finally succumbing to the most powerful adversary it has ever had to face: critical relativism.

viii

Literature and value, the second of Wimsatt's irreducible critical factors, must now be considered. The question of relativism versus absolutism is, I believe, the most important issue facing literary studies today, and, probably because of that importance, it is rarely confronted squarely. The problem of relativism, however, is not confined to literary criticism, but poses a threat to the whole intellectual life. The magnitude of the threat validates, I believe, such an otherwise alarmist statement.

The concept of relativism is extremely difficult to grasp, and, despite its obvious importance, literature on the subject is anything but extensive. One recent theorist did, however, present an adequate definition of its opposite, absolutism, which he also calls objectivism:

> Absolutism typically holds that a definite amount of value resides intrinsically in the object in the sense that the value has ontological subsistence and is independent of any human relationship. It follows that the objectivist critic will believe in the existence of absolute, ultimate standards which lie outside or above human evaluations, will maintain that there is one and only one correct taste, and will strive for that objective rightness of judgment which, given his assumptions, must exist. To be sure, because of human finitude and fallibility, these ultimate standards can never be known and the absolute goal of correct judgment never be attained.[12]

A relativist, on the other hand, believes that no objective values exist, that all value judgments are necessarily subjective, are relative only to the individual. This does not mean that he merely recognizes a problem of subjectivity inherent in judgments—that personal prejudices and human shortcomings tend to dilute objectivity, for the absolutist recognizes this problem of subjectivity. Rather, a relativist believes that all value judgments by their very nature are only individual opinion and that is all that they *can* be. If a relativist follows his position out to its logical end, he must conclude that all discussion and interchange of ideas are meaningless, since there is little point in exchanging what he will allow to be only subjective predilections.

The form of relativism most often encountered can be called historical relativism, a subspecies.[13] The historical relativist argues that values are given by one's society and change from age to age, and he usually points to anthropology to substantiate his claims. Theoretically, however, the absolutist position does not depend on uniformity of particular value judgments, since, as one theorist has put it, "a specific value is ontologically there"; and yet the absolutist would likely also insist that, in the field of morals for example, not all that much vacillation is present: murder for gain within a society has never been condoned.[14]

In any event, the objectivity supposedly afforded to values by the agreement of the members of a society proves delusionary, since, on consideration, such a social group is merely a collective subjective.[15] Absolutism and relativism are diametrically opposed, although compromises have been confidently put forward. Relativism and absolutism ultimately come to an either/or distinction, and no compromise is possible.[16]

Part of the difficulty in understanding the problem concerns terminology once again. *Absolutist* sounds equivalent to "dogmatic," "unbending," "narrow-minded," even "obtuse." In popular use, this is precisely what is often intended; the following is an excerpt from a recent newspaper editorial:

[He] is an absolutist. Everything is black or white. He sees no shades of grey. This is fine in most areas of police work. A fingerprint either matches or does not match. There is no in between. But when [he] wanders into subjective fields such as child rearing or teaching he should leave his absolutist views behind.[17]

In fact, however, absolutism need have nothing to do directly with dogma. There is no such thing as an "absolute judgment"; there are only judgments made with an appeal to absolute values. It is a matter of philosophical basis only—that which allows judgments to be more than *merely* individual.

For the absolutist, objective values exist, and these allow for discussion. No one is infallible; all should be searching for what is true. Anyone can be wrong; no one has direct access to the truth. For example, the question might be raised whether a judgment is valid or an action moral. Either case can be argued using reason and appeal to experience, both that of the individual and of mankind. But it is not a matter of whether I believe, or our society believes, a proposition, but whether it is so—*sub specie aeternitatis.* Values, if they are absolute, never change; what is true or immoral today will be so tomorrow, whatever we think. What we thought was true may prove to have been false all along, but that is another matter. One must in fact attempt to distinguish the accidental from the permanent.

Being an absolutist does not make judgments any easier; on the contrary, as far as forming judgments is concerned, there is no real reason for a thoroughgoing relativist to think at all, for he can only end in solipsism. But absolutism does make the business of judging meaningful. The task of literary evaluation is immensely difficult; one must try to avoid prejudices, the strictly contemporary bias of the times, but it is also immensely worthwhile to distinguish the good from the not-so-good or the bad, for one thus encourages the good. But only an absolutist, of course, will acknowledge that "the good" is a meaningful term.

The entire problem is quite difficult to grasp. While reading this disquisition, you are presupposing some kind of objective values; you are trying to determine the objective validity of my remarks. Perhaps the human mind simply works along absolutist lines, or perhaps we are all culturally conditioned to think in such a way. What usually results from an innate absolutism combined with a carelessly contracted relativism is fuzzy thinking. In another recent newspaper clipping, entitled "Truth Is a Subjective Thing," occurs the following statement:

> As I see it, the only hope for our civilization lies in the ability of this and following generations to sort from the tangled flow of information only the truth. We must bring ourselves to the realization that truth is a subjective thing and not try to force our philosophies on our fellow human beings.

Here you have the common confused mixture of an absolutist conception ("only the truth") with a relativist ("truth is a subjective thing").

For these and perhaps other reasons, thoroughgoing relativists are hard to come by. In my experience, most relativists are actively such only when it is to their advantage, interrupting a discussion with "That's your opinion" or "It's just a matter of taste." At other times they pursue an issue just as if they believed they were after an objective truth. Relativism has obvious attractions for those who prefer to be liberal at any cost: if no objective truth or values exist, then everyone is "right," whatever that can mean under the circumstances. Relativism also consorts well with the misology of our age.

In a sense, the metaphysical basis of absolutism can be separated from the discussion here; the ontological basis for absolute values could easily form another inquiry altogether, and I am not qualified to pursue the matter in any case. But one point is worth mentioning. Absolute values, if they exist, are unchanging; consequently, they must be in some sense supernatural, change being characteristic of the natural world. A materialist, therefore, should inevitably be a relativist if he wishes to be consistent. In the Greco-Christian scheme, which is of course transcendental, absolute values exist in God or the One. Plato himself had to confront relativism, as we see in his *Protagoras*; and it is possible that his whole idealistic metaphysic originated as a means of explaining the existence of absolutes and thus of avoiding the intellectual chaos of relativism.[18]

In any case, an alternative to full acceptance of absolutism exists in what might be called "agnostic absolutism"—the recognition that absolute values *must* exist joined to an ignorance as to *how* they do. Something like this occurs in an introduction to F. R. Leavis's criticism written by Eric Bentley:

> Judgement is the summation of criticism. And some degree or kind of objectivity is presumed by it. For if all judgements are equally valid, there is just my predilection and yours and the other man's, and we are not in the human realm at all; we are in a sub-human chaos. Whether "order" is interpreted by the philosophers to be something pre-existing or something man-made we have to insist on having it. Aesthetic judgement is difficult and risky, but scarcely more difficult and risky than judgement in other realms, where we grant its necessity.[19]

Leavis himself prefers to ignore the problem of relativism, apparently in order to avoid antagonizing readers.[20]

Relativism is a historical phenomenon as well as a philosophical position, and in the realm of literary criticism its historical aspects have been the subject of a recent monograph. Emerson R. Marks found that relativism took rise in the eighteenth century and came to flower in the later nineteenth century.[21] I find Marks's treatment confusing at points, both as to logic and terminology, but his scheme does translate neatly into my own terms. He separates the problem into the means and ends of literature. Absolutism of means, which he also calls

"Rymerism," is equivalent to my Neoclassical Rationalism.
Relativism of ends, on the other hand, is what I have described
simply as critical relativism. Marks claims that this relativism
is confined in the eighteenth century to minor figures such as
Blackmore and Bysshe, but received more support later. His
final category, absolutism of ends (and relativism of means)
is the same as the absolutism practiced by what I call the Aristotelian tradition. In the view of "several critics," such as John
Dryden,

> the ends are absolute, but the means to their attainment
> necessarily vary with changing circumstances. Quite logi-
> cally, this does not imply an abandonment of rules, does not
> negate the means-end view, does not, in short, question that
> literature is an "art." It does insist, however, that no set of
> rules can be universally and eternally binding, for their effi-
> cacy as means to a contemplated end depends upon preva-
> lent conditions of time and place many of which are extra-
> literary. Frequently this resulted in subjecting the rules to
> a test essentially pragmatic: only those which perform the
> job are valid.[22]

The "rules" mentioned in the quotation are, of course, the
formal, technical modes of composition.

The historical rise of relativism, however, had other manifestations than literary. The religious implications of relativism
have been observed already. It is thus no coincidence that theis-
tic belief and absolutism have declined together since the seventeenth century, nor that relativism and Romanticism have
risen during the same period. Another way of considering Romanticism is as a sort of surrogate for religion, and Romanticism is based on feeling, nothing being more subjective, more
relative to the individual.

It is impossible to "refute" either relativism or absolutism,
but at least the implications involved in the acceptance of either can be described. And in any event, it is far easier to argue
the problem negatively. To show the disastrous consequences
of relativism is easier, that is, than to show the advantages of

absolutism. In terms of literary criticism only, with relativism, theory is impossible, and no evaluation points beyond oneself or the predilections of one's age; thus critical activity becomes inevitably frivolous, which point is exactly what its detractors have always argued. As one recent commentator on the subject remarked, relativism does not allow us to defend the critical teaching of literature.[23] There exists no valid basis on which to argue with a student who prefers Mickey Spillane to William Shakespeare. There is even no explanation possible for why we read one poet's works rather than another's. (I have myself witnessed a relativist teacher resort to dogmatism.) Without objective values, only opinion, feeling, and statistics remain.

ix

If a constant pattern of basic literary theory does extend from Aristotle to the present, as I maintain it does, the agreement on fundamentals alone argues for the possibility of permanence in literary principles and thus of the existence of objective values.

But agreement about the existence of a tradition may prove difficult. There has been a tendency to discover sources and borrowings of specific ideas between the figures I have placed in the Aristotelian tradition, and even to discern general similarities in their wider literary views. But no one, I believe, has argued in favor of a tradition sharing rock-bottom literary principles, such as mimesis, universality, and morality, as well as common methods, such as empiricalness and flexibility. No one especially has discerned a tradition that continues right down to the present.

Only one of the theorists, Aristotle himself, wrote what could be described as a theoretical treatise or poetic. The others wrote verse letters or defenses or autobiography, and so on. Consequently, much of their fundamental theories has been obscured, and attention absorbed by their positions on such particular topics as the use of rhyme in drama or the existence of poetical diction. Only when the basic theories that necessarily underlie such subordinate matters are examined does a distinct tradition emerge.

The similarities between the figures examined are, I believe, of substantially more importance than their differences. Therefore, I have proposed the existence of an Aristotelian tradition. Other theorists have belonged to the tradition; I have concentrated on the high points, on those figures in which the tradition is most alive, and I have limited myself, partly for convenience, to the later tradition as it exists in England. Walter Jackson Bate, who likewise emphasized English criticism, argues, however, that English critics tend to be more representative and even superior in most regards to those of other literatures.[24] I would agree, but I do not wish to stress the point as the basis of my selection.

What I have attempted in this study, in any event, is not merely speculation about a particular thesis, but a history of literary criticism as well. With this in mind, I have ventured to supply information on each critic that summarizes current scholarship. This study, moreover, is not intended to replace the reading of the critical documents discussed. Unlike some histories of literary criticism, I have not tried to recapitulate the entire contents of a critical work nor to mention every specific theory of each critic, but only those which illuminate the fundamental theories. On the other hand, this study *is* intended to supply an intelligible approach to some of the greatest literary thought ever written.

It is doubtful if literary theory has ever interested a wide number of people; today there is certainly less than an enthusiastic audience for it. And yet, as R. S. Crane has observed, this does not bode well for our culture; rather, the opposite case might trumpet in a bright future:

> I cannot but think that the cult of the "concrete" in contemporary criticism—when the "concrete" is opposed to a concern with theoretical analysis—is a counterpart of the state

of affairs in medicine when the so-called "empirics" ruled; and we all know that the period of greatest progress in detailed observation and understanding in the medical arts began only after their reign was ended. It has been so, too, with the notable advances of the present century in physics, genetics, psychology, economics, political science, and linguistics: they have all been preceded and accompanied by theoretical revivals; and in any university the subjects which are now most alive are those in which there is the least indifference to general ideas and the least inclination to find an incompatibility between a concern for them and the pursuit of particular facts.[25]

There is, of course, no need to argue that literary theory should be allowed to continue. As long as literature is produced and read, it will be discussed, and as long as literature is discussed, theory will underlie that discussion. The more articulate literary theory becomes, however, the more likely it is that it will produce the vitality envisioned by Crane.

Consequently, there is a practical end in view in the following attempt to trace a functioning tradition of theory that has survived some twenty-three centuries. An age that insists on seeing itself as wallowing in a chaos of theories and antitheories is prey to charlatanism and is not likely to produce much enduring literary theory or evaluation, or even literature for that matter.

NOTES

1. George Saintsbury, *A History of Criticism,* 3 vols. (New York, 1950), 1:3-4
2. George Watson, *The Literary Critics,* 2d ed. (New York, 1964), pp. 11-15.
3. Meyer H. Abrams, *The Mirror and the Lamp* (New York, 1953). Since Abrams is dealing with various forms of literary theory, he usually means by *criticism* "theory;" and when this is the case, it is only the incompatibility of this meaning with the etymological one (judgment) that leads to confusion. For example, on p. 10 occurs the statement: "Aristotle's criticism . . . is not only criticism of art as art." Elsewhere, the term can well have other meanings than "theory"; for example, on p. 16, Abrams mentions "the critical essays of Dryden" and the rules that were intended to guide

"the critics in judging any future product." In the last section, on "Objective Theories," the term seems often to refer to judgment.

4. Abrams does occasionally qualify the exclusive nature of his categories, speaking of dominant roles and primary orientations (Ibid., p. 14). Nevertheless, his categories do tend to divide theories firmly where they ought not to be divided at all.

5. T. M. Raysor, *Coleridge's Miscellaneous Criticism* (London, 1936), p. 373.

6. Walter Bagehot, *The Collected Works of Walter Bagehot,* ed. Norman St. John-Stevas, 8 vols. (Cambridge, Mass., 1965), 2:56.

7. René Wellek and Austin Warren, *Theory of Literature,* 3d ed. (New York, 1956), p. 29.

8. Murray Krieger, ed., *Northrup Frye in Modern Criticism* (New York, 1966), p. 79,

9. For a discussion of the tradition, see Walter Jackson Bate, *From Classic to Romantic* (New York, 1961), chap. 2. Bate continually uses the term *Neoclassical Rationalism,* and, although he does not treat it as a tradition, his description of the phenomenon is adequate to present what I have in mind. I have seldom seen the term *Neoclassical rationalist* used; see, however, Baxter Hathaway, *Marvels and Commonplaces* (New York, 1968), p. 59; Thomas Hanzo, *Latitude and Restoration Criticism* (Copenhagen, 1961), pp. 55-56; and Samuel Taylor Coleridge, *Shakespearean Criticism,* ed. Thomas M. Raysor, 2 vols. Everyman ed. (London and New York, 1960), 1:xxix.

10. A. O. Lovejoy, "On the Discrimination of Romanticisms,"*PMLA* 39 (1924): 229-53

11. Bate, *From Classic to Romantic,* especially chaps. 1, 5, and 6.

12. Bernard C. Heyl, *New Bearings in Esthetics and Art Criticism* (New Haven, Conn., 1943), p. 93.

13. The most outspoken proponent of this view is Frederick A. Pottle, *The Idiom of Poetry* (Bloomington, Ind,., 1963).

14. Heyl, *New Bearings,* p. 94. The anthropological argument based on the analogy of primitive tribes could be dismissed as Romantic primitivism, inasmuch as one should go to a civilized society (one highly developed enough for its members to realize their full potential) to find out what man is like, not to a group of savages, noble or otherwise.

15. For further refutation of Pottle's position, see Cleanth Brooks, *The Well Wrought Urn* (New York, 1947), app. 1.

16. In agreement with this statement are both Brooks,*Well Wrought Urn,* p. 234 and Yvor Winters, *In Defense of Reason* (Denver, Colo., 1947), p. 10.

17. Why child rearing and teaching must be considered subjective fields is never explained.

18. See A. E. Taylor, *Plato* (New York, 1966), pp. 244-51; Bate, *Criticism,* p. 39.

19. Eric Bentley, ed., *The Importance of Scrutiny* (New York, 1948), p. xxiii

20. See F. R. Leavis, "A Reply, by F. R. Leavis," in *Importance of Scrutiny,* ed. Bentley, pp. 30-40.

21. Emerson R. Marks, *Relativist and Absolutist* (New Brunswick, N. J. 1955), pp. 7, 25.

22. Ibid., pp. 35-36.

23 Winters, *In Defense of Reason,* p. 10.

24 Bate, *Criticism,* pp. ix-x.

25. Ronald S. Crane, *The Languages of Criticism and the Structure of Poetry* (Toronto, 1953), pp. xiii-xiv.

2

Plato and Aristotle

i

Aristotle has often been called the Father of Literary Criticism, and with a good deal of reason. Plato, Aristotle's teacher for some twenty years might with similar point deserve the title of "Stepmother of Literary Criticism"; for not only was he probably the efficient cause of much of Aristotle's literary theories and thus shared in the parentage, but Plato is also well known for his rejection of poetry from his ideal republic, for abusing, in stepmotherly fashion, the thing he ought to have loved.

Most of what Plato had to say about literature occurs in his *Republic*, but scattered comments are present in his other works. What might even be considered as creative theory occurs in his *Ion* in the form of a claim that poetry comes from inspiration, even from the possession of the poet by the gods:

> Not by art does the poet sing, but by power divine. Had he learned by rules of art, he would have known how to speak not of one theme only, but of all; and therefore God takes away the minds of poets, and uses them as his ministers.[1]

The discussion in the *Ion* is negative—poetry is not a source of useful knowledge and requires no skill; but the brunt of his attack on the poets can be found in books 2, 3, and 10 of his *Republic*. Plato objects to poetry on three grounds, two ethical and the third intellectual: (1) that the poets tell corrupting lies about the gods and about such other things as the happiness of unjust men (bks. 2 and 3); (2) that poetry indulges, and thus encourages, the passions (bk. 10); and (3) that poetry, as imitation, merely presents a copy of objects of sense perception, themselves "copies" of the ideal forms that compose reality.

The first objection amounts to an exaggerated demand for poetic justice whereby everything imitated must be good and just and conducive to goodness and justice in the "reader." Socrates, concerned that Hesiod's stories of the battles of the Titans might corrupt the ideal state, comments in book 2:

> Neither, if we mean our future guardians to regard the habit of quarreling among themselves as of all things the basest, should any word be said to them of the wars in heaven, and of the plots and fightings of the gods against one another, for they are not true. No, we shall never mention the battles of the giants, or let them be embroidered on garments; and we shall be silent about the innumerable other quarrels of gods and heroes with their friends and relatives. If they would only believe us we would tell them that quarreling is unholy, and that never up to this time has there been any quarrel between citizens; this is what old men and old women should begin by telling children; and when they grow up, the poets also should be told to compose for them in a similar spirit. (2, 75)

This morally didactic view of literature has been variously blamed on Socrates himself and the moralist legacy of fifth- and sixth-century Greece. Plato has even been defended on the grounds that the problems of censorship have still to be solved, but, in fact, on this first objection Plato is least defensible.

That art encourages man's passions, Plato's second objection, has perhaps more to be said for it. For example, "literature" on the order of the typical best-seller, with its falsified view of the world and its sentimentality, could be legitimately attacked as detrimental to the mental and emotional health of readers. As it appears in book 10 of the *Republic*, however, the objection seems to partake merely of Plato's distrust of emotions in general. Socrates, after noting the debilitating effect of buffoonery and of giving way to sorrow, as well as the assistance given to this effect by poetry, adds (bk. 10):

> And the same may be said of lust and anger and all the other affections, of desire and pain and pleasure, which are held to be inseparable from every action—in all of them poetry feeds and waters the passions instead of drying them up; she lets them rule, although they ought to be controlled, if mankind are ever to increase in happiness and virtue. (2, 396)

The first extant use of the term *mimesis* (or imitation) with regard to literature occurs in Plato's works, although there were most probably earlier instances of such a use. And thus the concept of mimesis, which was to assume such importance in the history of literary theory, got off to a bad start. Plato combined it with his idealist view of existence—that only ideal forms exist, all material objects being merely appearance—to conclude that poetry led one away from reality and truth. Mimesis for Plato was strictly a matter of exact copying, exact enough in the case of painting to delude the observer, and so it was inevitable for him to consider poetry or any mimetic art as a mere copy of an appearance. In Plato's example (in bk. 10 of the *Republic*), the artist paints a picture of a bed that is only an image of the essential form, bedness. Thus, by means of what is called the classical or inclusive manner of counting, the painting or poem is said to be three removes from the truth. This metaphysical objection depends on a delusionist theory of mimesis; the Neoplatonists avoided the problem by claiming that the artist paints the ideal form (bedness) and not the bed itself. Aristotle, as we shall see, chose still another alternative.

There have been a number of attempts to defend Plato on one or another grounds, usually that some misunderstanding has arisen; Sir Phillip Sidney's is only the most famous of these. And there are some very good reasons why such defenses should arise, for considerable evidence exists that Plato's seeming

aversion to poetry was at best only theoretical. Even the heated
dismissal of poetry in book 10 has been explained as perhaps
generated by Plato's agonized but necessary choice between
philosophy and literature at precisely that moment of his life.
Plato himself was a great writer, especially in the early dialogues, and there are numerous remarks, even in book 10, that
he liked poetry a great deal and felt only too well its attractions.
In the *Phaedrus* and the *Laws*, written after the *Republic*, Plato
even softens his strictures. Furthermore, several extenuating
circumstances have been offered: that Plato was reacting
against the Sophists of the time and against the decay of literature. By the beginning of the fourth century B.C., the great
literary age had passed; drama under the influence of Euripides was turning into melodrama.

ii

The same sort of controversy that plagues Platonic commentators obstructs a clear discussion of Aristotle's literary theory
as well. The situation in fact worsens. Not only is there no difin-
itive Greek text of the *Poetics*, but the composition of those parts
usually taken to be Aristotle's authentic work is often poor,
and both of these factors give rise to widely divergent translations, which lead in turn to widely divergent interpretations.
Even the frequent references to other of Aristotle's works have
nurtured arrogant and contradictory readings of the *Poetics*.

There is so much controversy, even anarchy, connected with
almost every point made by Aristotle that paradoxically one
is not chastened into more modest assertions, but rather em-
boldened into more eccentric interpretations. The tendency
indeed among commentators on the *Poetics* is toward extremes,
often involving total dismissal of previous scholarship. When
charting the headwaters of a great literary tradition, this situation creates large, but not insuperable, difficulties.

Even the date of composition of the *Poetics* is controversial;
and depending on whether early or late in Aristotle's career—

that is, whether written during or after the period when he was under Plato's instruction—much of the *Poetics* can be seen as refuting the objections to poetry raised by Plato. On this general point, too, depends a number of interpretations of particular passages. Today some scholars place the date of the *Poetics* late and therefore question the issue of rebuttal. And yet, as one scholar has commented, "We cannot afford to forget that Aristotle was under the necessity either of answering Plato's accusations against poetry or of remaining silent on the subject of poetry.[2]

That there are substantial differences between Aristotle and his teacher in their literary theories has been questioned. Their metaphysical views provide the fundamental distinction between them, for Aristotle offered an alternative to Plato's thoroughgoing idealism. Put most simply, Aristotle accepted the Platonic ideal forms but insisted that these essences were inherent in material things as a dynamic principle. This distinction was important, as we shall see, when Aristotle turned to the question of mimesis.

The approach each took to philosophical problems is a still more important distinction with regard to the *Poetics*. Although largely a question of tendencies, it is still possible to describe Plato as more rationalistic, more dependent on abstract logic, on deduction. Aristotle, on the other hand, was more empirically minded; his bent was more toward concretes and inductive logic. Another way of pointing up the same thing would be to repeat the often-expressed dictum that Plato's scientific preference was the mathematical, Aristotle's the biological.

Aristotle's classifying bent can be seen in his choice of the kind of work he wrote. The *Poetics*, like his other works, is a treatise, for Aristotle was out to reorganize all knowledge and so divided it into sciences and subsciences. The three main groups of sciences were the theoretical, the practical, and the productive, the *Poetics* falling into the latter category. Plato, on the other hand, wrote in the dialogue form, which offers different kinds of approaches to the truth; it is in fact a literary form. This distinction in forms is important; it limits what Aristotle will concern himself with. In the *Republic*, for example, Plato was concerned with religion, politics, poetry, and ethics; Aristotle's *Poetics* deals with poetry and stays as clear of ethical and political considerations as possible. For his views on these other matters, one must refer to his *Politics* and the *Nicomachean Ethics*.

And yet, given Aristotle's categorizing approach, the *Poetics* seems surprisingly disorganized. Although not always visible through the smoothness of translations, the style itself often gets in the way, being crabbed, abrupt, and digressive, and there are even some contradictions in the text for good measure. The *Poetics* as we have it is, furthermore, thought to be incomplete, for there are indications that a second volume once existed that treated comedy, iambic poetry, and perhaps even the much-disputed subject of catharsis.

Other omissions noted in the present *Poetics* were probably not contained in a second volume. The lyric may well have been considered by Aristotle to be part of music; he would not have been much interested in the lyric in any case since it had no plot, which was the "soul" of tragedy, for Aristotle the highest form of poetry. Descriptive poetry might also seem to have been ignored, but the Greeks had none as such, probably because of their anthropocentric bias. Whatever there is of omission or of improper emphasis is perhaps largely owing to the absence of another literature with which Aristotle could compare his own.

Sometimes a case is made for the discernible organization of the material of the *Poetics*. Such a case, however, usually depends upon rejecting certain parts as later interpolations. Chapter 12, which contains a boring digression on the technical parts of tragedy, is usually so dismissed. Even with such interpolation removed, the structure inevitably appears out of proportion when the *Poetics* is chopped into large and small consecutive sections, although this might seem the most logical way of analyzing its structure. A recent ingenious attempt by

O. B. Hardison eschews such an approach in favor of finding a pattern that follows Aristotle's categorizing bent.[3] Aristotle is seen as moving from general to particular, with the most important subcategory treated first. Thus tragedy is discussed first as being the most important genre. Plot, being the most important subcategory of tragedy, is mentioned next, then character, thought, and so on, until Aristotle returns to epic, the second most important genre. This scheme has the added advantage of placing comedy and iambic poetry in a missing second book, where they would logically follow epic as less important genres. Hardison's reading does, however, depend on translating the opening of the *Poetics* not as the usual "Let us discuss the art of poetry," but as "Let us discuss the art of making itself," which difference provides a more general position from which to start the breakdown. Hardison, nevertheless, provides a very convincing analysis of the structure of the *Poetics*.

Because of the condition in which the *Poetics* is now found, most scholars have speculated that it probably began as a lecture series. This explanation has the additional support of the tone, which often has a magisterial ring to it. Another explanation is that the *Poetics* is an *esoteric* work—that is, one that was "published" only within the Lyceum and meant to circulate among students who would be familiar with Aristotle's other writings. Both views would explain the lack of transitions and the uneven density of explanation and illustration.

Regardless of problems involved in its form, the contents of the *Poetics* are easy to describe, at least in general. There is very little practical criticism of particular works, and what there is is strictly illustrative. As for creative theory (the psychology of composition), one passage in which it might be found occurs in chapter 17, where Aristotle comes out against the dependence of the poetic composition on madness, although because of a probable flaw in the text Aristotle has often been thought to agree with Plato on this issue in spite of Aristotle's emphasis on artistic technique. The *Poetics* consists instead of two things. One is what one historian of literary criticism, George Watson, would call "legislative criticism." Part of the *Poetics*, that is, consists of practical advice on how to write a tragedy (e. g., chap. 17), and the very name most often applied to Aristotle's work, *Poetics* (compare *Rhetoric*), suggests such a function. The bulk of the *Poetics*, however, consists of literary theory. In Aristotle's work, in fact, can be seen the real beginnings of literary theory, not to mention the initiation of the whole tradition of literary thought that it is the purpose of this study to trace.

iii

Probably the most important characteristic of this tradition is a belief that literature is mimetic (or imitative). In terms of the *Poetics*, the importance of mimesis can be seen in its use as the differentia between nature and art, between the useful and the fine arts, between one fine art and another, and even as distinguishing the various literary genres. As Aristotle remarks in chapter 9, the poet is "a poet by virtue of the imitative element in his work."[4]

Despite its importance, however, mimesis is never adequately defined in the *Poetics*, and seems to have more than one meaning. Aristotle apparently borrowed the term from Plato; in Aristotle's use, it could easily be an attempt at an answer to Plato's objection that poetry was merely a copy of a copy. Aristotle's metaphysics, which views essential form as inherent in particulars, would allow for this reading.

Aristotle's metaphysical views might even allow him to discuss mimesis in two ways. First, like Plato, he could talk of it as a copy of a particular object or event. Aristotle, in chapter 4, for example, explains the pleasure we receive from imitation as deriving from recognition of an object:

> The reason of the delight in seeing the picture is that one is at the same time learning—gathering the meaning of things, e. g. that the man there is so-and-so; for if one has

not seen the thing before, one's pleasure will not be in the picture as an imitation of it, but will be due to the execution or colouring or some similar cause. (p. 11)[5]

Aristotle, I believe, is able to discuss mimesis in this way because mimesis *is* mimicry *and* something more. Put in scholastic terms, mimicry is a necessary but not sufficient part of literary mimesis.

That mimesis does involve something more is not difficult to see; one has only to dip into the *Poetics* almost at random. In chapter 24 we learn that "a likely impossibility is always preferable to an unconvincing possibility" (p. 79), and in the following chapter this idea is repeated. In chapter 2 Aristotle remarks that tragedy can be distinguished from comedy: "The one would make its personages worse, and the other better, than the men of the present day" (p. 7). Clearly, something more than a mere copy is involved.

This observation receives further substantiation from a look at the kind of imagery that Aristotle uses, especially when contrasted to Plato's. When speaking of mimesis, Plato uses the metaphor of a mirror. It is true that later in the tradition this image would be used in a different way, but when used to mean something more than a copy it has an inherent problem in that the normal mirror gives off an exact image of whatever is reflected in it. Of course, as we have seen, this would be no problem for Plato, for it was precisely the meaning of exact copy that Plato wished to convey through the analogy. If, however, one wishes to find a figure that conveys the idea of representation *and* something more, what is available?

The analogy of a painting is the only one that comes to mind; in a painting one can *represent* an object and still vary the representation to some extent. Significantly, Aristotle uses just this figure of the painter several times, and most often in a context that makes it clear that more than exact copying is involved. In chapter 15, for example, he comments:

We in our way should follow the example of good portrait-painters, who reproduce the distinctive features of a man, and at the same time, without losing the likeness, make him handsomer than he is. The poet in like manner, in portraying men quick or slow to anger, or with similar infirmities of character, must know how to represent them as such, and at the same time as good men, as Agathon and Homer have represented Achilles. (P. 45)

That the alternatives to the mirror image are seriously restricted is clear from Aristotle's choice of the painting image, for such an image can become confusing if one stops to consider that for Aristotle painting is itself a mimetic art that is being used as an analogy for the working of mimesis (plus) in literature. In the *Republic* Plato also uses the painting figure, but in Plato painting is considered strictly realistic and delusionist; he even uses the image to reinforce his delusionist view of mimesis:

A painter will paint a cobbler, carpenter, or any other artist, though he knows nothing of their arts; and, if he is a good artist, he may deceive children or simple persons, when he shows them his picture of a carpenter from a distance, and they will fancy that they are looking at a real carpenter. (2: 383)

The analogy of a mirror is not, moreover, the only problem with the term *mimesis*, or imitation. The very word *imitation* in most languages conveys the idea of copying a previous work, and this confusion can easily lead to the sort of sterile "imitations" produced by some of the minor writers of the Renaissance. To avoid other problems of English idiom, one scholar has suggested that, instead of using the verb *imitates*, we say *makes an imitation of.*[6]

A final problem must also be dealt with—the distinction that Aristotle makes between mimesis and narration in chapter 24:

Homer, admirable as he is in every other respect, is especially so in this, that he alone among epic poets is not unaware of the part to be played by the poet himself in the poem. The poet should say very little in *propria persona,* as he is no imitator when doing that. Whereas the other poets are perpetually coming forward in person, and say but little, and that only here and there, as imitators, Homer after a brief preface brings in forthwith a man, a woman, or some other Character—no one of them characterless, but each with distinctive characteristics. (P. 77)

The poet, it would appear, is not an imitator while speaking in the first person. This view has its source in book 3 of Plato's *Republic,* where imitation seems to be equivalent to dramatic form.[7] This equation consorts well with Plato's delusory view of art.

The distinction would likewise seem to call for a more narrow interpretation of mimesis in the *Poetics* than I have given Aristotle credit for. And yet it is, I believe, possible that Aristotle, and Plato, are merely being naive in assuming that first-person narrative or lyrical forms must represent the author himself and are therefore "real" in some sense, like a memoir or a diary; that is, mimicry would not be involved. The question might even resolve itself into the absence of the concept of a persona (the use, by the author, of a fictitious first-person narrator who does not represent the author). If the concept of this literary device were beyond the reach of Aristotle, the first-person narrator would always be the actual author himself, and, as such, he would always be too particular, not sufficiently universalized. Another question that might be raised is whether this problem is similar to Aristotle's narrow view of history as simple chronicle (*vide infra*) or whether the problem is merely another way of approaching the issue of determining where literature shades off into document—what, for example, makes a memoir literature?

iv

Gerald O. Else, a recent commentator on the *Poetics*, has remarked that the transition from Plato's to Aristotle's view of mimesis was in effect a move from copying to creating.[8] There is a great deal of truth in this observation: the "something more than mere copy" allows for creativity. It is necessary, however, to distinguish this creativity from the sort that the Romantics believed in, creation out of nothing; Aristotle saw art not as in competition with nature, but as its fulfillment. Clearly, too, this creative mimesis, or rather mimetic creativity, does not allow for either expressionism or the *poésie pure* dear to the hearts of nineteenth-century advocates of art for art's sake.

Universality, another characteristic of the tradition, is the "something more than copy" that Aristotle had in mind. But before speaking of universality and mimesis separately, I should insist that the two are inextricably joined in reality and can only be distinguished for the sake of discussion. The concept of universality in any event is set forth in chapter 9 in the well-known distinction between history and poetry: history

> describes the thing that has been, and the other a kind of thing that might be. Hence poetry is something more philosophic and of graver import than history, since its statements are of the nature rather of universals, whereas those of history are singulars. By a universal statement I mean one as to what such or such a kind of man will probably or necessarily say or do—which is the aim of poetry, though it affixes proper names to the characters; by a singular statement, one as to what, say, Alcibiades did or had done to him. (P. 27)

Aristotle's view of history here and in chapter 23 depends on considering it as the merest sort of chronicling, totally without interpretation or more than chronological organization. One recent scholar has suggested that Aristotle's contemporaries were just such historians.[9]

Mimesis and universality are inseparable; both, in Aristotle's view, are essential to literature. Mimesis indeed might even have been seen as the basis of universality, in much the same way as in Aristotle's metaphysics the material world is the necessary basis for ideal forms to inhere. Without mimesis, Aristotle informs us in chapter 1 and again in chapter 9, poetry would be merely didactic verse:

> It is the way with people to tack on 'poet' to the name of a metre, and talk of elegiac-poets and epic-poets, thinking that they call them poets not by reason of the imitative nature of their work, but indiscriminately by reason of the metre they write in. Even if a theory of medicine or physical philosophy be put forth in a metrical form, it is usual to describe the writer in this way; Homer and Empedocles, however, have really nothing in common apart from their metre; so that, if the one is to be called a poet, the other should be termed a physicist rather than a poet. (P. 5)

Didactic verse is perhaps one extreme avoided by Aristotle through his mimesis. The other would in that case be the "pure poetry" of the nineteenth-century decadents, which they see as having no necessary meaning. For there is one thing evident: whatever else mimesis means to Aristotle, it involves a close relationship between literature and life.

That the mimesis involved in literature is of men in action Aristotle tells us early in the *Poetics*, and in the comparison quoted above between poetry and history he places the emphasis just there, on "what such or such a kind of man will probably or necessarily say or do." The question of probability and necessity brings up the universality of literature as well, for the probable and the necessary *are* universality as regards action. The merely possible, which Aristotle rejects, partakes of the chaos of particularity.

The phrase *kind of man*, which Aristotle uses, introduces us to a further controversy, probably the most important with regard to universality—whether the *Poetics* is type-dominated in its views of characterization. The second point to be aimed

at in characterization (chap. 15), appropriateness, would seem
unmistakably to call for types: "The Character before us may
be, say, manly; but it is not appropriate in a female Character
to be manly, or clever" (p. 43). This is surely not far from the
decorum of type found in Horace (lines 153-78 of *Ars Poetica*).
But if we proceed to the third point—that the character should
be "like" (usually translated "like life"), we see this emphasis
on types qualified in the direction of mimesis. O. B. Hardison,
the commentator most insistent upon Aristotle's dominance
by types, points outside the *Poetics* to the *Rhetoric* and to the
Ethics as showing Aristotle's involvement with the idea of
types; and yet even Hardison claims that Aristotle also wished
to "particularize the character, to give him idiosyncrasies that
soften—without obscuring—the general outline."[10]

There is a clue here, I believe. Perhaps, as was the case with
mimesis, universalizing when treated separately from mimesis, tends to take on a misleading importance. Both are important, and neither can exist without the other. A character
pushed too far toward the typical loses its reality, its mimetic
quality. If through the concept of mimesis/universality literature presents at once a copy and not a copy, then it also presents a type that is not a type.

v

The combination of mimesis and universality would seem
to point to some purpose for literature; in other words, they
do not appear to be sufficient ends in themselves. Aristotle,
however, is never explicit on the point of the purpose of literature except to indicate that it gives pleasure. We are told early
that imitation is in itself pleasurable and later that tragedy
has its "own proper pleasure" (p. 39). Some scholars are content to let it go at that; this is especially true of such art-for-
art's-sake commentators as S. H. Butcher, who would prefer
to keep Aristotle a hedonist, or at least to keep him from
seeming to espouse a moral purpose for literature.[11] A good

deal of what Aristotle says in the *Poetics*, others point out in disagreement, obviously involves moral issues, and even points to a moral view—that is, one that sees literature as in some way *improving* the reader.

Catharsis is one of the points often discussed as moral. The term itself occurs but once in the *Poetics*, at the end of the famous definition of tragedy in chapter 6:

> A tragedy, then, is the imitation of an action that is serious and also, as having magnitude, complete in itself; in language with pleasurable accessories, each kind brought in separately in the parts of the work; in a dramatic, not in a narrative form; with incidents arousing pity and fear, wherewith to accomplish its catharsis of such emotions. (P. 17)

Problems of interpretation concerning the last few lines of the definition are legion, but most interpretations work with something very like the phrasing rendered in the translation above.

The interpretations can be classified under three headings. The first, which is often considered a rebuttal to Plato's objection on the score of corrupted emotions, has been called the "medical" reading, as well as the "hygienic" and "therapeutic." According to this interpretation, catharsis is a simple purgation of pity and fear, involving a medical analogy of evacuation. Thus, in answer to Plato, tragedy, the highest form of poetry, does not encourage the passions; it rids the spectator of them. A reference is, moreover, often made to a passage in Aristotle's *Politics* (bk. 7), where purgation by music is discussed:

> Music should be studied . . . with a view to . . . purgation (the word "purgation" we use at present without explanation, but when hereafter we speak of poetry, we will treat the subject with more precision). . . . In education the most ethical modes are to be preferred, but in listening to the performances of others we may admit the modes of action and passion also. For feelings such as pity and fear, or, again, enthusiasm, exist very strongly in some souls, and have more or less influence over all. Some persons fall into a religious

frenzy, whom we see as a result of the sacred melodies—when they have used the melodies that excite the soul to mystic frenzy—restored as though they had found healing and purgation. Those who are influenced by pity or fear, and every emotional nature, must have a like experience, and others in so far as each is susceptible to such emotions, and all are in a manner purged and their souls lightened and delighted. [12]

The case for the medical interpretation is strong. There is even a similarity in the purgation theory to Freud's psychoanalytical theory of the purging of childhood memories as a way of eliminating neurosis and to his general theory of the eradication of repression.

The second, the religious interpretation of catharsis, differs from the medical in seeing the emotions not as eliminated but as purified. The following passage from book 2 of the *Nicomachean Ethics* is often quoted to reinforce this theory:

If . . . virtue is more exact and better than any art, as nature also is, then virtue must have the quality of aiming at the intermediate. I mean moral virtue; for it is this that is concerned with passions and actions, and in these there is excess, defeat, and the intermediate. For instance, both fear and confidence and appetite and anger and pity and in general pleasure and pain may be felt both too much and too little, and in both cases not well; but to feel them at the right times, with reference to the right objects, towards the right people, with the right motive, and in the right way, is what is both intermediate and best, and this is characteristic of virtue. [13]

In this interpretation, pity and fear are often seen as merely representative emotions. This view, moreover, has the advantage of being consistent with Aristotle's respect for the emotions, in contrast to Plato's distrust of emotions, reflected more by the purgation theory.

The third and last interpretation of catharsis might be called "intellectual" and constitutes a relatively recent approach to the explanation of catharsis. The most revolutionary theory of this group belongs to Leon Golden, who argues that a third possible translation of *catharsis* is "clarification."[14] Following Gerald Else, Golden claims that catharsis depends on the structure of the play, not on the psychology of the spectator of a tragedy. By presenting pitiable and fearful incidents in certain ways to bring out universal truths, the result will be the enlightenment of the spectator. A similar theory in many respects was suggested some years ago by W. F. French. Literature, if any good, gives a sense of order and significance to human fate. "Actual experiences," he explained,

> arouse in us pity and fear, often disturbingly, deleteriously: art may arouse in us the same emotions. Actuality leaves us thus deleteriously perturbed; art resolves the perturbation into peace. Actuality gives us the disparate, the inchoate, of the phenomenal world; art joins together the disparate in harmony, builds the inchoate into unity, because it deals with the universal, the abiding.[15]

Both Golden's and French's interpretaions do not depend on other of Aristotle's works but of course neither are they supported by any. In any event, both have the advantage of fitting in organically with the concept of mimesis and universality and provide that concept with a meaningful function.

W. K. Wimsatt finished his discussion of catharsis by dismissing the whole matter as belonging to "experimental psychology" rather than to literary criticism.[16] And yet the catharsis clause, coming as it does at the end of the definition, may well be equivalent to the final cause of tragedy in Aristotle's view. If this is the case, catharsis surely has a place in the *Poetics*. And no matter how the term is interpreted, it must point to the improvement of the spectator, in other words, to a moral view.

Another thorny topic with regard to the moral purpose of literature centers upon Aristotle's use of the word *hamartia*. The main passage in which the term occurs is in chapter 13, in his discussion of the tragic hero in relation to plot:

There remains, then, the intermediate kind of personage, a man not preeminently virtuous and just, whose misfortune, however, is brought upon him not by vice and depravity but by some error of judgement [hamartia], of the number of those in the enjoyment of great reputation and prosperity; e. g. Oedipus, Thysestes, and the men of note of similar families. The perfect plot, accordingly, must have a single, and not (as some tell us) a double issue; the change in the hero's fortunes must be not from misery to happiness, but on the contrary from happiness to misery; and the cause of it must lie not in any depravity, but in some great error [hamartia] on his part; the man himself being either such as we have described, or better, not worse, than that. (Pp. 35, 37)

The only thing agreed upon, however, is that hamartia is unconscious, which makes "recognition" and "discovery" (for Aristotle the keys to a successful plot) natural outgrowths of hamartia. As for the rest, interpretations are for the most part split between the most common reading of "moral error" and an intellectual rather than moral rendering, "miscalculation," reflected in the above translation. In a complicated linguistic argument Martin Ostwald has convincingly argued that hamartia is an intellectual affair, not an act of the hero but part of his disposition, an ignorance of particular circumstances. [17]

Almost every other commentator, no matter which of the two interpretations he chooses, makes reference to the *Nicomachean Ethics*. In general, Aristotle believed in the complete interdependence of action and morality. Virtue, in this view, is a habit or bent, and "character" in the *Poetics* means just such a bent. This disposition of the hero is seen only in the action; it is not a static thing he possesses.

A moral interpretation of hamartia is not difficult. The rest of the quotation above emphasizes moral qualities: "not preeminently virtuous and just," "not by vice and depravity." It would indeed be odd if hamartia were a totally amoral concept. And, if hamartia is not a matter of depravity, it can be explained in moral terms as a temporary aberration—temporary to avoid shocking the spectator.

Hamartia, however, need not be a moral concept in order for a moral purpose to be attributed to Aristotle in the *Poetics*. Ostwald's argument in favor of the interpretation of "ignorance of a particular circumstance" may well be valid. But the classification of the tragic hero in chapters 2 and 15 at least shows Aristotle's moral concern.

Rather than get embroiled in controversies over translations and interpretations of such possibly moral concepts as catharsis and hamartia, I have preferred to remain largely descriptive of past efforts. Now for some general observations and tentative conclusions about Aristotle's view of the purpose of literature.

Catharsis, whatever the interpretation, almost always is seen to involve (at least indirectly) some effect on the spectator of a tragedy, an effect of a positive sort. (Aristotle, however, never claims that one would go to a tragedy for catharsis; pleasure would seem a more likely motive.) And yet if literature can have such a positive effect, it could be called its purpose, and since human behavior is involved, it could be called a moral purpose. Hamartia likewise can be interpreted morally and occurs in the midst of clearly moral criteria of the tragic hero, found elsewhere in the *Poetics* as well.

A moral purpose for literature, is, then, a distinct possibility. But the moral purpose must be qualified. If Aristotle did believe that literature was moral, at least it was not moral in a didactic way. As we have already seen, Aristotle had very little use for versified treatises; he also comes out at the end of chapter 13 against a form of poetic justice, where there is "an opposite issue for the good and the bad personages." A plot with such an ending "is ranked as first only through the weakness of the audiences" (p. 37) and actually belongs to comedy. Aristotle's rejection of didacticism is the more remarkable in that in the traditional Greek view poetry was educational, a form of practical knowledge.

Although through the concept of mimesis Aristotle upheld literature's close connection with life, he made some distinctions between literature and other facets of life—distinctions that can only be called aesthetic. At the end of chapter 19, for example, he dismisses a criticism of Homer based on purely rhetorical considerations "as appertaining to another art, and not to that of poetry" (p. 57). Perhaps even more to the point, near the beginning of chapter 25 he makes a distinction between an aesthetic and a technical error:

> It is to be remembered, too, that there is not the same kind of correctness in poetry as in politics, or indeed any other art. There is, however, within the limits of poetry itself a possibility of two kinds of error, the one directly, the other only accidentally connected with the art. If the poet meant to describe the thing correctly, and failed through lack of power of expression, his art itself is at fault. But if it was through his having meant to describe it in some incorrect way (e. g. to make the horse in movement have both right legs thrown forward) that the technical error (one in a matter of, say, medicine or some other special science), or impossibilities of whatever kind they may be, have got into his description, his error in that case is not in the essentials of the poetic art. (P. 81)

It would be difficult, however, to argue from these statements that Aristotle took an extreme aesthetic position, such as art for art's sake, and saw literature as set aside in its own special world without purpose and without values. For clearly Aristotle is here only objecting to the other extreme view of literature as a slavish copy of life incurring a need for technical accuracy.

As we have seen, Aristotle did not consider literature to be only a copy; he went beyond this Platonic concept to one in which mimesis and universality merged. In much the same way, Aristotle, I believe, went beyond Plato's simple view of the morality of literature as an instrument that changes one in very immediate ways for better or worse (usually, in Plato's view, for worse). And it was precisely Aristotle's concept of mimesis/universality that allowed him to view literature as working *indirectly* in a moral way. "Moral" should here be understood, as Matthew Arnold later put it, in "a large sense": "whatever bears upon the question, 'how to live,' comes under it."[18] That is, literature indirectly conveys to us moral knowledge; this is its purpose.

Such a view is not, of course, set forth even in so many words in the *Poetics*, but it does not conflict with Aristotle's other comments, and it does provide the concept of mimetic universalizing with a purpose—knowledge. Knowledge, Aristotle tells us, gives pleasure, and, according to the *Poetics*, pleasure is a definite part of the poetic experience. In view of the probable origin of the *Poetics* as a lecture published within the Lyceum, it is possible that Aristotle did not feel the need to spell out his moral views. This "moral" interpretation of the *Poetics*, moreover, is not novel, although it is fairly modern.

In any event, whether or not Aristotle believed that literature served an indirect moral purpose is not a crucial question with regard to the tradition of literary theory he began. As we shall see, direct moral instruction became the traditional view from Horace on; the theory of indirection submerged, to appear only in the early nineteenth century. But Aristotle was at least not amoral in his treatment of literature, nor was the tradition that he fathered.

vi

Just as Aristotle did not consider literature as cut off from life, neither did he sever his literary theory from experience. His empirical bent is in fact another of the major characteristics that he left to the tradition. An empirical approach behind literary theory is a source of vitality; it keeps theory flexible and open to change. Without it, dogma and (paradoxically) arbitrariness render literary theory worthless.

The process whereby literary theory comes into being and

evolves is simple enough in outline. Reason and intuition are applied to experience, including literature, to arrive at principles. These principles are in turn applied to the literary experience and are gradually refined. Any principle found not to conform to extended experience is abandoned and replaced with a principle that does conform.

Aristotle, in the *Poetics*, has a reputation for being inductive—that is, for arguing from particulars to generals—but this reputation has been seriously questioned by a recent scholar. In his commentary on the *Poetics*, O. B. Hardison insists that the method of the *Poetics* is deductive, basing his argument on the overall organization and on several passages.[19] Perhaps the case for induction has been exaggerated, for Hardison's structural analysis does support his argument; and, as we saw above, the analysis itself is convincing. Certainly, too, his example of Aristotle's prehistory of satire in chapter 4 is valid; since the facts did not exist, only theoretical speculation was possible.[20] But Hardison's claim that the definition of tragedy is based, not on examination of many tragedies, but on theory, is suspect. According to Humphrey House, Aristotle had written a history of Greek poetry, and traces of this study are to be found in the *Poetics*, evidence of an underlying inductive method.[21]

This controversy might continue indefinitely, I believe, because the question of induction and deduction is in reality only one of direction of thought processes. Both directions are essential if any intellectual progress is to be made. Elder Olsen indeed claims this in a special way for Aristotle.[22]

Even the question of which of the methods preponderates in the *Poetics* is not as significant as the proposal that both methods are clearly present. Aristotle's literary principles are at least empirical. There is none of the large-scale theorizing based on abstract reasoning such as is found in Plato's argument about poetry as a copy of a copy or in Renaissance theories of the Unities. In the *Poetics* we are never far from data, from fact and experience. There are, for instance, constant references to the reader's own experience. In chapter 4, when speaking of the pleasure derived from mimesis, Aristotle remarks: "The truth of this second point is shown by experience" (p. 9), and then proceeds to give an example and an explanation. In chapter 13 Aristotle stops to comment several times that "fact also confirms our theory," and that "the best proof is [that] on the stage" it is as he has said (p. 37). Examples are likewise continually given to bring the theory close to experience; an instance of this occurs in chapter 7 where Aristotle explains the proper magnitude for beauty by means of an appeal to one's view of animals. [23] One aspect of his theory may also help considerably to keep him empirical—his emphasis on pleasure as one result of poetry. He commented in chapter 9 that tragedians do not have to use known names, giving Agathon's *Antheus* as an example and adding that "it is no less delightful on that account" (p. 29). Such a hedonistic premise always allows one to fall back on the simple, practical question, Which works give pleasure?

Aristotle's empiricalness naturally keeps him flexible. He is seldom, if ever, dogmatic, although occasionally his lecture tone may cause him to seem so. Time and again he evinces an exemplary open-mindedness. An improbable event is said in chapter 18 to be probable, inasmuch as there is a "probability of even improbabilities coming to pass" (p. 55), and in chapter 25 we are told that even impossibilities are permissible, "if they serve the end of poetry itself" (p. 81). Both examples represent exceptions to literary principles Aristotle is propounding, and reflect the tone of moderation that pervades the *Poetics*. This tone is especially noticeable when contrasted to the kinds of critical objections Aristotle attempts to meet in chapter 25; apparently, his contemporary critics were prone to verbal niggling and to a technical view of art that demanded that literature be scientifically accurate in details.

Unlike those critics, Aristotle has survived and managed to remain vital and fresh despite all the controversy and hordes of commentators down the centuries. There is, of course, a wealth of principles and insights in the *Poetics* to sustain it. Some of those singled out for praise by modern scholars are his expounding for the first time the concept of evolution in literary history, his categories of genres, his recognition of the importance of poetic diction and metaphor, and his belief in the organic unity of a literary work. The last principle can be found anticipated in Plato's *Phaedrus*, but it became in the *Poetics* a basic tenet.[24] And yet even more important than these principles, I believe, are those fundamental characteristics I have already discussed at some length, especially the fusion of mimesis and universality.

After Aristotle, there occurred what amounted to a break as far as Greek literary theory went. There was no one disciple at hand to take up Aristotle's principles and refine them. Instead, his theory continued to be taught at the Lyceum, and a new school of literary thought arose in Alexandria in competiton to it. Both of these filtered down to Horace, the next great theorist of the tradition, through various intermediaries. Aristotle had little direct influence on the tradition until the Renaissance, when the *Poetics* was virtually rediscovered. And yet his influence is present all along. Carried by the tradition, it shows up strongly in the theory of Horace. It would indeed be strange if Aristotle's ideas about literature, with all their scope, vitality, and soundness, had been solely dependent on the *Poetics* for survival.

NOTES

1. Plato, *Ion*, in *The Works of Plato*, trans. B. Jowett (New York, n. d.), 4:287. All quotations from Plato are from this edition; subsequent references to his works appear in parentheses in the text.

2. R. K. Hack, "The Doctrine of Literary Forms," *Harvard Studies in Classical Philology* 27 (1916): 53

3. O. B. Hardison, Jr., in Leon Golden and O. B. Hardison, Jr., *Aristotle's "Poetics"* (Englewood Cliffs, N.J., 1968), pp. 74-78.

4. Ingram Bywater, trans., *Aristotle on the Art of Poetry* (Oxford, 1909), p. 29. All quotations of the *Poetics* are from this edition; subsequent references to this work appear in parentheses in the text.

5. Watching a one-year-old child intensely involved with a picture book reinforces one's agreement with Aristotle's explanation of the human attraction to imitation.

6. Gilbert Murray, "An Essay in the Theory of Poetry, "*Yale Review* 10 (1921): 483.

7. Plato *Republic* 2. 94-102.

8. Gerald Else, *Aristotle's "Poetics": The Argument* (Cambridge, Mass., 1957), p. 322; see also Hardison, *Aristotle's "Poetics,"* p. 291.

9. G. M. A. Grube, *The Greek and Roman Critics* (London, 1965), p. 84.

10. Hardison, *Aristotle's "Poetics,"* p. 203. Hardison in fact claims that the four points in chapter 15 follow Aristotle's customary pattern in moving from the general to the more particular.

11. S. H. Butcher trans., *Aristotle's Theory of Poetry and Fine Art*, 4th ed. (New York, 1951), p. 238. Even Butcher, however, concludes that Aristotle was not entirely free from traditional moralistic views.

12. Aristotle, *Politica*, trans. B. Jowett, rev. ed., in *The Works of Aristotle*, ed. W. D. Ross (Oxford, 1921), 10. 1341b36-42a17.

13. Aristotle, *Ethica Nicomachea*, trans. W. D. Ross, in *The Works of Aristotle*, ed. W. D. Ross (Oxford, 1921), 9. 1106b14-24.

14. Leon Golden, "Catharsis," *Transactions of the American Philological Association* 93 (1962): 51-60. Still another interpretation is perhaps arguable. If *catharsis* is translated as "clarification," the function of tragedy might be to clarify pity and fear—that is, to put them in the proper perspective. Since timidity and foolhardiness so often take the place of fear, and hardheartedness and sentimentality the place of pity, this clarification or dramatization of what pity and fear really consist of would be at least a fitting function for tragedy. Aristotle is certainly concerned to distinguish what is and is not pitiable and fearful elsewhere in the *Poetics*. The passage from book 2 of the *Nicomachean Ethics* (quoted above), moreover, would more than encourage such interpretation.

15. W. F. French, "The Function of Poetry According to Aristotle," *Studies* 19 (1930): 562.

16. William K. Wimsatt, Jr., and Cleanth Brooks, *Literary Criticism: A Short History* (New York, 1965), p. 37.

17. Martin Ostwald,"Aristotle on *Hamartia* and Sophocles' *Oedipus Tyrannus*," in *Festschrift Ernst Kapp* (Hamburg, 1958), pp. 93-108.

18. Matthew Arnold,"Wordsworth," in *Matthew Arnold's Essays in Criticism*, ed. Thomas M. Hoctor (New York and London, 1964), p. 301.

19. Hardison *Aristotle's "Poetics."* The most important arguments and examples occur on pp. 68, 76, 90, 97, 99, 113, 183.

20. Ibid., p. 97.

21. Ibid., p.113; Humphrey House, *Aristotle's "Poetics": A Course of Eight Lectures* (London, 1956), pp. 32-33.

22. Elder Olson, "The Poetic Method of Aristotle," *English Institute Essays, 1951* (New York, 1951), pp. 72-73.

23. Bywater, trans., *Aristotle on the Art of Poetry*, pp. 23-25.

24. An interesting point with regard to organic unity is Atkins's comment (*Literary Criticism in Antiquity* [Gloucester, Mass., 1961], p. 87) that all of Aristotle's concern to determine whether plot or character was more important is pointless if a tragedy is truly organic.

3

Horace

i

Nearly three hundred years after Aristotle, Horace made his contribution to literary thought. He proved in fact to be second only to Aristotle in influence in the history of literary criticism; during certain eras he was even more influential.

It is perhaps difficult to understand this rivalry, for at first glance Horace does not seem to have anything like the scope and liberality of Aristotle. Horace seems more conventional or, to put it positively, more polite and urbane. He is also said to be negative, sometimes even moralistic.

Justice would be better served, however, if we avoid for the moment a direct confrontation with Horace's literary theory and turn instead to consider the historical context out of which that theory arose. For in the case of Horace, writing in what was in some respects a more complicated literary era, it would naturally be more important to consider context and intention, provocation and motive. In the Augustan period, with its peace, prosperity and power, there was indeed a new interest in literature, and poets, such as Horace, had a new prestige. There was patronage of the arts—the Pisos to whom Horace addressed his *Ars Poetica* were most likely patrons; literary coteries, further evidence of affluence, had also sprung up. There were now literary positions to be taken and battles to be fought.

J. W. H. Atkins has sketched out the three literary points of view that obtained. [1] These three attitudes, which belonged not to distinct groups and were not even well defined, were concerned largely with the question of models for Roman literature. The Atticist point of view favored the Greek classics as models. Most Augustan writers shared this view, Horace included, as a look at lines 268-69 of the *Ars Poetica* will substantiate. The later Hellenistic or Alexandrian school fostered another literary attitude. This school was representative of the recurrent Romantic theory and creative work that dominates world literature from time to time. The characteristics are familiar: capriciousness of form, novelty of content, emphasis on emotions, detachment from real life, and subjectivism. Appolonius's *Voyage of the Argo* is a good example of the Romantic products of the Hellenistic age. Some of the literary theories propounded were not, however, specifically Romantic, nor even un-Romantic. For instance, there was a demand for meticulous craftsmanship and an emphasis on short verse forms (in the latter point there is a remarkable similarity to the theory of a later Romantic, Edgar Allan Poe). This Alexandrian tradition was strong enough to have influenced the best Augustan writers, including Virgil. Horace himself stressed polished writing, but he resisted other Hellenistic influences: he was very much in favor of longer verse forms and even emphasized epic and drama in the *Ars*. In this resistance, too, he was not alone among the Augustans.

The third attitude was reactionary and nationalistic, and belonged to what might be called the Older Latin School. It included a preference for earlier Roman poets, such as Ennius, for whom exaggerated claims were made. Such a nostalgic point of view was apparently strong, for Horace protests against it in his "Epistle to Augustus." Accompanying this attitude was a purist streak with regard to poetic diction, an objection to neologisms and Greek borrowings; the *Ars Poetica*, of course, contains a rejection of such an extreme view.

Horace joined battle on these general issues in three satires and three epistles, in addition to the *Ars Poetica*. The fourth and tenth satires of book 1 and the first of book 2 of Horace's *Satires* form a kind of series. They contain literary comments limited to consideration of satire as genre, its moral purpose, and appropriate style. His *Epistles* followed the *Satires*, although otherwise their dating is uncertain. The nineteenth epistle of book 1 and the first ("The Epistle to Augustus") and second ("The Epistle to Florus") of book 2 contain most of what there is of literary concern. The last two are especially important for discussion of poetic standards and style ("To Florus") and of the position of the poet and poetry at Rome ("To Augustus").

The "Epistle to the Pisos," or the *Ars Poetica*, as it is most commonly called, is related in its literary theory to Horace's comments elsewhere and yet goes far beyond them. It provided a framework for his literary ideas and filled out his literary program. It is his major work of literary criticism.

More compact and impersonal in approach than his other epistles with literary subjects, the *Ars* has been said to show Horace viewing literature from without, that is, not as an active poet. Indeed, Horace himself backs off (lines 305-6): "Though I write nothing of my own I will teach the office and the duty."[2] The date of composition of the *Ars* is uncertain, although the tone, maturity, and comprehensiveness point to a late date, probably sometime after the other literary epistles. It was addressed to L. Piso, possibly later a city prefect but never definitely identified. The title *Ars Poetica* was applied to the epistle three generations later by Quintillian, possibly by someone else earlier, but almost certainly not by Horace himself. Most commentators reject the newer title as inappropriate and misleading, but the *Ars* is a manual at least in the sense that in it literary art is seen as the capacity to produce a given end.

The longest of Horace's poems, the *Ars Poetica* presents a clear problem of organization. At least on the surface, its structure is, like Aristotle's *Poetics*, not all it might be. Its desultory quality was remarked by Alexander Pope in his *Essay on Criticism* (lines 653-54):

> Horace still charms with graceful negligence,
> And without method talks us into sense.

Very few have missed the opportunity to make similar com-

ment or to point out the incompatibility of Horace's demand
for order and unity with his own practice in the *Ars*.

But, as with the *Poetics*, perhaps more method is involved
than is at first apparent. Horace was, after all, something like
what one scholar named him—"one of the most architectonic
of poets."[3] And as many others have pointed out, the *Ars Poetica* is essentially a verse letter and must be viewed partly in the
context of Horace's other epistles. The versified epistle was
used by Horace for serious subjects; the abrupt beginning and
ending of the *Ars* should not be allowed to mislead one. The
epistles are generally casual in tone. They were in fact intended as letters to actual correspondents with their personalities
and needs in mind. What turned out to be a treatise in the
largest sense began at least as a letter.

And a structure of sorts has been discerned in the *Ars*. Por-
phyrio, a commentator of the third century A.D., claimed that
Horace had copied a Hellenistic treatise on poetry written by
Neoptolemus of Parium, a literary scholar, grammarian, and
poet-critic. Neoptolemus lived probably in the third century
B.C. (at least pre-180 B.C.), and probably had strong Aristotelian
leanings. His extant work is fragmentary, but the consensus
now is that Horace got his overall construction of the *Ars* from
a work by Neoptolemus. With the dividing line-numbers dependent on the scholar performing the division, the *Ars* is seen
to have a tripartite structure: (1) *poesis* or poetry, dealing with
content;(2) *poema* or poetics, dealing with style (techniques,
language, and versification); and (3) *poeta* or poet, containing miscellaneous ideas concerning poets. Even with this
overall tripartite structure, however, the *Ars* does not emerge
as a neatly packaged treatise.

C. O. Brink offers a still more acceptable view of the structure of the *Ars* in his recent study of Horace's literary criticism.
He begins by quarreling with the distinction "*either* order *or*
disorder" as descriptive of the *Ars*. For Brink the work is somewhere in between—in between, to put it another way, a treatise
and a poem. He accepts the tripartite division but splits the

poem along different lines. After a forty-line introduction, which is outside the divisions and contains the underlying principles for the following sections, comes the first section (lines 40–118), which deals with style, including arrangement. Lines 119-294 comprise the second section and contain general observations on poetry, especially comments on content and plot, and these observations are illustrated by the epic and particularly by the drama. The final section (lines 295-476) contains miscellaneous general principles of poetry. These sections are joined by subtle transitions, but contemporaries, familiar with rhetorical theory, would have recognized the triad.[4]

The *Ars Poetica* also has, in the words of Brink, the "coherence of poetry," and contains structural elements most often connected with poetry.[5] For example, Brink points out that concepts are often joined by juxtaposition rather than by argument, that motifs are used deliberately and economically, and that the poem begins and ends with caricatures, which thus afford a kind of poetic unity. H. L. Tracy pointed out in 1948 that the *Ars* was very like the earlier epistles in using a "lyrical method" in contrast to a didactic method, with a good many concrete images, epigrams, anecdotes, and a lyrical structure.[6]

ii

The kind of "criticism" contained in the *Ars* likewise divides into three parts, but here the divisions are unequal in amount and importance. Evaluation (or practical criticism of particular works) is even more vague in application than was Aristotle's in the *Poetics* and, like Aristotle's, it is incidental to other purposes. It is, furthermore, confined largely to stylistic errors. Horace's criticism of older Latin writers, such as that of Plautus in lines 270-74, has been called by one scholar "strangely biased and unfair," but Horace did champion elsewhere the new school of poetry of which Virgil was a member.[7] There was little creative theory (psychology of creation) in the *Ars*;

like Aristotle, however, Horace did insist (lines 101-3) that the poet must feel the emotions that he seeks to communicate. And as in his other works, Horace emphasizes (lines 408-18) the need for poetic training in poets.

The overwhelming bulk of the *Ars Poetica* is literary theory. There is less of such theory on the surface of the *Ars*, less outright statement of principle and more discussion of topical issues than is found in Aristotle's *Poetics*. Those who claim that the *Ars* contains little literary theory can mean no more than that; for there is of necessity literary theory underlying and supporting every word of the piece.

A large number of sources have been detected for Horace's theory, especially early in this century when *Quellenforschung* was so popular. Among the specific candidates for the bits and pieces are Lucilius, Cicero, Neoptolemus of Parium, and Aristotle. Horace was not, indeed, especially original in his literary theory, and yet many of the concepts in the *Ars* were pervasive in the Augustan period; thus we need not view the *Ars* as a mere patchwork of direct borrowings. Horace, moreover, made the concepts his own; as C. O. Brink put it, the *Ars Poetica* is "unmistakably personal."[8]

Two of the influences widely noted are, nevertheless, of immense importance—Aristotle and Neoptolemus. For Horace's theories are largely Aristotelian in basis, and he came by his Aristotelian ideas probably through the works of Neoptolemus. Thus transmitted were Aristotle's *Rhetoric* and *Poetics,* possibly even his *De Poetis*, of which only a fragment survives. There is no evidence of firsthand knowledge of the *Poetics* in the Augustan period, and, although it is likely that Horace was "Aristotlized" by Neoptolemus, others were possibly involved as middlemen as well. There is too little left of Neoptolemus's literary theory to be certain of such matters; Brink's scrutiny of the pertinent documents merely shows Neoptolemus's role, especially in adapting Aristotle's views (as in the *Rhetoric*) in the direction of more strictly literary concerns.

Many similarities exist between Horace's *Ars Poetica* and

Aristotle's *Poetics*. There are parallels and even occasional echoes. Most obvious, of course, are the large peculiarities shared by both. There is, for example, the concept of organic unity, so strong in the *Poetics*, right in the opening of the *Ars* in the image of the inorganic monster. Then there is the emphasis on drama and the limitation of genres discussed, even more surprising in the *Ars* since Horace was a poet practicing in the forms that he all but ignored as a theorist. Other more specific similarities have also been pointed out. Among them is the praise of Homer and the rejection of the concept of *ars metrica*; Horace's remarks on characterization are, moreover, very much like those in chapter 9 of the *Poetics*, although Horace has one fewer category. And these examples by no means exhaust the likenesses.

iii

Even more important, however, are the general characteristics shared by Aristotle and Horace. Horace was in fact squarely in the Aristotelian tradition.

On the question of the purpose of literature, Horace was much clearer than Aristotle; Horace might even be said to have diverted the tradition for many centuries on this point, positing a more direct moral purpose than Aristotle would have subscribed to. In any event, Horace was so straightforward on literary purpose that he has given his name to the concept that art teaches and pleases—the Horatian formula. The passage in which it occurs reads as follows (lines 333-34): "The aim of the poet is either to benefit, or to amuse, or to make his words at once please and give lessons of life" (p. 357). In a passage shortly thereafter, Horace adds (lines 341-46):

> The centuries of the elders hunt off the stage what lacks profit. The proud Ramnes [i. e., young aristocrats] will have nothing to say to dry poems. He has gained every vote who has mingled profit with pleasure by delighting the reader

at once and instructing him. This is the book that makes the fortune of the Sosii [booksellers], that crosses the seas, and gives a long life of fame to its author. (P. 357)

The point here is unmistakable: if one wishes to appeal to the widest audience--if one wishes to sell widely--one must instruct *and* please. The irony (unintentional) of this statement following the strong anticommercialism of the previous passage (lines 323-32) has, as far as I know, never been pointed out.

It has been remarked, however, that the distinction "to teach *or* to please" has provided a sort of theoretical foothold for later hedonists to get a purchase on. The moral view of poetry was apparently not strong in Horace's own times; at least Brink claims that few Augustans would have looked to literature for moral enlightenment.[9]

A moral view was in any case consistent with Horace's literary beliefs in his other works. In the *Satires*, Horace claimed that the satiric genre has a moral purpose; and in the *Letter to Augustus* he defended poetry by spelling out its utility as educator of the young and its usefulness to the state (a parallel passage occurs in the historical sketch given in the *Ars* [lines 391-407]). Even in the *Odes*, Horace saw a moral function in poetry.

The Horatian formula, as we have seen, was not contained in Aristotle's *Poetics* in so many words. The formula could have been borrowed by Horace from Neoptolemus.[10] But the instruction part of the formula, the view of the educational value of literature, was a traditional Greek view, adopted by the Stoics from more recent Greek critics and preserved during the Alexandrian period by Stoics such as Strabo. Lines 309-16 of the *Ars* show that Horace considered moral thought to be part of poetic composition:

Of writing well the source and fountain-head is wise thinking. Matter Socratic pages will be able to set before you: and when the matter is first found, the words will not be slow to follow. He who has learnt what he owes to his country and what to his friends, with what affection a parent, with what a brother and a guest should be loved, what is the duty of a conscript father, what of a judge, what the functions of one sent as a captain to the war, he, you may be sure, knows how to give his fitting part to each character. (P. 356)

The reference to "Socratic pages" in the above quotation illustrates the Stoic involvement in Horace's moral views of literature, for the Stoics claimed to be Socratic.

The Stoics held to a thoroughgoing didacticism; that is, they believed that literature teaches directly by precept and example. Pleasure is permissible as the sugarcoating of the pill. Horace, however, while he accepted the instructive nature of poetry, did not downgrade the pleasure of literature to the subordinate role the Stoics assigned it. His view of literature as direct instruction is clear enough in any case: the chorus

should take the side of the good, and give friendly counsels, and rule the angry, and cherish the law-abiding. It should praise the fare of a modest table, it should praise health-bringing justice and law and peace with her open gates. It should keep secrets, and pray and beseech the gods that fortune may return to the sad and desert the proud. (P. 350)

Lines 335-36 likewise favor a strictly didactic view: "When you wish to instruct, be brief; that men's minds may take in quickly what you say, learn its lesson, and retain it faithfully" (p. 357).

There is, nevertheless, some evidence of a belief in an indirect moral working elsewhere in Horace's works. The second epistle of book 1 begins with the following statement (lines 1-4): "While you have been practising declamation at Rome, Lollius Maximus, I have been reading again at Praeneste the story-teller of the war of Troy; who shows us what is fair, what is foul, what is profitable, what not, more plainly and better than a Chrysippus or a Crantor [moral philosophers]" (p. 267). But the Horatian formula undoubtedly stands out among Horace's pronouncements on the purpose of literature, and there is an unmistakable tendency in the *Ars* and elsewhere toward a view of the morality of literature that is directly didactic. It is precisely this loss of Aristotle's indirect moral view of literature sometime between the *Poetics* and the *Ars* that is the most serious loss to the tradition Aristotle initiated.

iv

The loss of the concept of moral indirection even affected other of the characteristics Horace possessed as part of the Aristotelian tradition. For with a view of direct moral working, the purpose of literature is already explained; consequently, it is unnecessary to emphasize the mimetic-universalizing aspects of literature with their *indirect* moral function. This is precisely what happened: the mimetic concept so fundamental to the *Poetics* is never spelled out in the *Ars Poetica*.

Imitation had by Horace's time even taken on another meaning—the imitation of past models. Such imitation was a primary rule of Hellenistic theory and was urged by the rhetoricians. Horace himself deals specifically with imitation of models in the short nineteenth epistle of book 1 and in the *Ars* (lines 128-35); the concept is basic to Horace and can be found, at least implicitly, frequently in his works. But it is imperative that no misunderstanding arise concerning this kind of "imitation"; living after the Romantics we tend to think of originality as a prime value in literature. Horace and the other classical theoristis had no such rage for novelty, and yet they saw literary imitation not in a narrow sense of copying, but as re-creation. Horace was decidedly against any concept of slavish reproduction, as the following lines from the *Ars* (131-35) illustrate:

> You may acquire private rights in common ground, provided you will neither linger in the one hackneyed and easy round; nor trouble to render word for word with the faithfulness of a translator; nor by your mode of imitating take the "leap into the pit" out of which very shame, if not the

law of your work, will forbid you to stir hand or foot to escape. (P. 347)

Some recent scholars have even charged that such literary imitation had taken over, that Horace does not hold to a mimetic view of literature. And yet another scholar, J. W. H. Atkins, has claimed that mimetic theory is implicit in Horace's literary theory.[11] I believe that Atkins's claim is correct, that it can be shown that Horace believed in a close relationship of literature and life. But, like Aristotle on the matter of moral purpose, Horace apparently felt no need to be explicit on the subject.

The concept of mimesis is rarely very far beneath the surface of Horace's stated theory. In the "Letter to Augustus" Horace praises Virgil and Varius (and through them all poets) for mimetic ability (lines 248–50): "And features copied in bronze do not show more clearly than the manners and souls of heroes of renown in the poet's work" (p. 327). In the *Ars Poetica*, even the opening image of the inorganic monster contains an implicit appeal to the reader's sense of reality. Later in the section on the four ages of man (lines 153-78), the point is made that dramatic characters ought to be true to life. The same point recurs at lines 310–18, mimesis becoming explicit in lines 317-18: "My advice to one who is to pass as a trained artist will be to take as his model real life and manners, and from thence to draw the language that will seem like that of real life" (p. 356). Earlier in the poem (lines 182-88) Horace objects to showing outrageous or miraculous events on stage on the grounds that they will be abhorrent and *discredited* (*"incredulus odi"*). Again later in the poem (lines 337-40), Horace becomes explicitly mimetic: "Fictions intended to please must keep as near as may be to real life. The plot must not ask our credence for anything that it chooses: it must not draw a live boy from the belly of a Lamia who has just dined on him" (p. 357). This profusion of examples is meant to point up what is clearly an underlying principle in Horace's literary theory.

V

As with mimesis, Horace's views on the universality of literature are not spelled out; but, as with mimesis, those views
are not far to seek. C. O. Brink, following the lead of Rostagni,
has found the concept of universality in lines 128-35 of the
Ars, said to be adopted from Aristotle's *Poetics* (chap. 9), probably by Neoptolemus.[12] As usual, Neoptolemus had likely
adapted Aristotle's concept for the practical use of a writer,
and it shows up in Horace as practical advice on plot construction. But both the universal and the individual are still present
in the concept.

The concept of universality also appears under the guise
of decorum, where decorum is concerned with the preservation
of types. The passage especially concerned occurs at lines
152-78, where the characteristics of childhood, youth, maturity, and old age are briefly sketched. Standard character
types result, and these clearly share in the idea of universality,
even though in the *Ars* there is nothing like Aristotle's metaphysical pondering.

When the passage on the four ages was discussed above in
connection with mimesis, truth-to-life was said to be Horace's
intention. Brink has remarked that the passage should not
be taken as a "logical analysis" but as "a descriptive sketch";
in fact it seems to be a borrowing from Aristotle's *Rhetoric*.[13] But
even if taken in this way, its tendency is to some extent away
from realism, whatever Horace's intention. There is doubtless
something valid in Horace's concept; that is, a major character
who was egregiously unlike others of his same age would most
likely be considered a flaw in a literary work. And yet Horace's
sketch is too narrowly drawn, too restrictive; it overlooks all
variables and, by pushing the typical, makes all the ages sound
stereotyped.

The extent to which Horace's literary theory is empirical has never attracted much attention. J. W. H. Atkins, who did consider the matter, concluded that Horace was too derivative to be inductive, too reliant on Greek and Hellenistic theory to really look at literature at firsthand. And yet in the middle of his discussion, Atkins remarks of Horace: "What he does is to select from earlier authorities principles in accord with those convictions of his which were the outcome of his own experience and thought." [14] This latter view, is, I believe, closer to the truth.

Horace does not simply appeal to previous theorists as authorities; as in the opening of the *Ars* and elsewhere, he resorts to examples as illustrations of his principles. His poetic technique, as was noted earlier, relies heavily on imagery and anecdotes. There is, in addition, a constant reference to the audience's response, especially to its delight. The double attraction of instruction and delight is only one example of such reference. At lines 112-13 we are told: "If the speaker's language rings false to his circumstances, all Rome, front seats and back alike, will join the laugh against him" (p. 346). At lines 222-25 Horace says that "the attention of the spectator fresh from sacrifice, well drunk and in lawless mood, had to be kept by the attraction of pleasant novelty" (p. 352). So much insistence on actual response to literary work could not, I submit, coexist with a distinct a priori approach.

Horace in fact seldom indulges in abstract reasoning and only occasionally resorts to dogmatic statements of supposedly self-evident truths. The section (lines 189-201) espousing the necessity of five acts, rejection of the deus ex machina, and proper use of the chorus is one of the few instances of such. On the other side of the ledger, Horace bases his remarks on diction squarely on usage, that is, on linguistic experience (lines 71-72)—a principle many have yet to learn.

Like Aristotle, Horace does, however, turn to a priori logic to trace literary origins; since he, like Aristotle, had no access to historical fact, Horace quite naturally resorted to deductive speculation. But on the whole, Horace shares with Aristotle an empirical approach to literature, although Horace is not so interested in speculation as in pragmatic concerns and contemporary issues.

An empirical approach leads naturally to flexibility, and Horace's theory has the latter quality in good measure. This contention runs counter to the view often held, but a look at the contemporary literary situation will help to substantiate my claim. It is not that Horace's contemporaries were less flexible in contrast; rather some were *too* flexible. Tenney Frank earlier in this century examined Horace's contemporary writers in some detail, pointing out the literary controversies and the extremes taken by many. [15] As far as diction went, there was a good deal of "fine writing" by the Alexandrian advocates, and Maecenas, a writer and influential patron, in particular indulged in wild diction for effect. At the other extreme were the purists of the old school. The chorus, moreover, was constantly misused through Hellenistic influence, and the relationship between subject and genre was disastrously ignored by some writers. Organic unity was likewise missing from much of the older Latin and neoteric literature. Classical meter, much more sensitive and restricted than English, was also abused by the neoterics. There was, in short, sufficient provocation for many of the strictures contained in the *Ars Poetica*, and without this information available, someone like Horace, combating this array of abuses, is not likely to seem especially liberal. Indeed, he could be quite liberal and yet appear negative and narrow-minded under the circumstances.

Horace was no perfectionist; he realized the human limitations to art. He was in fact fluid on the question of the "law of the genre," the restriction of particular meters and subjects to particular genres. On the question of diction, as we have already seen, Horace appealed to usage—a fact that ought to be as well remembered as his pronouncement of the five-act law. Such an appeal to linguistic experience was the more remarkable in view of the codified rhetorics of the time. Horace even practiced his preachment with four coinages in the *Ars Poetica* itself.[16] It is ironic that Horace was perhaps least influential on the matter of diction. Then there are the frequent compromises, such as between training and native genius or between teaching and pleasing, that argue for a moderate, flexible approach. And perhaps best known is Horace's tolerance of the few flaws found in Homer.

Horace has been frequently accused of a certain aloofness, a lack of enthusiasm in approaching literature, an acute formalism. He is supposed to see poetry as versified prose composed according to hard-and-fast rules. If such is the case, what is to be done with the following passage (lines 99-103)?

> It is not enough that poems have beauty of form: they must have charm, and draw the hearer's feelings which way they will. Men smile—such is human nature—on those who smile: on the same terms they wait on those who weep. If you wish to draw tears from me, you must first feel pain yourself. (P. 346)

In the famous passage rejecting mediocrity in poetry (lines 366-90), Archibald Campbell, moreover, finds evidence of the ultimate flexibility. In the rejection of mediocrity, Horace was in effect repudiating the golden mean, was saying that all the rules and all the training he insists upon are insufficient for poetry if "distinction" is absent. Campbell calls this "the last discovery," for

> it leaves the fundamental problem once more where it was (and where it always will be); for this "distinction" no recipe can be given, no hint even. Originality in writing always means creation in some degree and no man can tell you how to create; you can only do it by creating. Horace, naturally, does not attempt to give any such recipe.[17]

And yet, with all his flexibility, Horace leads inexorably

to the Neoclassical Rationalists of the late Renaissance. These later rule-ridden theorists were to misinterpret Horace's pronouncements in the direction of dogma and would carry Horace's concept of decorum to excess. Horace, of course, cannot be held wholly responsible for what later critics would do to his theories, but the seeds of such mischief are present in Horace's works. His five-act rule (lines 189-90) is a case in point. It does not derive from literary experience; although its source is uncertain, it probably originated in Hellenistic theory and is based on a misunderstanding of the term *act*, apparently thought to be, but certainly not, a Greek concept. This adoption by Horace is not much different from later Renaissance adoption of the so-called Unities.

Horace has, then, this tendency toward inflexibility, but too much can easily be made of it, and, in any event, it is not the whole story. Several general points ought always to be kept in mind. In the *Ars* and elsewhere Horace is presenting his literary ideas in verse, and the tone may sound more dogmatic because of the terseness and concision of the epigrammatic style. Second, although he is partly responsible for the dogmatism of his Renaissance admirers, Horace should never be confused with them. The comparison with Aristotle, furthermore, is not entirely fair. Horace is, it is generally agreed, more limited than Aristotle, but there are good reasons for his comparative limitations. As heir not only to Aristotle's theories but to those of his followers and other theorists in the three centuries since Aristotle's death, Horace found that, unlike Aristotle, he could assume a great deal of basic agreement. Thus there is lacking in Horace's literary theory the basic probing found in the *Poetics*. Horace was embroiled in topical disputes as well, and this contemporary involvement was a further obstacle to discussion of ultimate literary issues. Horace was a good deal more flexible than he is often given credit for.

Again in contrast to Aristotle's case, Horace's treatise was never lost. We know, for example, that his works were read by Jerome, Augustus, and Dante. His influence became especially strong and widespread in the Renaissance. Queen Elizabeth began a translation of the *Ars*, and Ben Johnson completed one. Horace was, to be sure, misread; his more dynamic qualities were ignored and the *Ars Poetica* became a kind of sourcebook for maxims and dogma. Aristotle himself, after the virtual rediscovery of the *Poetics* in the Renaissance, was misinterpreted in the light of Horace's works, which had the appeal of greater simplicity. In the early eighteenth century, Horace was even more influential than Aristotle, and, although that influence was beginning to ebb during the latter part of the century, even Longinus, with all the appeal of his vitality and enthusiasm, never dislodged him. For better or worse Horace was, then, for many centuries the main torchbearer of the Aristotelian tradition.

NOTES

1. J. W. H. Atkins, *Literary Criticism in Antiquity*, 2 vols. (Gloucester, Mass., 1961), 2:50-53. See also Henry Nettleship, *Lectures and Essays*, 2d ser., ed. F. Haverfield. (Oxford, 1895), p. 69

2. E. C. Wickham, trans., *Horace for English Readers* (Oxford, 1903), p. 355. All quotations from Horace are from this edition; subsequent references to his works appear in parentheses in the text.

3. Charles O. Brink, *Horace on Poetry*, 2 vols. (Cambridge, 1963-71), p. vii.

4. Ibid., p. 245.

5. Ibid., p. viii. See also pt. 4, chap. 2.

6. H. L. Tracy, "Horace's *Ars Poetica*: A Systematic Argument," *Greece and Rome* 17 (1948):104-15.

7. Atkins, *Literary Criticism*, 2:94. See also 2:95-96.

8. Brink, *Horace on Poetry*, pp. 154-55.

9. Ibid., p. 200.

10. J. D. Boyd, *The Function of Mimesis and Its Decline* (Cambridge, Mass., 1968), p. 44, has remarked that the tripartite function of rhetoric (to teach, to please, and to move) probably is also behind the Horatian formula. He also mentions that Stoic views are probably involved as well.

11. Atkins, *Literary Criticism*, 2:75.

12. Brink, *Horace on Poetry*, pp. 103-9. Lines 128-35 read as follows: "It is a hard task to treat what is common in a way of your own; and you are doing more rightly in breaking the tale of Troy into acts than in giving the world a new story of your own telling. You may acquire private rights in common ground, provided you will neither linger in the one hackneyed and easy round; nor trouble to render word for word with the faithfulness of a translator; nor by your mode of imitating take the

'leap into the pit' out of which very shame, if not the law of your work, will forbid you to stir hand or foot to escape. (Wickham, *Horace for English Readers*, p. 347).

13. Ibid., pp. 111-13.

14. Atkins, *Literary Criticism*, pp. 97-98.

15. Tenney Frank, "Horace on Contemporary Poetry," *Classical Journal* 13 (1917-18) :550-64.

16. Ibid., p. 558.

17. Archibald Y. Campbell, *Horace: A New Interpretation* (London, 1924), p. 253.

4

Longinus

i

By the time Dryden came to write his "Apology for Heroic Poetry" in 1677, there was a third literary theorist whose classical authority could be invoked, a third member of a "Classical Triumvirate of Criticism." Aristotle and Horace were by that time joined by the renascent Longinus, and, although the history of his reputation and influence has had its ups and downs ever since, Longinus has never quite been deposed. By more recent scholars he is most frequently seen as second only to Aristotle in Greek critical thought and sometimes even as the fulfillment or reconciliation of Plato and Aristotle.

The problems encountered in the dating of the *Poetics* and the *Ars Poetica* are far surpassed by Longinus's *Peri Hupsous*. In his case they are complicated by a still murkier problem; even the authorship of the *Peri Hupsous* is very much in doubt—the name *Longinus* is used only as a matter of convenience. Only one actual historical figure—the man to whom the treatise has traditionally been ascribed—has much support for authorship: Cassius Longinus, a Greek writer and scholar of the third century A.D. After that attribution was called into question in the early nineteenth century because of manuscript inconsistencies in the author's name, a first-century writer, possibly also named Longinus, was seized upon as fitting the evidence best.

The first century A.D. is now generally agreed upon; some scholars seem to think the matter settled, even though others have seriously cast doubt upon the new evidence and the conclusions. If the *Peri Hupsous* does not belong to Cassius

Longinus of the third century, however, the author is entirely unknown, for there are no references to him or to his work by classical writers. With the issue so uncertain, it seems best to leave both the date and the authorship of the treatise as unknown, to say it was written sometime in the early Christian era and to call the author Longinus for sake of expedience.

Of the other personages mentioned as involved in the text, two are historical. Caecilius of Calacte, to whose treatise Longinus is objecting, was a teacher of rhetoric at Rome under Augustus; he was a friend of Dionysus of Halicarnassus and most likely a Jew. Theodorus of Gadara, mentioned in chapter 3, was a Greek who also lived during the Augustan era. Theodorus was the founder of a school of rhetoric that was apparently less rigid than most; Longinus may have been a disciple of his school, possibly was actually one of Theodorus's students, and may have been influenced by him in the direction of flexibility. The other figure, Postumius Terentianus, was the addressee of the treatise and is unknown. But the forms of address used by Longinus provide some evidence, however tentative—evidence that Terentianus was a patron, probably a student-patron, a Roman of elevated, perhaps senatorial, rank, aged from twenty to forty.

Like the dating and authorship, the organization of the treatise brings to mind Aristotle and Horace, especially the missing second book of the *Poetics*. For the *Peri Hupsous* is a fragment; depending on the authority performing the calculation, either two-fifths or one-third of the original is now missing. The lacunae are in seven sections, six fairly long ones, with probably a short passage missing at the end. Omissions are not indicated by the present chapter numbers, which were added to the manuscript later by a different hand.

In spite of the lacunae, however, the organization is at least a little more discernible than in the case of the *Poetics* and the *Ars*. Roughly, there is an introductory section, a discussion of four of the five sources of the sublime, and an ending lamenting the decline of great writing. In the body of the work, the discussion of the five sources, vestiges of the traditional rhetorical scheme of progression (from invention to expression to delivery) have been pointed out. If the last category, delivery, is dropped as inapplicable to literature, we are left with *res* and *verba*, "content" and "form," and this division can be seen in the split between the first two sources and the last three.

Longinus, however, treats the sources separately; consequently, the traditional division remains vestigial. And there are problems of organization in the five-source scheme. For example, the summary of the treatment of the first source given at the end of chapter 15 is incorrect, and material in chapters 10 and 11, which is not covered by the summary, seems out of place. Chapters 60-63, moreover, are disconnected, probably indicating Longinus's lack of interest in technical detail. There has been a further question raised as to the appropriateness of the last chapter, but at least it clearly has ties with Longinus's concern about the personality of the author. And it also is consistent with Longinus's general "philosophy."

More general objections to Longinus's organization have also been voiced. The first two and last three sources, although divided along lines of author and style, are not mutually exclusive and do in fact become confused. Longinus also becomes so enthusiastic while discussing the various sources of *hupsous* that he begins to treat each as the *only* source. There are, furthermore, a number of digressions, such as the comparison of the *Odyssey* and the *Iliad* in chapter 9. Longinus, it would be fair to conclude, was not rigid in his structure of the *Peri Hupsous*, and the variety of his approaches—the ranging from one element of the triad author-reader-work to another—serves, I believe, to make the basic framework of the treatise even less noticeable.

Not only do the date, authorship, and organization present problems, but there is also no general agreement on what the treatise is about. This quandary can even be seen in the various attempts to translate the *hupsous* of the title. In Greek the word literally means "height," and *sublimitas* is a valid Latin equivalent. One of the only points of general agreement is that the English translation "sublime" is vastly inadequate and, in view of various connotations of calm or obscurity assumed by that word in the eighteenth century, inevitably misleading. By studying the term *sublime* one may end up understanding eighteenth-century usage, but not Longinus's meaning.

And yet all ten English translations after 1739 rendered *hupsous* as "sublime." Even today, *sublime* is the identifying term for the treatise, just as *Longinus* is given as the author's name. In any case, there have been numerous suggestions of alternate English terms. William Wordsworth showed the difficulty involved by proposing a series of terms: "animated, empassioned, energetic, or if you will, elevated writing"; George Saintsbury, closely adhering to the literal meaning, in some respects preferred "the height of eloquence," used by John Hall in his translation of 1652; Arthur Quiller-Couch likewise preferred an earlier version, "On the Sovereign Perfection of Writing," a title used in 1712; Allen Tate, following his New-Critical linguistic bent, chose "elevation of language"; and "Heightening of Style" was the choice of scholar C. S. Baldwin.[1]

G. M. A. Grube, a recent translator of the *Peri Hupsous*, after examining the synonyms used in the treatise, concluded that *hupsous* involved two main considerations—"the metaphor of height, and greatness or vigour of conception."[2] Placing emphasis on the second, he translated the title as *On Great Writing*, which probably is as good as any of the other attempts and better than most. Longinus never defines *hupsous*, but only describes the phenomenon. The term itself had been used previously by rhetoricians to designate the grand style, but this is obviously not what Longinus had in mind. Great writing, he tells us in chapter 31, can reside in the plain style.

"Great writing," then, probably gets close to Longinus's meaning if the above qualification—that great writing is not necessarily high-flown—is kept in mind, and if we remember that *hupsous* is not exclusively a verbal or literary concept. Although writing is Longinus's main concern in the treatise, he also tells us that *hupsous* can reside in silence (chap. 9) and in nature (chap. 35). *Hupsous* appears to be in these contexts an effect or quality, perhaps a force.

In spite of this indefinable aspect of the topic, the *Peri Hupsous* is nevertheless a treatise on rhetoric, at least to a certain extent. In the opening chapter we learn that Longinus is in search of something that "may be useful to public speakers."[3] The treatise is, among other things, clearly meant as a kind of textbook. The discussion of the third and fourth sources, which is the main section to survive, is technical in a rhetorical way. Rhetorics in this period were codified and influential; consequently, it is the more surprising that Longinus can be relatively so liberal in his treatment of the subject.

But, if as Aristotle says in his *Rhetoric* (1355b), the end of rhetoric is persuasion, we discover in the first chapter of *Peri Hupsous* that Longinus is pursuing a different quality, transport. And Longinus constantly distinguishes devices used to produce great writing and those used for rhetorical purposes. In themselves, these two differences are unusual enough in a rhetoric, and the appearance of abnormality increases when we consider that Longinus centers upon a single quality. This approach was too generalized for the traditional rhetoric; that is, normal categorizations necessarily fell by the way. Longinus, for example, does not bother with considerations of that time-honored categorization, genre.

Longinus also deals with poetry to a large extent, but, as W. J. Bate observes, the borderline "between the style of prose-rhetoric and that of poetry" is "thin in most classical writing."[4] Many quotations in the treatise are taken from Homer and the Greek tragedians, as well as from Demosthenes, Cicero, Plato, and the Greek historians. Longinus, in fact, makes the extraordinary attempt to combine in one study technical rhetoric and an examination of an indefinable, je-ne-sais-quoi quality. At the end of chapter 35 he remarks: "We might say of all such matters that man can easily understand what is useful or necessary, but he admires what passes his understanding" (p. 48). Longinus is clearly doing more than usual; he is going beyond technical aspects, and yet he also shows that a certain amount of system is involved as well. Otherwise, of course, a treatise on the subject would be pointless; like a modern scholar studying literary symbols, he had to follow the subject as far as discursive reason could take him.

ii

The *Peri Hupsous* is a different kind of work than the *Poetics* or the *Ars Poetica*. The difference, however, is not so much a matter of ends—all three are to some degree both treatises and manuals—but of means. The triple approach Longinus used (to author, reader, and work) has already been mentioned. Unlike Aristotle and Horace, who were largely concerned with the last two categories, Longinus spent some time discussing the author.

In other words, in the *Peri Hupsous* there is considerably more creative theory, a commodity not often found either in rhetorics or in any classical discussion of literature. Perhaps one reason for the scarcity of creative theory elsewhere in classical criticism is that the concepts of mimesis and universality tend to lead away from the author to the work and its relation to life. Why Longinus, who shared a belief in those concepts, should find room for further considerations is a matter for conjecture.

Longinus's creative theory is contained partly in surface similarities to discussions in the *Poetics* and the *Ars*. All three theorists, it is true, share a belief that both genius and training, nature and art, are necessary for a successful writer. Longinus, even here, however, significantly gives more emphasis to genius, both in chapter 2 and in the following remark in chapter 36: "Since the avoidance of error is mostly due to the successful application of the rules of art while supremacy belongs to genius, it is fitting that art should everywhere give its help to nature." (p. 49).

But Longinus resembles Plato in going beyond this conventional discussion to a concern with the process of creation in the poet's mind. A genuine psychological interest is evident in his selection of the first two sources of great writing, set forth in chapter 8: "Vigor of mental conception" and "strong and inspired emotion" (p. 10).

Chapter 15 concerns itself with "imagination," which was to be central to discussions of creative theory in the eighteenth and nineteenth centuries. Here, however, *imagination* is synonymous with *image-making*: "In the general sense, any thought present in the mind and producing speech is called imagination, but in its now prevailing sense the word applies when ecstasy or passion makes you appear to see what you are describing and enables you to make your audience see it" (pp. 23-24). "Imagination" appears to be the ability to summon up a vivid picture and communicate that picture to the reader. Nothing, that is, on the order of Coleridge's creative, fusing imagination seems to be meant by Longinus.[5] And yet Longinus is the only theorist to deal with this creative aspect of literature to any extent before the eighteenth century.

When Longinus turns from the author to the work, we find what we might have expected—a further variety of approaches. In chapter 9 alone, Longinus uses at least five different approaches—all of which are now loosely denominated "criticism."

After discussing the workings of a Homeric passage, he enthuses:

Here Homer blows upon the fires of battle like a directing wind, and his own feelings can be described as:

Mad, as Ares is mad when hurling his spear,
As is deadly fire raging on the hills
Or in the forest deep; and from his lips
Foam started. . . . (Pp.14-15)

Such a passage reminds one of Pope's comment (following Boileau) that Longinus was "*himself* that great *Sublime* he draws."[6] Or, more pertinently, of Gibbon's remark:

> Till now, I was acquainted only with two ways of criticizing a beautiful passage: the one, to show, by an exact anatomy of it, the distinct beauties of it, and from whence they sprung; the other, an idle exclamation, or a general encomium, which leaves nothing behind it. Longinus has shown me that there is a third. He tells me his own feelings upon reading it and tells them with such energy that he communicates them. I almost doubt which is most sublime, Homer's battle of the gods, or Longinus's apostrophe to Terentianus upon it.[7]

Such enthusiastic displays by Longinus are indeed similar at times to Hazlitt's impressionism, and yet Longinus never lets the tendency get out of hand, never, for all his figurative style, attempts to turn his treatise itself into a work of art.

In the passage following the enthusiastic praise of Homer occurs Longinus's comparison of the *Odyssey* and the *Iliad*. His very attempt to determine which of the works was written first is an example of literary history, albeit of the speculative variety, and the comparative approach itself is characteristic of Longinus, as well as of a later critic, T. S. Eliot. The analysis of literary techniques to describe their role in producing great writing likewise occurs in chapter 9 and throughout the *Peri Hupsous*. Very little of this sort of detailed scrutiny of passages would occur again outside of straightforward rhetorics until the New-Critical movement of the twentieth century.

In a final literary approach, the evaluative, Longinus was less of a pioneer and more like Aristotle and Horace. For although Longinus is prone to say what he thinks of each author, his criticisms are incidental to his discussions of great writing in general; that is, they are not judgments in their own right. There is, nevertheless, a good deal more evaluation in Longinus than in his predecessors. Longinus is likewise in a sense more modern in his criticism than Aristotle, who is interested more in the overall structure of longer works. Longinus sticks mostly to short passages, which perhaps places him in an extreme position beyond the modern exegetic critic; the only poem he treats in entirety is Sappho's "Ode." Longinus, however, follows Aristotle and Horace in emphasizing organic unity, as a look at chapter 10 or 40 will substantiate.

iii

Underlying the evaluations in the *Peri Hupsous* is literary theory. Although the treatise is ostensibly concerned with one literary quality, it is the quality that is productive of great literature, and so Longinus is really dealing with what might be called literature at its best. That is, the focusing in this case does not actually narrow the scope of the treatise. Most works of literary theory are concerned primarily with literature worthy of the description "great."

On the face of it, much if not all of the *Peri Hupsous* may seem to fall outside the tradition begun by Aristotle and transmitted by Horace. Emphasis on passion and feeling, not to say enthusiasm, seems perhaps to point to a place for Longinus in the Romantic tradition. Favoring this view is Longinus's concern with the personality of the poet, his notion of the inspired bard, and his frequent metaphors of enthusiasm. His occasional critical impressionism, mentioned above, is also evidence of Romantic tendencies.

But although Longinus was admired by the eighteenth-century "Pre-Romantics" and obviously influenced them, he was clearly not a proponent of Romantic license. In chapter 2, for example, he leaves little doubt as to where he stands:

> Great qualities are too precarious when left to themselves, unsteadied and unballasted by knowledge, abandoned to mere impulse and untutored daring; they need the bridle as well as the spur. (P. 5)

And, as Saintsbury points out, Longinus is basically commonsensical even in pursuit of the mystical.[8] What impressionism there is, furthermore, is held under control. It is with good reason that the nineteenth century, during which the Romantic tradition flourished, had little use for Longinus; the *Peri Hupsous* might as well have never been written for all the stir it then made.

This lack of interest is ironic, for Longinus is easily the most open-minded of the classical theorists. He did in fact serve as a liberalizing influence in the eighteenth century; he was a major force in restraining the rule mongering of Neoclassical Rationalism, so rampant early in the century. Longinus was even put to use in the struggle against the Rules.

One of the insistent notes sounded in the *Peri Hupsous* is that rules are insufficient to produce greatness. Longinus is especially flexible when it comes to diction (chaps. 31-32), but the best-known instance of his critical liberalism occurs in chapter 33:

> Preciseness in every detail incurs the risk of pettiness, whereas with the very great, as with the very rich, something must inevitably be neglected. It is perhaps also inevitable that inferior and average talent remains for the most part safe and faultless because it avoids risk and does not aim at the heights, while great qualities are always precarious because of their very greatness. Nor am I unaware of this further point: that in all human endeavors it is natural for weaknesses to be more easily recognized; the memory of failures remains ineffaceable while successes are easily forgotten. (Pp. 44-45)

W. K. Wimsatt, Jr., on the evidence of passages like the above, goes as far as to suggest that Longinus was a bit *too* open-minded, that he never considers that a mediocre writer might be riddled with faults and the great writer have very few of them[9]

Longinus's overall flexibility, nevertheless, is not really flexibility born of chaos; he has no lack of principles. He stands, in fact, between the extremes of lawlessness and rule-mongering; his literary theory is based on principles and is nurtured by an empirical approach. The principles must be sought out and will be examined shortly. The empiricalness on the other hand is quite explicit at points (as in chap. 39): "Perhaps it is foolish even to question matters so generally accepted, for experience is sufficient proof" (p. 52).

For purposes of evaluation, Longinus set forth some empirical criteria in chapter 7:

> Our soul is naturally uplifted by the truly great; . . . we are filled with delight and pride. . . .
>
> Any piece of writing which is heard repeatedly by a man of intelligence and experience yet fails to stir his soul to noble thoughts and does not leave impressed upon his mind reflections which reach beyond what was said, and which on further observation is seen to fade and be forgotten—that is not truly great writing, as it is only remembered while it is before us. . . .
>
> Consider truly great and beautiful writing to be that which satisfies all men at all times. (P. 10)

Longinus gives no abstract definitions of great writing; he here provides the reader with practical tests: (1) which works or passages please? (2) which please again and again? and (3) which have continued to please down through the ages? Each question provides a greater degree of empirical reliability.

Longinus, moreover, generally sticks close to a text and seems to wish to illustrate every observation. Rarely are we asked to take anything on faith. Over eighty quotations in the extant manuscript invite the reader to judge for himself, and the main approaches used—close analysis and comparison—both have that same effect.

iv

That the reader *can* judge for himself often depends on the concept of mimesis, on discerning a close relationship between the literature in question and life. In other words, besides the triad author-reader-work, Longinus pays a good deal of attention to a fourth element—the universe as represented in a work of literature. Longinus's mimetic principle is most explicit in his discussion of hyperbaton in chapter 22. He begins by explaining that this figure, a dislocation of word order, is effective because it reflects the way the speech of men "in real life" is affected by emotions; then he comments: "The best writers imitate this aspect of real life by means of hyperbata. For *art at its best is mistaken for nature*, and nature is successful when it contains hidden art" (p.33, italics added). Later in the chapter Longinus speaks of the "impression of actuality" (p. 34), an expression repeated in the following chapter. Besides the discussion of hyperbaton, Longinus makes a constant appeal to the conditions of real life in his analysis of literary devices; in the tradition of mimetic theorists, he often finds that poetic devices are used to reflect the poetic situation.

As in Horace, imitation can also refer to imitation of past literary models. The most prolonged passage occurs in chapter 13:

> Plato shows us . . . that there is another road to greatness . . . , the emulation and imitation of the great prose writers and poets of the past. This . . . is an aim we should never abandon. Many a man derives inspiration from another spirit in the same way as the Pythian priestess at Delphi, when she approaches the tripod at the place where there is a cleft in the ground, is said to inhale a divine vapor; thus at once she becomes impregnated with divine power and, suddenly inspired, she utters oracles. So from the genius of the ancients exhalations flow, as from the sacred clefts, into the minds of those who emulate them, and even those little inclined to inspiration become possessed by the greatness of others. (P. 22)

Longinus is still more liberal about such imitation than Horace, who is quite liberal in his own right. With Longinus, however, imitation involves a complex mental, perhaps even spiritual, process, and might even be called simply "inspiration." Any sense of copying has disappeared. Connected with this imitation is another passage in the following chapter (14): "And it is right for us, too, whenever we are laboring over a piece of writing which requires greatness in thought or expression, to imagine how Homer might perchance have said it, how Plato or Demosthenes, or in history Thucydides, would have made it great" (p. 23). We have here almost a prefigurement of Matthew Arnold's touchstones, except that here the comparison of passages is to be performed by the writer, not the critic, and it is unnecessary to have in mind specific passages from the past.

Just as mimesis is not set forth in so many words as a literary principle, so, too, with universality. In fact, the universality of literature is the most elusive of Longinus's basic views and must be found largely by implication. While there is enough evidence to conclude that Longinus believed in mimesis, for example, there is every reason to believe from his remarks on great writing that it would not stop at a simple realism. Great writers, he tells us in chapter 36, "reach a more than human level. Other qualities prove writers to be men, greatness raises them close to the nobility of a divine mind" (p. 48).

Another indication of Longinus's belief in the universality of literature is the test of time. We have already seen that in chapter 7 Longinus gives us the endurance of a work as a criterion of its greatness; in chapter 14 he claims that the work of a potentially great author "looks beyond his own life and time" (p. 23), and, in chapter 36 that the greatness of the best writers will endure. This conviction of the endurance of great writing points to a belief in literary universality in the existence of enduring types, or of other elements in literature that transcend the accidents of any age and appeal to every age. Nothing that emphasizes the particular and the topical could have this quality. The method of comparison between authors and works separated in time, moreover, illustrates a belief in this transcendent quality.

V

Poetry, according to Horace, should both teach and please. The category of pleasure in Longinus's theories is perhaps easiest to discover and recall, for great writing leads, we are told, to the transport of the reader. In chapter 7, Longinus observes: "Our soul is naturally uplifted by the truly great; we receive it as a joyous offering; we are filled with delight" (p. 10). But the teaching complement is also not far to seek. At the opening of chapter 36, we are told that the greatness of writers "is ever of use and benefit to us" (p. 48). And when we turn back to chapter 7, we find something very like the Horatian formula if we combine the following with the quotation on pleasure (above), which directly precedes it: great writing when "heard repeatedly by a man of intelligence and experience" is said "to stir his soul to noble thoughts" and to "leave impressed upon his mind reflections which reach beyond what was said" (p. 10). The instruction is apparently accomplished in a more indirect way, more like Aristotle's view of the matter than Horace's. It presents, in addition, a kind of prefiguring of the course the moral view of literature would take in the early nineteenth century. There is also, it should be noted, a more narrow view of instruction and of the morality of literature in general in chapter 9, where Longinus comments on a Homeric quotation: "These things are terrifying; yet from another point of view they are, *unless understood allegorically,* altogether impious and transgress the boundaries of good taste" (p. 13, italics added).

Morality in any event is certainly a major consideration in Longinus's concept of great writing. He is concerned especially with the character and moral values of the writer (chap. 9):

A true writer's mind can be neither humble nor ignoble. Men whose thoughts and concerns are mean and petty throughout life cannot produce anything admirable or worthy of lasting fame. The authors of great works are en-

v Critical variety, complete with an organic view of struc-
e.[15]

Longinus was part of the tradition begun by Aristotle, and
later influenced that tradition, especially by his flexibility.
e Aristotle's *Poetics*, his *Peri Hupsous* dropped from sight
many centuries, and the tenure of his importance and in-
nce was relatively short, especially when compared to
t of either Horace or Aristotle. And yet there is a freshness
l a vigor to his work that have stood his own test of time
ter than the others.

NOTES

William Wordsworth and Dorothy Wordsworth, *The Letters of William and
hy Wordsworth: The Later Years* ed. Ernest De Selincourt (Oxford, 1939), 1:194;
ge Saintsbury, *A History of Criticism*, 3 vols. (New York, 1950), 1:154; Arthur
ler-Couch, *Studies in Literature*, 3d ser. (New York, 1930), p. 143; Allen Tate,
nginus and the 'New Criticism,' " *Collected Essays* (Denver, Colo., 1959), p. 509;
rles S. Baldwin, *Ancient Rhetoric and Poetic* (Gloucester, Mass., 1959), p. 123.
  G. M. A. Grube, "Notes on the *Peri Hupsous*," *American Journal of Philology* 78
7):359.
  Longinus *On Great Writing*, trans. G. M. A. Grube (New York, 1957), p. 3. All
ations from the *Peri Hupsous* are from this edition; subsequent references to this
appear in parentheses in the text.
  Walter Jackson Bate, ed., *Criticism: The Major Texts* (New York, 1952), p. 59.
  Something like Coleridge's distinction between fancy and imagination could,
ever, perhaps be seen in a remark made early in chapter 10: "There are, in every
ation, a number of features which combine to make up the texture of events.
elect the most vital of these and to relate them to one another to form a unified
le is an essential cause of great writing. One writer charms the reader by the
tion of such details, another by the manner in which he presses them into close
ionship" (p. 17).
  Alexander Pope, *Essay on Criticism*, line 680, in the Twickenham edition of the
s of Alexander Pope*, ed., John Butt, 6 vols. (New Haven, Conn., 1961), 1: 316.
  Edward Gibbon, *Journal*, ed. D. M. Low (London, 1929), 3 October 1762,
155-56.
  Saintsbury, *A History of Criticism*, 1:159.
  W. K. Wimsatt, Jr., and Cleanth Brooks, *Literary Criticism: A Short History* (New
k, 1965), p. 106.
). F. R. B. Godolphin, "The Basic Critical Doctrine of Longinus' *On the Sublime*,"
sactions of the American Philological Association* 68 (1937):172-83; Charles P. Segal,
psous* and the Problem of Cultural Decline in the *De Sublimitate*," *Harvard Studies
lassical Philology* 64 (1959):137, 139.

dowed with dignity of mind, and literary excellence belongs
to those of high spirit. (P. 12)

In this same vein is the well-known ending of the *Peri Hupsous*,
where a moral argument is preferred to a political. The moral
fiber of the writer is for Longinus clearly the ultimate source
of great writing, an idea that is close to Buffon's "The style
is the man," except that Longinus is concerned with more
than just style. Several scholars even consider Longinus's
moral position as part of a larger world view. F. D. B. Godolphin points up Longinus's religious beliefs, which do occur
in the text and have been ignored; C. P. Segal claims that
Longinus finds in *hupsous* "cosmic principles" with moral
implications, part of a " 'philosophy' of rhetoric."[10]

vi

Many of the particular literary views in the *Peri Hupsous*
are not original; in fact, Longinus was in this regard quite
eclectic. A good deal of his treatment of devices is in the rhetorical tradition, even though much is also his own—for example,
his reversing the order of treatment to deal with figures before
diction. The traditional organization of rhetoric is, as we have
seen, also discernible in the structure of the *Peri Hupsous*.
Caecilius's treatise, against which Longinus is arguing, is
known, moreover, to have contained a comparison of Demosthenes and Cicero, and it was probably from Caecilius that
Longinus learned of Genesis.

The two most important sources, however, were probably
Horace and Plato. Horace provided the test of time, the danger
of making one error when avoiding another, the limits of correctness, and even the occasional nodding of Homer. Plato
afforded the aspiration for the divine, the moral ideal, concern
for the poet, and interest in imagination and inspiration; even
the questioning in chapter 2 probably has it origins in Socratic
questioning in the dialogues. The organic view of literature,

originated by Plato but emphasized by Aristotle, might also be mentioned.

But these are merely individual literary ideas found here and there in the *Peri Hupsous*. Vastly more important are the underlying literary principles, especially Longinus's moral and mimetic concepts. It is on the basis of these that Longinus rests securely in the Aristotelian tradition.

vii

The history of the *Peri Hupsous* is easier to trace than that of either the *Poetics* or the *Ars Poetica*. The main influence of Longinus's treatise was confined pretty nearly to a 125-year span. Like the *Poetics*, the *Peri Hupsous* was resurrected in the sixteenth century. Robortello brought out an edition as early as 1554, but, in spite of numerous translations and commentaries, no real interest was aroused for over one hundred years. During that time the work was treated as just another classical rhetoric.

Then, in 1674, Boileau published his French translation, and that translation, especially his famous preface, popularized Longinus throughout Europe. Longinus from 1674 until about the end of the eighteenth century was an important critical force. As has been mentioned, his treatise had a liberalizing influence on the period, perhaps even helped to contain the Neoclassical Rationalist tradition. The height of his reputation occurred about 1783, with a gradual decline to the end of the century.

His influence was not confined to literary theory, however. His ideas were probably behind the rage for periphrasis in eighteenth-century English poetry, even though he warned against the abuse of the device as well as promoted its use. Josephine Miles goes so far as to call one poetic mode of the period in England the "Sublime Mode," a title that implies a good deal of Longinian influence.[11] Longinus was also adopted by the aestheticians in England, but in their case

his influence was indirect. They treated Lo[...] as a guide, but as a point of departure. E[...] example, never deals with Longinus in h[...] *Beautiful* (1757). By the time of Kant, Lon[...] universality had been transformed into i[...] jectivism.

Although Longinus's influence can per[...] as one of the causes of the new impressionisr[...] in creative theory found in the nineteenth c[...] but ignored in the century as far as public[...] Arthur Quiller-Couch has suggested severa[...] slight—namely, that Longinus's acceptance[...] counter to the new Romantic love of freed[...] completeness of his treatment of the subjec[...] was not conducive to further comment.[12] D[...] ulates on an additional reason—that Longi[...] inspiration were commonplace by the nine[...] Another reason might be found in his major[...] izing influence. In the nineteenth century, w[...] tradition well under way, there would no l[...] for a liberalizing force—quite the contrary.[...]

In the twentieth century, there has been [...] like a revival of the *Peri Hupsous*, but Longi[...] a good deal of scholarly attention, and reco[...] given to his compatibility with modern lite[...] cially those of the New Criticism. T. R. He[...] a follower of I. A. Richards at the time, pub[...] study of the applicability of Longinus's views[...] ature. Henn pushed the organic concept and[...] ginus's idea of transport as a prefiguremer[...] psychological synthesis.[14] Allen Tate, a New[...] very nearly transforms Longinus's views in[...] doctrine. For example, Longinus is said to di[...] texture and structure in a manner similar[...] Ransom; and Tate finds in Longinus's app[...] of tension or paradox, as well as a linguistic[...]

11. Josephine Miles, *Eras and Modes in English Poetry* (Berkeley, Calif., 1964), pp. 48-49.

12. Quiller-Couch, *Studies in Literature*, pp. 157-61.

13. D. A. Russell, *Longinus on the Sublime* (Oxford, 1964), p. xlviii.

14. T. R. Henn, *Longinus and English Criticism* (Cambridge, 1934), pp.135-136.

15. Allen Tate, "Longinus and the 'New Criticism,' " *Collected Essays* (Denver, Colo., 1959), pp. 512, 520.

Sir Philip Sidney

i

Between Longinus in the early Christian period and Sir Philip Sidney in the English Renaissance, there was not much written about literature beyond rhetorical treatises. No one at least has made a claim for the greatness of literary theory written by any figure in the intervening period. Sidney, however, brings the fallow period to an end, for he is clearly an important figure in the history of literary criticism, with the testimony of modern scholars sufficient to establish his high reputation. Praise abounds for Sidney not only as the first great and lasting critic in English, but he is also seen as a kind of epitome of the best in English Renaissance criticism.

Joel E. Spingarn went beyond such an estimate to claim that Sidney was "a veritable epitome of the literary criticism of the Italian Renaissance."[1] This claim reinforces Sidney's representative quality while it underlines two points that must be made early in a discussion of Sidney: that the literary theory of the Italian Renaissance had a tremendous influence on English Renaissance theory and that Sidney was especially eclectic in his main literary thought, was especially influenced by continental theory.

A good deal of work has been done tracing Sidney's debts, which are as considerable as Spingarn suggests. For instance, Sidney apparently borrowed the concept of the Unities from Scaliger and Castelvetro, the idea of the poet as second creator from Scaliger, and the point that tragedy evokes "admiration" from Minturno. Besides these main Italian sources, Sidney dipped into the works of a list of theorists that resembles a roll call of the Italian Renaissance: Boccaccio, Robortello,

Landino, Tressino, Daniello. Classical theory also had a profound influence on Sidney, but that influence on the whole was exerted indirectly through the Italian commentators on classical treatises, especially on those of Plato and Aristotle. Horace had a more direct influence, as seen in Sidney's borrowing of such concepts as the poet as seer and the Horatian formula. Sidney, furthermore, relied largely on Latin translations of Aristotle and Plato made by Italians, and misrenderings sometimes affected his own ideas of what Aristotle and Plato had said.

The French had little influence on Elizabethan criticism, but Sidney was possibly affected by the new dialectical approach of Ramus (*vide infra*). Something like an English "tradition" also existed, for there was a new nationalism in England that resisted outside cultural domination. Traces of borrowings from Sir Thomas Elyot, Thomas Lodge, and George Whetstone are to be found here and there in the *Apology*.

It is not surprising, then, that Sidney is considered less than original in the outlines of his main ideas and even in some of his less important points. But he is generally esteemed for what he does with all his borrowings, for forming of them a coherent and forceful defense of poetry. There have, nevertheless, been a few adverse comments even on the organization. J. W. H. Atkins complained that Sidney does not always assimilate his material well. As evidence, Atkins cites Sidney's inconsistencies on the subject of *ars metrica*. Indeed, Sidney had followed Aristotle in his concept that versification is inessential to poetry and then combined that concept with the three categories of poetry borrowed from the Italians. According to his first position, Sidney's second category of poetry—philosophy versified—should not have been considered poetry at all.[2] Sidney's mixture of Platonic concepts with Aristotelian mimetic theory proved unsatisfactory too, as we shall see.

As with all the works containing literary theory examined so far, the date of the composition of Sidney's *Apology* is uncertain. It was probably not written before 1579, and the most likely years are 1581-83. The latter date, 1583, is the one usually given. The *Apology* was first published posthumously in 1595 but undoubtedly circulated in manuscript soon after written.

The title of Sidney's treatise likewise follows the pattern so far encountered in the Aristotelian tradition. In this case, we are confronted, not with a popular title nor one that is misleading, but with two titles, both of which are correct. In 1595 Sidney's work was published in two separate editions, one by William Ponsonby entitled *The Defence of Poesie* and the other by Henry Olney entitled *An Apology for Poetrie.*

Both titles serve to place the general form of Sidney's work. The Renaissance was preeminently a literary culture, and literary discussions took many forms. Of these, W. K. Wimsatt, Jr., has discerned four major genres: (1) versified arts of poetry, such as Vida's *De Arte Poetica* (1527); (2) treatises on poetics, such as Scaliger's *Poetice* (1561); (3) prefaces and treatises retorting against specific classicist objections, such as Tasso's *Discorsi* (1594); and (4) apologetic essays answering classicist objections to vernacular literature or puritanical outcries against the immorality of literature.[3] Sidney's *Apology* obviously falls into the last category.

Such defenses were a popular form in Renaissance England, others being written by Willis, Lodge, Rainolds, and Puttenham. In itself the popularity of the form should warn one against supposing that the literary defense was an affected genre, contrived merely as just another way of setting forth one's views on literary matters. Attacks on literature were in fact prevalent in the period. Some better-known attacks on the continent were Savanarola's in Italy (1492) and Cornelius Agrippa's in Germany (1527). In England there were attacks by Thomas Drant (1567) and Stephen Gosson (1579). Gosson was answered directly by Thomas Lodge in the same year, and Gosson's pamphlet, *School of Abuse,* has traditionally been assumed to be the primary occasion of Sidney's *Apology,* with note usually taken of the heavy irony that Gosson dedicated his work to Sidney. J Bronowski, in *The Poet's Defence*, admits that Sidney does not really answer Gosson and that the bases of both writers were the same, but proceeds anyway to examine closely Sidney's arguments as rebuttals to Gosson's, and even claims that we cannot understand Sidney without Gosson.[4]

Other scholars, however, have remarked that no direct connection necessarily exists between the two works. And in the most recent large-scale treatment of the *Apology*, Geoffrey Shepherd rejects the idea of Sidney's rebuttal of Gosson altogether, observing that Gosson was "an Oxford hack" unworthy of such attention and that their attitudes were in general alike.[5] Gosson was not a Calvinistic Puritan, as is so often claimed, but, like Sidney, was a sort of puritanical Anglican. There were, furthermore, other attacks (mentioned above), and Sidney could just as well have had any one of them or the whole lot in mind, or perhaps no written attack at all. He followed the traditional lines of argument in defense of poetry and differs from other apologists mainly in attempting a complete statement.

Of the major texts of literary theory examined so far, the *Apology*, moreover, is the first document both complete and orderly. In 1935 K. O. Myrick demonstrated that the basic form of the *Apology* belongs to a rhetorical tradition for centuries parallel to but outside that of literary criticism.[6] In the Renaissance there was a particularly close relationship between poetry and rhetoric; often, in fact, little distinction was made between them. Thus there should be no surprise at finding that the construction of the *Apology* in its entirety follows a classical form of oration—the judicial. Even the language reflects this legal genre, and transitions dividing the various sections show that the *Apology* was written according to recipe. There are seven sections, each with its traditional title, plus a recommended digression (on English poetry). Minor rhetorical precepts are also followed.

Myrick's scheme is now generally accepted. In fact, only

one scholar has challenged it. G. W. Hallam has recently argued that Sidney was not following a traditional rhetorical plan, but that he organized the work under the influence of Peter Ramus, a French logician of the sixteenth century. Instead of the seven-part rhetorical division, Hallam finds ten "topical places" in the *Apology*.[7] Others, moreover, have discerned what appear to be nonstructural divisions in Sidney's work, cutting the *Apology* into either three or four parts. Geoffrey Shepherd has observed the difficulty involved in remembering Sidney's argument, partly due to the ease with which he makes his case.[8] Indeed, Sidney practiced what was called *sprezzatura*, "artless art"; and thus, in spite of following a fairly complex plan of organization, that plan is not apparent.

ii

Like Aristotle and Horace before him, Sidney intended a great deal more by the word *poetry* than mere verse. Following them, he rejected the concept of *ars metrica*:

> The greatest part of Poets have apparelled their poeticall inuentions in that numbrous kinde of writing which is called verse: indeed but apparelled, verse being but an ornament and no cause to Poetry, sith there haue beene many most excellent Poets that neuer versified, and now swarme many versifiers that neede neuer aunswere to the name of Poets.[9]

And yet, when discussing contemporary poetry, Sidney sticks closely to works in verse.

His evaluation of particular literary works, in any event, is still largely incidental and is confined for the most part to his digression on English poetry. In order to appreciate adequately what there is, however, one should recall (1) that the Renaissance as a whole was antagonistic toward medieval literature, and (2) that if Sidney seems to sell Elizabethan literature short, it is probably because the great works of the period had yet to be written.

Turning from practical criticism to creative theory, we find that Sidney does see the poet as to high degree creative, but that even less of such theory than literary evaluation turns up in the *Apology*. For, in spite of his interest in creativity, Sidney never examines nor describes the process itself. At one point he even tells us his interests lie elsewhere: "I speak of the Arte, and not of the Artificer" (p. 169). The creativity of the poet is nevertheless involved in Sidney's concept of mimesis (to be discussed later). Sidney's view of poetic creation is more limited than it may seem to us living after the nineteenth century, and yet surely W. K. Wimsatt is correct in assuming that that view must have encouraged the later idea of the creative imagination.[10]

iii

No one has more right to be called the Father of English Criticism than Sir Philip Sidney, if by *criticism* we mean *literary theory*. The *Apology* had, of course, a practical purpose and a specific form to fit that purpose, but, although it was not a theoretical treatise, literary theory must underlie Sidney's arguments.

Much of that theory, as we have seen, was derivative. The sources of Sidney's ideas are difficult to sort out—although most of the source hunters do not like to admit it—because many of those ideas were commonplaces of the time. This is especially true of the literary ideas of Aristotle and Horace, which were available to Sidney in original form, in translations of varying accuracy, and by intellectual osmosis.

The literary theory that underlies the *Apology* in fact falls in the tradition begun by Aristotle and continued by Horace. But Sidney stands at a fork where the Neoclassical Rationalist tradition branches off to become a tradition almost in its own right. Sidney, in other words, shows signs of influence by the Italian Aristotelians (especially Scaliger), whose theories were beginning to harden into dogma and rules. Although Sidney's theories had by no means "set" in the concrete forms of the English Neoclassical Rationalists under the French influence of the later seventeenth century, a crust was beginning to form.

Sidney's concept of mimesis—the close relationship of literature to life—was relatively unaffected by this influence except on incidental points, such as the Unities, arising from the hardening of mimesis into strict verisimilitude. But Sidney himself tampered with Aristotle's theory of mimesis. As noted above in chapter 2, that theory involves creativity from its connection with Aristotle's concept of the universality of literature. Possibly to avoid the new trend away from such creativity toward a more static realism in the interpretation of mimesis, Sidney attempted to intermix Plato's concept of ideal forms, not, as in Aristotle's metaphysical solution, as imminent in the concrete, but as forming "another nature," a "golden" world created by the poet.

As C. S. Lewis has demonstrated, Sidney performs a bit of a juggling act when he comes to define poetry.[11] First he stresses what amounts to "Platonic creativity":

> Onely the Poet, disdayning to be tied to any such subiection, lifted vp with the vigor of his owne inuention, dooth growe in effect another nature, in making things either better then Nature bringeth forth, or, quite a newe, formes such as neuer were in Nature, as the *Heroes, Demigods, Cyclops, Chimeras, Furies,* and such like: so as hee goeth hand in hand with Nature, not inclosed within the narrow warrant of her guifts, but freely ranging onely within the Zodiack of his owne wit. (P. 156)

Then, since this view might be considered "too sawcie," Sidney decides to give "a more ordinary opening" of the poet's function:

> Poesie therefore is an arte of imitation, for so *Aristotle*

termeth it in his word *Mimesis,*, that is to say, a representing, counterfetting, or figuring foorth : to speake metaphorically, a speaking picture: with this end, to teach and delight. (P. 158)

After thus dropping Aristotle's name as an authority, Sidney nevertheless reverts to the concept of creativity with a Platonic cast. Of the third kind of poets, he remarks:

These third be they which most properly do imitate to teach and delight, and to imitate borrow nothing of what is, hath been, or shall be: but range, onely rayned with learned discretion, into the diuine consideration of what may be, and should be. (P. 159)

Notice that by adding "may be" to Aristotle's "should be" Sidney is subverting Aristotle's strictures against the merely possible. The whole idea of the three kinds of poetry, moreover, was taken from Minturno and Scaliger, and Scaliger also provided the idea of the second world created by the poet. This conflict between Aristotelian and Platonic views and that described above between Sidney's own anti–*ars-metrica* position and the second category of poets show this to be the section of the *Apology* in which sources are least well assimilated.

The imagery by which Aristotle and Plato illustrated their mimetic views was significant; so too in the case of Sidney. He did not use Plato's figure of the mirror, with its delusionist implications, but adopted Aristotle's figure of a painting as illustrating mimesis. In a passage quoted above he calls poetry "a speaking picture," and he uses the painting metaphor time and again in the *Apology*. Plato, as we saw, also uses the metaphor of a picture but viewed painting as strictly realistic. Sidney follows Aristotle instead in seeing painting as presenting an interpretative view of the world. In comparing the versifying philosophers and the imitative poets, he comments that they present such a kinde of difference as betwixt the meaner sort of Painters (who counterfet onely such faces as are sette before them) and the more excellent, who, hauing no law but wit, bestow that in cullours vpon you which is fittest for the eye to see : as the constant though lamenting looke of *Lucrecia* when she punished in her selfe an others fault; wherein he painteth not *Lucrecia* whom he neuer sawe, but painteth the outwarde beauty of such a vertue. (P. 159)

Poetry (and painting) conveys for Sidney Aristotle's idea of a heightened reality, one that is universalized.

That Plato's concept of ideal forms became involved in Sidney's essentially Aristotelian theory of mimesis was perhaps inevitable, for, according to Baxter Hathaway, the concept of the universal to most Renaissance theorists meant Plato's idealism.[12] In any event, Sidney otherwise follows Aristotle's concept of the universal as inherent in the particular; the *Apology* even mimics the *Poetics* with a comparison of poetry with history and philosophy. And when dealing with the question of universality, Sidney cites and quotes Aristotle as his authority:

Truely, *Aristotle* himselfe, in his discourse of Poesie, plainely determineth this question, saying that Poetry is *Philosopho-teron* and *Spoudaioteron,* that is to say, it is more Philosophicall and more studiously serious then history. His reason is, because Poesie dealeth with *Katholou,* that is to say, with the vniuersall consideration; and the history with *Kathekaston,* the perticuler: "nowe," sayth he, "the vniuersall wayes what is fit to bee sayd or done, eyther in likelihood or necessity, (which the Poesie considereth in his imposed names), and the perticuler only marks whether *Alcibiades* did, or suffered, this or that." Thus farre Aristotle. (P. 167)

In fact, Sidney renders for the Aristotelian tradition something like the classic phrasing of the universality of literature: the poet "coupleth the generall notion with the particuler example" (p. 164)

In a pinch, Sidney does fall back on Aristotelian univer-

sality. When confronted by the accusation that poetry consists
solely of lies, Sidney at first resorts to a simple argument—
namely, that "the Poet . . . nothing affirmes, and therefore
neuer lyeth" (p. 184). This argument, however, only means
that one should not confuse poetry with actual or historical
fact. He then continues his case by referring to Aristotelian
universals as containing the embodied truth of poetry: the
poet does not labor "to tell you what is, or is not, but what
should or should not be" (p. 185). But it is interesting that
Sidney neither relies on the essential truth of universality as
his sole argument nor even stresses it, as if he did not understand himself the full implications of his theory.

iv

Although under a great deal of pressure to resort to a priori
logic and to the potent voices of classical authority, Sidney
fortunately maintained an empirical approach, the kind de-
cribed by Sidney himself in the following passage:

> But when *by the ballance of experience* it was found that the
> Astronomer looking to the starres might fall into a ditch,
> that the enquiring Philosopher might be blinde in himselfe,
> and the Mathematician might draw foorth a straight line
> with a crooked hart; then loe, did *proofe, the ouer ruler of
> opinions*, make manifest that all these are but seruing Sci-
> ences. (P. 161, italics added)

Later on, Sidney makes it clear in an aside that he values
actual experience by pointing out that under discussion are
only those plays "that I haue seene" (p. 196). Sidney also relies
on "experiments" rather than posing as a self-made authority
expecting instant faith; in dismissing most of contemporary
poetry, he adds:

> For proofe whereof, let but most of the verses bee put in
> Prose, and then aske the meaning; and it will be found that
> one verse did but beget another, without ordering at the

first what should be at the last; which becomes a confused masse of words, with a tingling sound of ryme, barely accompanied with reason. (P. 196)

Additional evidence of an empirical approach is Sidney's constant use of examples to support his statements.

Sidney's reliance on experience, on the inductive method, provides a sound basis for a critical flexibility not always found in later or earlier Renaissance criticism. Sidney, for instance, indulges in generous praise of *Chevy Chase* in spite of his typical Renaissance disdain for the Middle Ages: he admires the ballad in spite of its "rude stile" and its "being so euill apparrelled in the dust and cobwebbes of that vnciuill age" (p. 178). At another point Sidney presents a sensible, empirical argument that is quite similar to one used later by Dr. Johnson in his demolition of the Unities:

> What childe is there that, comming to a Play, and seeing *Thebes* written in great Letters vpon an olde doore, doth beleeue that it is *Thebes*? If then a man can ariue, at that childs age, to know that the Poets persons and dooings are but pictures what should be, and not stories what haue beene, they will never giue the lye to things not affirmatiuely but allegorically and figuratiuelie written. (P. 185)

At still another point, Sidney takes a liberal stand in favor of poetic inspiration that is very like one taken later by John Keats: "For Poesie must not be drawne by the eares; it must be gently led, or rather it must lead" (p. 195).[13] And on the question of the imitation of past models, Sidney much more favors the unconscious, like Longinus, than the mechanical, like Horace:

> Truly I could wish, if at least I might be so bold to wish in a thing beyond the reach of my capacity, the diligent imitators of *Tullie* and *Demosthenes* (most worthy to be imitated) did not so much keep *Nizolian* Paper-bookes of their figures and phrases, as by attentiue translation (as it were) deuoure them whole, and make them wholly theirs. (P. 202)

Sidney's tolerance on the issues of quantitative verse and rhyme have also been noted.

Yet with all his hold on experience and all his flexibility, Sidney was a man of his times, probably more so than any other critic we shall deal with, and the times were moving in the direction of Neoclassical Rationalism.

v

Although partly a holdover from the Middle Ages, one example of the trend and Sidney's place in it is his stand on the purpose of literature. Horace, with his narrowly conceived view of the direct moral workings of literature, was here the obvious influence. The Horatian formula in fact is set forth again and again after its initial statement in Sidney's definition of poetry: "with this end, to teach and delight" (p. 158). But notice that the loophole in Horace's either/or formula has been plugged; here Sidney, following Scaliger, leaves no choice with his *and*.

In the Renaissance the Horatian formula was popular, with variety provided by a vacillation between emphasis on teaching and on pleasing. Only one theorist was strictly a Hedonist—Castelvetro. Sidney is nonetheless very enthusiastic in his attitude toward literature, and, while poetry must instruct, clearly the poet must delight, even excite, as well:

> With a tale forsooth he commeth vnto you, with a tale which holdeth children from play, and old men from the chimney corner. (P. 172)

Unlike the medieval and early Renaissance theorists, Sidney respects pleasure as a good per se. Indeed, one modern scholar was so struck by Sidney's views on aesthetic pleasure that she made the extraordinary claim that Sidney was sympathetic to art for art's sake.[14]

Instruction, however, the other side of the Horatian coin, gets even more attention from Sidney than does delight. Such

is perhaps to be expected in a defense of poetry from moral
attacks. In any case, the basis for Sidney's position is clearly
set forth: "The ending end of all earthly learning [is] vertuous
action" (p. 161). Within this larger view, teaching is accomplished almost solely by example:

> If the Poet doe his part a-right, he will shew you in *Tantalus,
> Atreus,* and such like, nothing that is not to be shunned; in
> *Cyrus, Aeneas, Vlisses,* each thing to be followed. (P. 168)

Sometimes, however, the teaching seems to be at one remove,
closer to one's forming a precept, or at least closer to understanding, than merely to following an example:

> Anger, the *Stoicks* say, was a short madnes : let but *Sophocles*
> bring you *Aiax* on a stage, killing and whipping Sheepe and
> Oxen, thinking them the Army of Greeks, with theyr Chiefe-
> taines *Agamemnon* and *Menelaus,* and tell mee if you haue not
> a more familiar insight into anger then finding in the
> Schoolemen his *Genus* and difference. (P. 165)

In any event, Sidney rejects a straightforward didactic pro-
cedure in literature; he prefers to have the stories of virtuous
men told to get at the morals, "which, if they had been barely,
that is to say Philosophically, set out, they [the listeners] would
sweare they bee brought to schoole againe" (pp. 172-73).

From traditional Ciceronian rhetoric, Sidney derived a
third purpose, to move, which is really an extension of the instruction portion of the formula within the ultimate purpose
of virtuous action. In Sidney's words,

> And that moouing is of a higher degree then teaching, it
> may by this appeare, that it is wel nigh the cause and the
> effect of teaching. (P. 171)

Delight fits into this operation by giving instruction the power
to move to action. Essentially it is the old concept of the sugar-
coated pill: delight provides the attraction, "euen as the childe

is often brought to take most wholsom things by hiding them in such other as haue a pleasant tast" (p. 172). The moving, however, sometimes takes channels other than strictly moral; literature can serve a social or political function, such as dissuading kings from tyranny (pp. 177-78). By and large, these attitudes of Sidney share with their Horatian source the condition of being fairly narrow ways of considering the morality of literature. Sidney rejects straightforward didacticism, the most direct means of inculcating morality, but he does accept the next most direct, teaching by example. These two views of the direct moral function of literature are in fact what people usually think of when literature and morality are said to have a connection. Sure enough, Sidney even takes the example method as far as it will go:

> Nowe, to that which commonly is attributed to the prayse of histories, in respect of the notable learning is gotten by marking the successe, as though therein a man should see vertue exalted and vice punished. Truely that commendation is peculiar to Poetrie, and farre of from History. For indeede Poetrie euer setteth vertue so out in her best cullours, making Fortune her wel-wayting hand-mayd, that one must needs be enamored of her. Well may you see *Vlisses* in a storme, and in other hard plights; but they are but exercises of patience and magnanimitie, to make them shine the more in the neere-following prosperitie. And of the contrarie part, if euill men come to the stage, they euer goe out . . . so manacled as they little animate folkes to followe them. (Pp. 169-70)

It is worth remembering that there is another, indirect view of the moral function of literature, that Aristotle utterly rejected the sort of poetic justice contained in the above quotation.

Sidney did, however, avoid the hard line at points. When confronted with immoral poetry, the kind that leads men "to wanton sinfulness and lustful love," there would appear no way for anyone ascribing to the direct moral working of literature to avoid rejecting such works from the ranks of literature (which is said to be moral). And yet Sidney accepts immoral works under the category "literature abused" (pp. 186-87).

vi

Besides the narrowness of theory reflected in Sidney's moral stance, there are incidental signs of the hardening of his literary theories, of the encroachment of Neoclassical Rationalism.

His stand on the Unities is one such instance. Based on misreadings of Aristotle and Horace, the doctrine of the Unities was already formulated in Italy by 1555. Sidney probably borrowed the doctrine from Scaliger or Castelvetro. Of *Gorboduc* Sidney comments:

It is faulty both in place and time, the two necessary companions of all corporall actions. For where the stage should alwaies represent but one place, and the vttermost time presupposed in it should be, both by *Aristotles* precept and common reason, but one day, there is both many dayes, and many places, inartificially imagined. (P. 197)

This is followed by a long castigation of contemporary drama as a whole, criticism likewise based, one must suppose, on classical authority and deductive reason. And yet, as we have already seen, Sidney himself had earlier in the *Apology* provided the Johnsonian empirical argument that would one day finish off the Unities once and for all: "What childe is there that, comming to a Play, and seeing *Thebes* written in great Letters vpon an olde doore, doth beleeue that it is *Thebes*?" (p. 185).

The concept of the Unities was part of a larger concept, decorum. Deriving from Horace, decorum became a major law for Renaissance criticism. Besides the Unities, decorum called for a certain typicality of characterization. In the *Ars*

Poetica such a stipulation occurs, and Sidney follows suit, praising art over nature for conceiving "so true a louer as *Theagines*, so constant a friende as *Pilades*, so valiant a man as *Orlando*, so right a Prince as *Xenophons Cyrus*, so excellent a man euery way as *Virgils Aeneas*" (p. 157). When dealing with comedy, moreover, Sidney discusses comic types. But the extent to which he believes characters should be typical beyond the concept of universality is not, I believe, clear.

Decorum also ruled over the concept of genres and, as the Renaissance waned, came more to insist on a rigid compartmentalization. Sidney held a traditional belief in genres, as his list of them in the *Apology* indicates, but the question of rigidity arises only with respect to tragicomedy. Basil Willey, for example, claimed that Sidney abhorred the mixing of the two genres.[15] In a passage attacking contemporary drama, Sidney cited

> how all theyr Playes be neither right Tragedies, nor right Comedies; mingling Kings and Clownes, not because the matter so carrieth it, but thrust in Clownes by head and shoulders, to play a part in maiesticall matters, with neither decencie nor descretion: So as neither the admiration and commiseration, nor the right sportfulnes, is by their mungrell Tragy-comedie obtained. (P. 199)

If, however, this passage and the one that follows it (comparing the more effective way tragic and comic elements are joined in classical examples) are examined closely, it becomes clear that Sidney is not objecting to the mixture of genres itself but only to the inept mingling of them. In an earlier passage, Sidney does indeed include "the Tragi-comicall" in a list of legitimate mixed genres, commenting as to their validity: "If seuered they be good, the coniunction cannot be hurtfull" (p. 175).

Also characteristic of the quickening trend toward Neoclassical Rationalism is the reliance on authority. Sidney is not free of the taint. In one form, early in the *Apology*, it is a harmless enough, if not in fact a valid, point of view.

> But since the Authors of most of our Sciences were the
> Romans, and before them the Greekes, let vs a little stand
> vppon their authorities. (Pp. 153-54)

Fitting in with this sentiment is Sidney's constant direct
reference to Plato, Aristotle, and Horace. Appeal to the past
is not by nature vicious; it *is*, I believe, of some significance
that what one says is in agreement with Plato or Aristotle or
Horace.

The use of authorities, however, is easily abused; the human
reluctance to get involved in the strenuous reasoning required
by argumentation does in fact draw one toward such abuse.
Later in the *Apology*, for instance, Sidney objects to Spenser's
use of archaisms with the following words:

> That same framing of his stile to an old rustick language
> I dare not alowe, sith neyther *Theocritus* in Greeke, *Virgill*
> in Latine, nor *Sanazar* in Italian did affect it. (P. 196)

Such passages are always embarrassing when encountered in
an otherwise empirical, sensible critic, but, to be fair to Sidney,
this is the worst instance of it. And Sidney in the humorous
ending to the *Apology* seems to be aware of the abuse of invoking
authority when he ironically indulges himself by composing
a litany to Aristotle, Bembo, Scaliger, Clauserus, Landino, and
himself as witnesses to various truths.

Sidney is both an epitome of Renaissance critical thought
and, with parts of his *Apology* beginning to harden, an example
of the encroachment of Neoclassical Rationalism on that
thought. But he is more than representative. Although of the
major critics we are dealing with he is the most reliant on direct
borrowings, the most clearly a part of his age, and the easiest
to place in time, his theory partakes of greatness in his distil-
lation of these elements and his informing them with life. He
is, moreover, part of a live tradition. One scholar has noted
Sidney's conservatism, another his prognostication of criticism
that followed.[16] In other words, Sidney is part of a tradition—
the central tradition leading from Aristotle to the present.

NOTES

1. Joel E. Spingarn, *A History of Literary Criticism in the Renaissance* (New York, 1963), p. 170.

2. J. W. H. Atkins, *English Literary Criticism: The Renascence* (London, 1947), p. 118.

3. W. K. Wimsatt, Jr., and Cleanth Brooks, *Literary Criticism: A Short History* (New York, 1965), pp. 156-57.

4. Jacob Bronowski, *The Poet's Defence* (Cleveland, 1966), pp. 21-22, 33, 38-39.

5. Geoffrey Shepherd, ed., *An Apology for Poetry* (London, 1965), pp. 2-3.

6. Kenneth O. Myrick, *Sir Philip Sidney as a Literary Craftsman* (Cambridge, Mass., 1935), chap. 2.

7. G. W. Hallam, "Sidney's Supposed Ramism, " *Renaissance Papers 1963* (Chapel Hill, N. C., 1963), pp. 11-20.

8. Shepherd, *Apology for Poetry*, p. 11.

9. G. G. Smith, ed., *Elizabethan Critical Essays*, 2 vols (Oxford, 1937), 1:159-160. All quotations from Sidney's *Apology* are taken from this edition; subsequent references to this work appear in parentheses in the text.

10. Wimsatt and Brooks, *Literary Criticism*, p. 171.

11. C. S. Lewis, *English Literature in the Sixteenth Century* (Oxford, 1954), p. 344.

12. Baxter Hathaway, *Marvels and Commonplaces: Renaissance Literary Criticism* (New York, 1968), p. 49.

13. Compare Keats's "If Poetry comes not as naturally as the Leaves to a tree it had better not come at all" (Keats to John Taylor, 27 February 1818).

14. Marguerite Hearsey, "Sidney's *Defense of Poesy* and Amyot's *Preface* in North's *Plutarch*: A Relationship," *Studies in Philology* 30 (1933) :536.

15. Basil Willey, *Tendencies in Renaissance Literary Theory* (Cambridge, 1922), p. 42. See also Walter Jackson Bate, ed., *Criticism: The Major Texts* (New York, 1952), p. 82.

16. F. E. Schelling, *Poetic and Verse Criticism of the Reign of Elizabeth* (Philadelphia, 1891), p. 96; Shepherd, *Apology for Poetry*, p. 17.

6

John Dryden

Early in his life of John Dryden, Dr. Johnson called him "the father of English criticism "; in this century T. S. Eliot echoed Johnson by naming Dryden "positively the first master of English Criticism."[1] Similar tributes are to be found in most of the commentators on Dryden's criticism, a fact that may at first surprise the reader new to Dryden's literary writings. Not that the *Essay of Dramatic Poesy* and its "Defense," as well as several other of his prefaces, are not most impressive. But it takes more exposure to Dryden's literary thought to recognize its scope and the extent to which Dryden established a sound basis for evaluation and actually practiced it. For there is a sufficient amount of literary evaluation in the bulk of his criticism to establish Dryden as the first practitioner in the history of literary criticism.

The extent of Dryden's organization of the literary theory underlying the evaluation is especially difficult to discern. Most of Dryden's literary criticism seems so clearly practical, either in the way of self-justification or in explanation of his own creative endeavors. The criticism is almost wholly contained in prefaces and usually concerns the subject matter prefaced, mainly drama and translation. The most important documents for literary theory are *An Essay of Dramatic Poesy*, "Defense of an Essay of Dramatic Poesy," "A Parallel of Poetry and Painting," and the "Preface to *Fables Ancient and Modern*."

The most famous and probably the most important of these is *An Essay of Dramatic Poesy*, which will be emphasized in the following discussion. It is the only critical work of Dryden published by itself, and it is the only one he ever revised, appearing in three editions during his lifetime. As a dialogue, it is also the most elaborate of his critical works. Pseudo-Platonic dialogues were popular at the time, but although the *Essay* has an overall dialogue form complete with setting and characters, it can only be said to be a dialogue in the widest sense, for there is no real exchange, no buildup of argument to speak of, only long expositions of critical views (which do, nonetheless, respond to each other). And the *Essay* is hardly Socratic either: there is nothing like Socrates' razor-sharp mind at work on a victim; in fact, there is no central figure in the dialogue at all. The beginning is more conversational, however, and both it and the lightly humorous ending are no doubt largely responsible for the lively quality so often ascribed to the *Essay*.

Some of the interest at the time the *Essay* was written possibly derived from recognition of the real people represented by those involved in the dialogue. First identified in print by Edmond Malone in 1800 and only lately questioned, the characters have recently been more or less firmly established: Lisideius (probably an anagram for the atticized "Sidleius"), Sir Charles Sedley; Crites, Sir Robert Howard, Dryden's brother-in-law; Eugenius (Greek for "wellborn"), Charles Sackville, Lord Buckhurst; and Neander (Greek for "new man" and almost and anagram for "Dryden"), John Dryden himself.

That not all of the characters' views are Dryden's is perhaps the most important point, for sometimes they are taken as such with the disastrous results that are easy to anticipate. And although Eugenius and Neander are sometimes with more logic considered to share the same views—and they are responsible for almost two-thirds of the bulk of the *Essay*—only Neander clearly represents Dryden. Neander by himself, nevertheless, has almost half the wordage, and, as has been observed, he has the advantage of speaking last.

The characters are also said to represent critical positions of the time; their stands in the Battle of the Books are especially notable. But they perhaps even can be placed on a sort of scale of basic literary theory from Neoclassical Rationalism (Crites) to the Aristotelian tradition (Neander). To the left of Crites, Lisideius might be seen as less strict with regard to the Unities and as more empirical; Eugenius would in this scheme be still less strict—he denies the Unities are classical, but argues (to the right of Neander) that the Ancients are not regular enough in their drama. If this view of a critical spectrum is valid, it is a testimony to Dryden's honesty that the other end of the scale is not represented as foolish or extremist, is not caricatured. Crites is not a bigot as one might possibly expect of a theorist holding Neoclassical Rationalist principles; he is quite reasonable in making concessions to the other side.

The extent of Dryden's justice in opposing Neander's views to the others' has been disputed. Allan H. Gilbert, for example, claims that the form of the *Essay* "is used less to present various sides of the truth than to make clear wrong positions to be refuted."[2] On the other hand, some scholars insist that Dryden was almost skeptical in his open-mindedness in presenting the other side. The truth, I believe, lies somewhere in between: since Dryden was a practicing playwright, and therefore personally concerned about arriving at some answers, there would be no point in misrepresenting positions or in setting up straw men. And yet Neander/Dryden's position is certainly not presented carelessly; Dryden was not all that skeptical.

ii

Dryden was, however, flexible in his literary theory. Perhaps that is what the claims of extreme and irresponsible skepticism amount to after all. His flexibility is important to establish for other reasons as well, for flexibility is a central criterion in distinguishing Dryden from those in the Neoclassical Rationalist tradition. By the time Dryden was writing, Neoclassical Rationalism had shifted from an Italian center of influence to France, and the return of the English Court from

France at the Restoration made the influence of that rigid tradition much more clearly felt in England than ever before. Several theorists succumbed more or less completely—for example, Thomas Rymer.[3]

Dryden's basic open-mindedness can be demonstrated in the *Essay* alone. Like Sidney, for example, Dryden was favorably disposed toward tragicomedy, thus rejecting a favorite Neoclassical Rationalist rule against so-called infractions against the unity of action: Neander makes a point in his defense of the English "that we have invented, increas'd and perfected a more pleasant way of writing for the Stage then was ever known to the Ancients or Moderns of any Nation, which is Tragicomedie."[4] And although Dryden argued that Restoration drama surpassed anything the Elizabethans did or could have done in verse drama, he still was sufficiently flexible to admit that the Elizabethans were nevertheless greater dramatists.[5] Such examples of critical flexibility abound elsewhere in Dryden's writings, but one more instance must suffice. In his "Heads of an Answer to Rymer" (1677, unpublished), Dryden demolishes a bulwark of Neoclassical Rationalist theory—appeal to authoritiy: " 'Tis not enough that *Aristotle* has said so, for *Aristotle* drew his Models of Tragedy from *Sophocles* and *Euripides*; and if he had seen ours, might have chang'd his Mind."[6]

There are even places in Dryden's essays where he seems too flexible, too ready to conform his theory to contemporary practice. An example in the *Essay* occurs where Neander apparently rejects Aristotle's strictures on spectacle and offers some remarks on mimesis that are surely beside the point: the English

will scarcely suffer combats & other objects of horrour to be taken from them. And indeed, the indecency of tumults is all which can be objected against fighting: For why may not our imagination as well suffer it self to be deluded with the probability of it, as with any other thing in the Play? For my part, I can with as great ease perswade my self that the blowes are given in good earnest, as I can, that they who strike them are Kings or Princes, or those persons which they represent.[7]

And yet in spite of such examples, Dryden can scarcely be categorized as licentious in his theory. Neander argues that the unity of time (twenty-four hours) is too constrictive, suggesting in less than an unrestrained manner that "two or three dayes" might be allowed.[8] I will discuss certain Neoclassical Rationalist tendencies in Dryden below.

At one time, Dryden's flexibility earned him the reputation of being extremely inconsistent. Either because of a weak character or the skepticism of the age, Dryden was seen to have vacillated widely in his critical career from one point to another and back again. One of the supposed inconsistencies concerned Dryden's opinions of Shakespeare's value; but Hoyt Trowbridge in 1943 successfully, I believe, refuted such a charge in an article on Dryden's "Essay of the Dramatic Poetry of the Last Age," a key work in the Shakespeare controversy.[9] Trowbridge simply points out that if Dryden's remarks on Shakespeare are read in context, without succumbing to bardolatry, Dryden's views amount to a qualification of previous (and subsequent) praise, not an about-face.

iii

The fundamental coherence of Dryden's literary theory is now generally admitted, with the kind of qualification necessary in dealing with theory spread out over a critical career of some thirty-six years. There are quite naturally some inconsistencies in particular literary pronouncements, for there is always some development in a literary theorist, even some simple change of heart. The best-known revisions in Dryden's views are the rather abrupt turnabouts in his views on rhyme and tragicomedy. But rarely does Dryden shift back and forth on issues; and on subordinate points, such as the need for an English prosody or the argument that poets make the best critics, Dryden can even be boringly repetitious if read in large doses.

Basic theory, such as the mimetic basis of literature and the Horatian formula, appears still more frequently in Dryden's essays, often with little variation in phrasing. These elements of basic theory will be discussed later separately and in more detail, but for the present it is important to see them as part of Dryden's whole literary method. Just above such rock-bottom theory as mimesis and purposiveness lies a second level of more specific (but still very general) literary principles, which Dryden calls "rules."

These "rules" are what Dryden is attempting to determine, for, as he says, "without rules there can be no art."[10] That is, some kind of rules or principles are not only useful but essential; without them, there is mere chaos in literary criticism, and each man must start from scratch to provide himself the means to speak intelligently about literature. I have already expended a good deal of effort to demonstrate Dryden's flexibility and must rely here on that demonstation to maintain that the rules for which Dryden is searching are not the hard-and-fast rules with which the Neoclassical Rationalists were so taken. What Dryden has in mind are the sort of loose rules he found in the wellspring of the tradition in which he was working:

> Aristotle raised the fabric of his *Poetry* from observation of those things in which Euripides, Sophocles, and Aeschylus pleased: he considered how they raised the passions, and thence has drawn rules for our imitation. (1:183)

The basis in observation is essential, for, in the words of the French theorist Rapin (quoted by Dryden), rules are "made only to reduce Nature into method" (1:228), and the process depends on observation, on the empirical method. Reason is applied to experience, in this case the experience of literature. The Cartesian and general scientific influences fostering such induction in the seventeenth century have often been remarked, and yet the method is at least as old as Aristotle, as Dryden's statement would suggest.

Whether a work pleases is the central criterion in this empirical approach. Pleasure is the basis both for judging present worth and for establishing the body of great literature of the past:

> For generally to have pleased, and through all ages, must bear the force of universal tradition. And if you would appeal from thence to right reason, you will gain no more by it in effect, than, first, to set up your reason against those authors; and, secondly, against all those who have admired them. (1:183)

"Right reason" has its place, of course, but the weight of universal admiration is not easily overturned. This is the basis of Dryden's respect for traditional points of view.

But although pleasure is one of the most important pieces of evidence to be considered in forming principles, it does not become an arbitrary matter, as might be imagined. For stability is afforded by human nature: "The rules have been drawn by which we are instructed how to please, and to compass that end which they obtained, by following their example. For nature is still the same in all ages, and can never be contrary to herself" (2:134). That Dryden continually takes a historical point of view in evaluating past writers likewise should not be taken as pointing to a kind of relativism in Dryden's criticism, for the proposition that one age is more encouraging to genius than another is used only as an extenuation in the judgments. Dryden is quite clearly an absolutist. A work may please and yet be inferior: "It follows not, that what pleases most . . . is therefore good, but what ought to please. Our depraved appetites, and ignorance of the arts, mislead our judgments, and cause us often to take that for true imitation of Nature which has no resemblance of Nature in it" (2:136-37). "To inform our judgments," Dryden continues, bringing us full circle, "and to reform our tastes, rules were invented, that by them we might discern when Nature was imitated and how nearly."

Such is Dryden's empirical method of arriving at principles to apply to literature. It is no different, as I have suggested already, from the methods used by Dryden's predecessors in the Aristotelian tradition. But as an Aristotelian working in a period in which literary theory tended partly toward codification into strict rules, on the one hand, and partly was dissolving in the hands of critical relativists such as Sir Robert Howard, on the other, Dryden was forced to consider publicly such basic methods to an extent unmatched by previous theorists.

Error crept into Dryden's theory, furthermore, as it must into any human endeavor. More specifically, Dryden's literary thought, like Sidney's a hundred years before, showed occasional tendencies toward Neoclassical Rationalist thought. Dryden, for example apparently had little use for the Unities, but early in his career he does describe his own plays as within their limits, and several times he criticizes other writers for being outside, although the issue is never made central. He does, moreover, speak slightingly of the Unities on occasion, even though he finally reversed himself and rejected the tragicomedy he had defended in the *Essay*, on the grounds of Unity of action (2:146-47). Finally, however, like Sidney, Dryden prefigured Johnson's famous dismissal of the Unities in the dedication to *Love Triumphant*, his last play, which itself went beyond the Unity of place:

> They who will not allow this liberty to a poet, make it a very ridiculous thing for an audience to suppose themselves sometimes to be in a field, sometimes in a garden, and at other times in a chamber. There are not, indeed, so many absurdities in their supposition as in ours; but it is an original absurdity for the audience to suppose themselves to be in any other place than in the very theatre in which they sit, which is neither chamber, nor garden, nor yet a public place of any business, but that of the representation.[11]

It would probably be more surprising, in any case, if Dryden's literary theory was not tainted by Neoclassical Rationalist thought, since he was heavily indebted to Frenchmen in that tradition, in earlier essays to Corneille, and to Bossu and Rapin later. Dryden was likewise much impressed, apparently sincerely so, by Thomas Rymer, the most typical Neoclassical Rationalist theorist writing in England. Dryden praised Rymer both publicly and in private correspondence, and, even though he fell out with Rymer at one point, in Dryden's last essay Rymer is described as "that great critic" (2:249).

The debts to the French show, I believe, Dryden's flexibility and his eagerness to establish working principles, even at the expense of some acceptance of very questionable theory. His admiration for Rymer, on the other hand, is a genuine cause for wonder. Whatever the reason and the extent of his debts and admiration, however, Dryden was clearly in the Aristotelian tradition, which a look at his view on mimesis and purposiveness will show.

But before such a demonstration it is worth remarking that his adherence to Aristotle's most basic theories did not keep Dryden from rejecting subordinate ideas contained in the *Poetics*. In the "Heads of an Answer to Rymer," Dryden placed characterization over plot and insisted that pity and fear were not the only passions involved in tragedy.[12] And in his "Dedication of the Aeneis," he argues that epic is superior to tragedy (2:158). On this ability to reject what seems invalid in past theory, in fact, depends the vitality of the tradition Aristotle began.

iv

On the question of the purposiveness of literature, Dryden clearly falls into the tradition. Throughout his essays the Horatian formula, the mainstay of the Aristotelian tradition for so many years, is repeated in any number of forms. It occurs in the *Essay of Dramatic Poesy* in the general definition of a play—"for the Delight and Instruction of Mankind"—to which all present assent.[13] Poetry is elsewhere said to be "agreeable and instructive" and "useful and . . . delightful,"[14] and to afford both "profit" and "pleasure" (2:87).

In his earlier essays, Dryden tended to emphasize pleasure. In his *Essay*, for instance, pleasure is very much involved in Neander's argument in favor of the "lively" over the "just" in the matter of mimesis, which will be dealt with below. The early importance of pleasure is also evident in "Defense of an Essay of Dramatic Poesy": "Delight is the chief, if not the only, end of poesy." But Dryden quickly qualifies his apparent exaggeration: "Instruction can be admitted but in the second place, for poesy only instructs as it delights" (1:113). Later Dryden emphasized the instructive purpose of literature, and in the preface to the *Fables* he even assumed a puritanical attitude toward literature. In general, however, Dryden thought of the two parts of the Horatian formula as a matter of ends and means: "The great End of the Poem is to Instruct, which is perform'd by making Pleasure the Vehicle of that Instruction."[15]

At one point Dryden discusses the pleasure of literature in a way that suggests a dismissal of didacticism:

> They who will not grant me, that pleasure is one of the ends of poetry, but that it is only a means of compassing the only end, which is instruction, must yet allow, that, without the means of pleasure, the instruction is but a bare and dry philosophy: a crude preparation of morals, which we may have from Aristotle and Epictetus, with more profit than from any poet. (2:112)

There are even signs in Dryden's essays that he sometimes saw the moral workings of literature as indirect. When discussing the ends of comedy in 1671, he observed of the writer:

If he works a cure on folly, and the small imperfections in mankind, by exposing them to public view, that cure is not performed by an immediate operation. For it works first on the ill-nature of the audience; they are moved to laugh by the representation of deformity; and the shame of that laughter teaches us to amend what is ridiculous in our manners. (1:143)

Later Dryden talks of the wish to "insinuate into the people" a moral precept (1:213)

But too many instances of the concept that literature teaches by example occur to exclude Dryden from the school of *direct* moral purpose. A number of times we are told something like the following: "To instruct delightfully is the general end of all poetry. Philosophy instructs, but it performs its work by precept: which is not delightful, or not so delightful as example. To purge the passions by example is therefore the particular instruction which belongs to tragedy" (1:209-10). Instruction by example leads, if not inevitably, at least naturally, to the concept of poetic justice. Dryden did in fact subscribe to that concept, which he gives Thomas Rymer the credit for;[16] this insistence on punishment of the wicked and reward for the good constitutes still another instance of the tendency in Dryden toward Neoclassical Rationalism. Dryden even reverses Aristotle's observation (in *Poetics*, 13) that poetic justice belongs to comedy: since "the first end of Comedy is delight, and instruction only the second, it may reasonably be inferred, that Comedy is not so much obliged to the punishment of faults which it represents, as Tragedy" (1:143).

v

That literature is mimetic is also part of the italicized definition of a play in the *Essay:* "*A just and lively Image of Humane Nature, representing its Passions and Humours, and the Changes of Fortune to which it is subject; for the Delight and Instruction of Mankind.*"[17] All those engaged in the dialogue give their assent to this mimetic definition, and Dryden himself insists upon mimesis in the "Defense": "I never heard of any other foundation of Dramatic Poesy than the imitation of Nature; neither was there ever pretended any other by the Ancients or Moderns, or me, who endeavor to follow them in that rule" (1:123).

The others in the dialogue, however, stressed the "just" part of the definition, while Neander/Dryden emphasized the "lively."[18] W. K. Wimsatt, Jr., claims that such emphases point up differences in concepts of mimesis.[19] He takes *just* to refer to an idea of verisimilitude, but Dryden's normal use of the word does not sustain such a reading. According to H. James Jensen's *Glossary of John Dryden's Critical Terms*, Dryden uses *just* in its French meaning to designate correctness and decorum.[20] *Lively* as applied to an image, on the other hand, is defined in the O. E. D. as "lifelike, animated, vivid." And thus it is more likely that, rather than degrees of mimesis, Dryden has in mind ways of writing, the correct versus the animated—it is perhaps even the traditional opposition of art versus genius. Neander indeed uses the distinction to place French drama below the English:

> For the lively imitation of Nature being in the definition of a Play, those which best fulfil that law ought to be esteem'd superiour to the others. 'Tis true, those beauties of the *French*-poesie are such as will raise perfection higher where it is, but are not sufficient to give it where it is not: they are indeed the Beauties of a Statue, but not of a Man, because not animated with the Soul of Poesie, which is imitation of humour and passions.[21]

The French may be more correct, but their plays do not stir with life, with vivid characterization. Dryden uses the terms *just* and (especially) *lively* elsewhere in his works, but never again in such strong contrast.

When Neander is defending rhyme, moreover, he claims that the imitation involved in tragedy is well above mere copying: tragedy "is indeed the representation of Nature, but 'tis Nature wrought up to an higher pitch."[22] And yet, although all elements of the play may be raised accordingly, this may be done only "with proportion to verisimility," which Jensen claims meant "probability." Dryden here does not seem to be setting up another standard in the way of special pleading, as he has sometimes been accused, but this cosmetic view of mimesis appears rather to be connected with the strong genre criticism of the Neoclassical Rationalists and is perhaps another indication of Dryden's tendencies in that direction. In the above passage from the *Essay*, tragedy is compared to comedy, which is not at all elevated, and in Dryden's later essays it is epics and heroic plays patterned on epics that are said to demand elevation—see especially "Of Heroic Plays." This matter of elevation, it should be noted, does not appear to be involved in the universality of literature.

Mimesis, in any event, is the keystone in Dryden's literary theory. The concept appears in one guise or another in practically every essay: either the terms *representation, imaging, imitation of nature, and following nature* are present, or their opposite numbers, *unnatural, impossible, monstrous,* or *out of nature.* The connection of mimesis and delight is made a number of times: "Nothing but Nature can give a sincere pleasure; where that is not imitated, 'tis grotesque painting; the fine woman ends in a fish's tail" (2:161). Dryden even quarrels at one point with Aristotle's psychological explanation for the attraction of mimesis by way of elevating the concept:

> Aristotle tells us, that imitation pleases, because it affords matter for a reasoner to inquire into the truth or falsehood of imitation, by comparing its likeness, or unlikeness, with the original; but by this rule every speculation in nature, whose truth falls under the inquiry of a philosopher, must produce the same delight; which is not true. I should rather assign another reason. Truth is the object of our understanding, as good is of our will; and the understanding can no more be delighted with a lie, than the will can choose an apparent evil. As truth is the end of all our speculations, so the discovery of it is the pleasure of them; and since a true knowledge of Nature gives us pleasure, a lively imitation of it,

either in Poetry or Painting, must of necessity produce a much greater. (2:137)

The concept of mimesis even becomes a criterion for eliminating farce from serious consideration as literature. In "Preface to an Evening's Love"(1671) he explains his detestation of farce by comparing it to comedy, which "consists, though of low persons, yet of natural actions and characters; I mean such humours, adventures, and designs, as are to be found and met with in the world" (1:135-36). Farce, on the other hand, "consists of forced humours, and unnatural events," works "on the fancy only," and presents "an impossible adventure" (1:136). It succeeds only because "to write unnatural things is the most probable way of pleasing them, who understand not Nature" (ibid.). This argument is repeated in "A Parallel of Poetry and Painting" (1695; 2:132-33).

And yet, although mimesis serves this exclusory function for Dryden, it is no narrow concept. In "The Author's Apology for Heroic Poetry" (1677), Dryden asks: "How are poetical fictions, how are hippocentaurs and chimeras, or how are angels and immaterial substances to be imaged; which, some of them, are things quite out of nature; others, such whereof we can have no notion?" (1:186-87). Dryden describes the practical solution to how these things are represented, and posits the underlying theory that such representation is possible because " 'tis still an imitation, though of . . . men's fancies" (1:187).

In spite of this fundamentally wide concept, however, Dryden at points seems to subscribe to a more narrow view of mimesis, very much like the strict verisimilitude of the Neoclassical Rationalists. In the *Essay* Neander seems to have confused literature and life in his defense of one of Jonson's characters: "I am assur'd from divers persons, that *Ben Johnson* [*sic*] was actually acquainted with such a man, one altogether as ridiculous as he is here represented."[23] In "Of Heroic Plays" (1672) he seems to argue in favor of artistic delusion: the poet is "to persuade [the audience], for the time, that what they behold on the theatre is really performed. The poet is then to endeavour an absolute dominion over the minds of the spectators" (1:154-55). And yet, on the whole, mimesis is a reasonable and flexible concept in Dryden's hands.

vi

The universality of literature is the most elusive of concepts in Dryden's essays. It is never spelled out precisely; there is no illuminating comparison of poetry and philosophy, as in Aristotle and Sidney, nor an insistence on "general nature," as in Dr. Johnson. Dryden does quote in "A Parallel of Poetry and Painting" a long Neoplatonic passage that claims that painters imitate "superior beauties," not corrupted nature itself (2:118). But several pages later (2:125) he rejects such "an idea of perfect nature" operative in comedy and tragedy, in which the characters "are never to be made perfect, but always to be drawn with some specks of frailty and deficience." "The perfection of such stage-characters," he continues, "consists chiefly in their likeness to the deficient faulty nature, which is their original." But, he adds two pages later, epic heroes often share in the perfection required of painting.

Something of a negative approach will perhaps be useful in uncovering the concept of universality. Mimesis, as I have shown, is the keystone of Dryden's theory, and yet rarely in his essays is there any evidence of a mere realism, photographic or otherwise, or of a strict verisimilitude. The alternative is a tacit belief in the closely knit concept of mimesis/universality. There was, furthermore, an idea of the transformation of reality by the writer in the cosmetic approach to mimesis—that is, in the heightening process discussed in the previous section—even though no reference to universal or permanent qualities in nature is present.

Dryden's use of the phrase *imitation of nature* and his insistence on the *naturalness* of mimesis perhaps provides further evidence;

for, as A. O. Lovejoy has observed, "That which is 'according to nature' meant first and foremost, that which corresponds to [the] assumption of uniformity; it is perhaps still necessary to repeat that in the most frequent of the normative uses of the word 'nature' in the Enlightenment, the principal element in the signification of the word *is* uniformity."[24]

From uniformity to universality is only a matter of extension in time, and there are additional indications that Dryden distinguished temporary from permanent or universal qualities. In "The Grounds of Criticism in Tragedy" (1679), he distinguishes "those things . . . which religion, customs of countries, idioms of languages, etc., have altered in the superstructures" from "the foundation of the design" (1:211). So too are the lasting aspects of Chaucer's characters admired in the "Preface to the Fables" (1700): "Their general characters are still remaining in mankind, and even in England, though they are called by other names than those of Monks, and Friars, and Canons, and Lady Abbesses, and Nuns; for mankind is ever the same, and nothing lost out of Nature, though everything is altered" (2:263). For Dryden universality in literature clearly depends on belief in the permanence of human nature; in fact, the two are here very nearly equated. Dryden's empirical approach to criticism also supports the universal concept. He appeals, in the "Preface to *Secret Love*" (1668), to something that all men have in common to defend the action of one of his characters:" It is indisputably that which every man, if he examines himself, would have done on the like occasion."[25] Spread out temporally, this appeal becomes the test of time: an inferior play may succeed "to effect a present liking, but not to fix a lasting admiration; for nothing but truth can long continue; and time is the surest judge of truth" ("Dedication of the Spanish Friar," [1681], 1:248-49).

Despite such evidence favoring Dryden's belief in the universality of literature, there is nonetheless some indication of a contrary stand. As regards the action of a play, universality exists as probability, and Dryden in his essay "Of Heroic Plays" so far forgot Aristotle as to comment: "This is indeed the most improbable of all his actions, but 'tis far from being impossible" (1:158). And yet Dryden is here defending one of his characters, and this could easily be special pleading and untypical.

Dryden has also been accused of being type-dominated in his theories of characterization. The major, if not the only, passage involved occurs in "The Grounds of Criticism"; in it Dryden indisputably calls for the typical: several of Fletcher's royal characters, for example, are said to have unkingly vices (1:218-19). Rymer is mentioned in the passage, which I believe can be dismissed as showing only the temporary influence of that Neoclassical Rationalist critic. Elsewhere in Dryden's essays, even in the passage in question, there is too much emphasis on lifelikeness to support his advocacy of literary types.

vii

Dryden was not much interested in creative theory. According to T. S. Eliot, this lack of interest was characteristic of his age and eminently praiseworthy. Passages of abstract theorizing about the creative act are indeed few. In the "Preface to *Annus Mirabilis*," Dryden makes the following observation, which he proceeds to use as the basis of comparison between Virgil and Ovid:

> So then the first happiness of the poet's imagination is properly invention, or finding of the thought; the second is fancy, or the variation, deriving, or moulding, of that thought, as the judgment represents it proper to the subject; the third is elocution, or the art of clothing and adorning that thought, so found and varied, in apt, significant, and sounding words: the quickness of the imagination is seen in the invention, the fertility in the fancy, and the accuracy in the expression. (1:15)

A similar passage occurs in "Parallel of Poetry and Painting"

(2:138), and in the same essay a passage of a more practical slant appears:

> For the moral (as Bossu observes) is the first business of the poet, as being the groundwork of his instruction. This being formed, he contrives such a design, or fable, as may be most suitable to the moral; after this he begins to think of the persons whom he is to employ in carrying on his design; and gives them the manners which are most proper to their several characters. The thoughts and words are the last parts, which give beauty and colouring to the piece. (2:127-28)

Whatever else may be said of Dryden's views on literature and creativity, they are clearly not organic.

The reason Eliot found Dryden's dearth of interest on the subject praiseworthy was that it left Dryden with a more single-minded approach to literature, one that was heavily evaluative. Several recent scholars have maintained that Dryden was the first of the evaluators in the history of literary criticism, and I believe there is sufficient evaluation in Dryden's essays to validate such a view. And yet there is little evaluation in its own right, little judgment of a particular author and work that is not incidental to some point being made. The prefatory nature of most of Dryden's essays would work against such independent criticism; we must turn to Dr. Johnson, especially his *Lives of the Poets,* for that.

Most of the evaluation to be found in Dryden's works, in any event, is concerned with verbal or stylistic matters. The two most famous judgments by Dryden—that of Shakespeare in the *Essay* and of Chaucer in the "Preface to the Fables"—are of course exceptions. A more typical example of Dryden's evaluation would be the following remarks on Virgil, from the "Preface to Sylvae" (1685): "Though he is smooth where smoothness is required, yet he is so far from affecting it, that he seems rather to disdain it; frequently makes use of synaloephas, and concludes his sense in the middle of his verse" (1:255-56).

Most of Dryden's evaluation also involves a comparison of two or more writers. This comparative urge, as well as the stylistic emphasis, probably manifests the influence of Longinus and perhaps of the French as well. Style is even discussed by Dryden several times in the manner of Longinus, that is, in terms of reflecting natural emotions (1:202, 256-57). Something like Longinus's expansive view of poetry is assumed by Dryden too: "The boldest strokes of poetry, when they are managed artfully, are those which most delight the reader" (1:183). Longinus is echoed (as well as Horace) in the observation that a writer can fall into one error in attempting to avoid another (2:117). And yet Dryden follows Longinus (chap. 2) likewise in recommending restraint, even using Longinus's metaphor: "No man should pretend to write who cannot temper his fancy with his judgment: nothing is more dangerous to a raw horseman than a hot-mouthed jade without a curb" (1:222). Furthermore, the test of time, spelled out by Longinus (chap. 7), has already been discussed as used by Dryden.

That Dryden was influenced by Aristotle, Horace, and Longinus needs no arguing; Dryden himself insists on the point: "Aristotle with his interpreters, and Horace, and Longinus, are the authors to whom I owe my lights" (1:207). But to my knowledge Dryden's influence on the following major figure in the tradition, Dr. Johnson, has never been pointed up satisfactorily. I have already shown Dryden's anticipation of Johnson's famous dismissal of the Unities. To this could be added the historical extenuation in Dryden's literary judgments (e.g., 1:165), and the test of time, so prominent in Johnson's preface to his edition of Shakespeare and in his *Lives of the Poets*. Other more specific echoes occur; both, for example, use the same simile to insist on the important elements in art: Dryden—"The painter is not to take so much pains about the drapery as about the face" (2:140); Dr. Johnson—"A poet overlooks the casual distinction of country and condition, as a painter, satisfied with the figure, neglects the drapery" (preface to Johnson's edition of Shakespeare).

But the main similarities between John Dryden and Samuel Johnson are, of course, those basic theories they share as members of the Aristotelian tradition.

NOTES

1. T. S. Eliot, *John Dryden* (New York, 1932), p. 51.
2. Allan H. Gilbert, *Literary Criticism: Plato to Dryden* (Detroit, Mich., 1962), p. 600.
3. Neoclassical Rationalist theory is described above in chapter 1.
Since Thomas Rymer serves as my main example of Neoclassical Rationalism in England, I would like to counter the most recent view of him as not really so rigid and rule-ridden, taken by Robert Hume in his *Dryden's Criticism* (Ithaca, N.Y., 1970), p. 107. Hume does, however, note that the main difference between Rymer and Dryden is the flexibility and empiricalness of the latter (p. 134). In fact, Rymer demonstrates most of the characteristics I have labeled as Neoclassical Rationalist (the following references are to Curt Zimansky's edition of *The Critical Works of Thomas Rymer* [New Haven, Conn., 1956]): Rymer coined the term *poetical justice* and affords a good example of its application at its most trivial—"Poetry will not permit an affront, where there can be no reparation" (p. 69); he demands strict decorum of character—women must always be depicted as modest (p. 64) and soldiers as soldierly (p. 134); he respects the Unities (p. 27), although he does not emphasize the concept; he also expects historical accuracy wherever pertinent (p. 165). Without some distinction between what I have called the Aristotelian and the Neoclassical Rationalist traditions, the differences between Rymer and Dryden must seem largely problematical, and if Hume waffles a bit in distinguishing the two critics, he has the additional excuse that Dryden has Neoclassical Rationalist tendencies.
4. John Dryden *The Works of John Dryden, vol. 17, Prose, 1668-1691: "An Essay of Dramatic Poesie" and Shorter Works,* ed. Samuel Holt Monk, A. E. Wallace Maurer, and Vinton Dearing (Berkeley, Calif. 1971), p. 46.
5. Ibid., pp. 72-73.
6. Ibid., p. 191.
7. Ibid., p. 50.
8. Ibid., p. 52.
9. Hoyt Trowbridge, "Dryden's 'Essay of the Dramatic Poetry of the Last Age,' " *Philological Quarterly* 22 (1943) :240-50.
10. John Dryden *Essays of John Dryden*, ed. W. P. Ker, 2 vols. (Oxford, 1900), 2:138. Most quotations from Dryden are from this edition; subsequent references to his works appear in parentheses in the text.
11. John Dryden *The Works of John Dryden*, ed. Sir Walter Scott, rev. George Saintsbury, 18 vols. (Edinburgh, 1884), 8:375. For some reason this dedication is contained in neither the Ker nor the Everyman editions.
12. Dryden, *Prose, 1668-1699*, pp. 185, 186.
13. Ibid., p. 15.

14. John Dryden, *"Of Dramatic Poesy" and Other Critical Essays*, ed. George Watson, 2 vols., Everyman ed. (London, 1962), 2:209, 214.

15. Dryden, *Prose, 1668-1691*, p. 192.

16. Dryden, *"Of Dramatic Poesy"and Other Critical Essays*, 2:48.

17. Dryden, *Prose, 1668-1691*. p. 15.

18. Ibid., p. 44.

19. W. K. Wimsatt, Jr., and Cleanth Brooks, *Literary Criticism: A Short History* (New York, 1965), p. 186.

20. H. James Jensen, *Glossary of John Dryden's Critical Terms* (Minneapolis, Minn., 1969), p. 70.

21. Dryden, *Prose, 1668-1691*, p. 44.

22. Ibid., p. 74.

23. Ibid., p. 59.

24. A. O. Lovejoy, *Essays in the History of Ideas* (New York, 1960), p. 80.

25. Dryden, *"Of Dramatic Poesy" and Other Critical Essays*, 1:106.

Samuel Johnson

i

Dr. Johnson is often seen today as a prominent figure in the history of literary criticism, but I believe he can lay claim to a still higher place than that. Within the scheme of this study, Samuel Johnson appears as a kind of culmination of the Aristotelian tradition. Not that he was in any sense the last of the tradition, as is sometimes suggested; but Johnson as both theorist and literary judge surpassed the others in ways that are peculiar to the tradition. There is almost a feeling when Johnson is read in this light that he was the critic at which the tradition was aiming. While those who came after had in some respects more valid positions to offer on such important points as the morality of literature, none ever has surpassed him in overall critical ability.

Johnson's reputation as a critic, nevertheless, has tended to vacillate from one extreme to the other. From his death until Macaulay's highly damaging essay in 1831, Johnson was very influential, especially with respect to the burgeoning literary reviews of the early nineteenth century. A period of low repute ensued until about the middle of the present century, when a number of studies, such as those by Jean Hagstrum and Walter Jackson Bate, managed to break though the encrusted bias to present what Johnson actually stood for.

Bias nevertheless disintegrates slowly. In an anthology published in 1962 (originally in 1941), Harry H. Clark could still remark: "Johnson's comments on Shakespeare are less touched by prejudice than *much* of his other criticism, which was *sometimes* weakened by his predetermined ideas" (italics added).[1] The confusion noticeable here probably indicates that the

quotation belongs to a transition period in Johnson's reputation. A more recent study by Emerson Marks shows no confusion: Johnson is presented as both hostile to literary principles and narrow-minded to boot.[2] My view of Johnson's
criticism, in any event, falls in with the larger trend (of Hagstrum and Bate) that is still afoot. Johnson, I would argue,
belongs clearly to the Aristotelian tradition and shares its
principles and open-mindedness.

Even though the bulk of criticism has increased enormously
from Dryden and other predecessors in the tradition, there
are no longer problems of dating or authorship. His criticism
can be found mainly in four works. Published in periodical
form between 1750 and 1752, some thirty of the *Rambler* essays
contain the bulk of Johnson's earlier critical efforts. (There
are also several critical essays in the *Adventurer* [1753-54] and
in the *Idler* [1758-60].) In 1759 Johnson published *Rasselas*
with its famous "Dissertation Upon Poetry," spoken by Imlac
in chapter 10. The third major locus of criticism is the preface
and notes to his edition of Shakespeare, published in 1765.

The most important critical work published by Johnson,
however, was his *Lives of the English Poets* (1779-81). These
lives are in the form of biographical and critical prefaces to
volumes of poetry published by thirty-six London booksellers.
The booksellers selected forty-eight poets, and Johnson was
allowed to add four more. The poets range from Cowley to
Gray and are arranged in order of death dates. Apparently
because the booksellers were reprinting the poets to protect
copyrights, there are no earlier poets included. Such poets as
Herbert and Herrick are also missing, presumably because
they were not sufficiently popular, although it is difficult to
believe some of the poets selected, such as Richard Duke or
William Walsh, could have been more popular; Johnson dismisses them in a page or two. As might be expected, the best
lives are the longest: Cowley, Milton, Dryden, Savage, and
Pope.

Despite the increase over his predecessors in sheer bulk of criticism, there is no increase in creative theory (the psychology of composition) in Johnson's works. There is, of course, an interest in authors, a first step toward such theory; Johnson could hardly have written the *Lives* otherwise. Even by following Dryden in attempting to place poets in historical perspective, he shows an interest in the poets beyond their individual works:

> To judge rightly of an author, we must transport ourselves to his time, and examine what were the wants of his contemporaries, and what were his means of supplying them. That which is easy at one time was difficult at another.[3]

But Johnson was not much interested in the creative process itself—that is, in how literature comes into being in the mind of a writer. There are several passages in which Johnson considers the "fantastic foppery" that writers can compose only at certain times, and in the life of Pope he briefly considers in Pope "all the qualities that constitute genius":

> He had Invention, by which new trains of events are formed and new scenes of imagery displayed, as in *The Rape of the Lock*, and by which extrinsick and adventitious embellishments and illustrations are connected with a known subject, as in the *Essay on Criticism*; he had Imagination, which strongly impresses on the writer's mind and enables him to convey to the reader the various forms of nature, incidents of life, and energies of passion, as in his *Eloisa, Windsor Forest*, and the *Ethick Epistles;* he had Judgement, which selects from life or nature what the present purpose requires, and, by separating the essence of things from its concomitants, often makes the representation more powerful than the reality. (*Lives*, 3:247)

Like Dryden, Johnson hardly had an organic view of creativity, nor actually much concern with poetic processes.

He was, moreover, suspicious of one of the above "qualities," the imagination; but, rather than rejecting it, he saw a necessary balance between imagination and the rational faculty. But a paucity of comment suggests that Johnson had almost no speculative interest in the imagination and certainly no concept of it as a central creative faculty, as Coleridge was to have. Even Johnson's interest in the author was, on the whole, subordinate to considerations of the response of the reader, as we shall see later.

iii

As is so often true of a large body of criticism, Johnson's literary theory is not set down in so many words in a neat treatise. And yet his theory can be ascertained by collecting scattered explicit remarks and by looking beneath other comments for the principles that necessarily underlie them.

Johnson's discussion of mimesis could well serve as the epitome of the Aristotelian tradition. Indeed, Johnson at one point specifically harks back to "the father of literary criticism" and his denomination of poetry as *"an imitative art"* (*Lives*, 1:19). Johnson even resurrects the analogy of the mirror in the preface to his edition of Shakespeare: "Shakespeare is above all writers, at least above all modern writers, the poet of nature; the poet that holds up to his readers a faithful mirrour of manners and of life."[4] This mirror image may seem to involve the same problems as when used by Plato (discussed in chap. 2, above); but, as Jean Hagstrum points out, Johnson in his dictionary had another meaning besides "looking-glass" for *mirror*: a "pattern; for that on which the eye ought to be fixed; an exemplar; an archetype." This second definition permits the image a meaning beyond delusionary art.

Literature, in any case, is seen time and time again as mimetic, as representing in a very close way life, "nature" (which usually signifies all of reality), or truth. Mimesis permeates Johnson's criticism as the basis for both positive and negative judgments. Shakespeare is preeminent as his ideal of mimesis fulfilled; romance writers, on the other hand, are perhaps his standard of the absence of mimesis. At one point in the preface, in fact, romance writers are used as a point of comparison:

> Whatever is remote from common appearances is always welcome to vulgar, as to childish credulity; and of a country unenlightened by learning, the whole people is the vulgar. The study of those who then aspired to plebeian learning was laid out upon adventures, giants, dragons, and enchantments. *The Death of Arthur* was the favourite volume.
> The mind, which has feasted on the luxurious wonders of fiction, has no taste of the insipidity of truth. (Yale ed., 7:82)

Mimesis is fundamentally a simple principle, but Johnson realized that simplicity often requires explanation and distinctions. It was, for example, the false pictures of humanity, and not the fabulous events, that undermined romances. Shakespeare could deal mimetically even with the marvelous:

> Even where the agency is supernatural the dialogue is level with life. Other writers disguise the most natural passions and most frequent incidents; so that he who contemplates them in the book will not know them in the world: Shakespeare approximates the remote, and familiarizes the wonderful; the event which he represents will not happen, but if it were possible, its effects would probably be such as he has assigned; and it may be said, that he has not only shewn human nature as it acts in real exigences, but as it would be found in trials, to which it cannot be exposed. (Yale ed., 7:64-65)

Another distinction Johnson found it necessary to make concerned dramatic presentations on stage. The Neoclassical Rationalists based their insistence on the dramatic Unities upon a principle that extended the concept of mimesis to an actual belief that what transpired on stage actually was happening—a theory not far from Plato's delusionary views.

Johnson answered that mimesis did not require delusion: "It is false, that any representation is mistaken for reality; that any dramatick fable *in its materiality* was ever credible, or, for a single moment, was ever credited" (Yale ed., 7:76, italics added).

Other distinctions point up the liberal manner in which Johnson applied the mimetic principle. The question of probability extends for Johnson, as it does for Aristotle, beyond what is actually probable. At one point, popular opinion is said to be sufficient to provide probability (Yale ed., 8:956); at others, probability is provided by the conventions of a genre: "That they exhibit a mode of life which does not exist, nor ever existed, is not to be objected; the supposition of such a state is allowed to Pastoral" (*Lives*, 3:324). And the absence of mimesis, the representation of human actions, is not in itself enough to reject a work, presumably if the picture presented is at least not false. Addison's *Cato* has "nothing that acquaints us with human sentiments or human actions," and yet "we place it with the fairest and the noblest progeny which judgment propagates by conjunction with learning," even if well below *Othello* (Yale ed., 7:84). A still more famous example is *Paradise Lost*, which presents "neither human actions nor human manners," but comes away with so much praise (*Lives*, 1:181).

"Poets, indeed, profess fiction," Johnson tells us, "but the legitimate end of fiction is the conveyance of truth" (*Lives*, 1:271), and he usually distinguishes the true to fact from the true to life, confining the mimetic demands of literature to the latter. But, as René Wellek has observed, not only is Johnson suspicious of fiction, but at times he loses the ability to distinguish literature from life. That is, Johnson, in his own unique way, sometimes loses control of his mimetic principles, which the history of literary criticism shows us is easy enough to do.

The confusion of mimesis with truth to fact takes two forms in Johnson's criticism. One of these is the preference for the historical over the purely imaginery. "History," Johnson at one point insists, "will always take stronger hold of the attention than fable" (*Lives*, 3:227). His praise of Pope's "Eloise and Abelard" provides a case in point: "The heart naturally loves truth. The adventures and misfortunes of this illustrious pair are known from undisputed history" (*Lives*, 3:235). Johnson's preference for biographies is also well known, but these few examples exhaust the subject. That history does have more appeal than do imaginary events seems to me questionable, but Johnson does not labor the issue.

The second, much more important problem concerns Johnson's view of the biographical role of the author and that critic's apparent ignorance of the use of personae. The side of literature that involves communication of emotion was of great interest to Johnson. The genres that most nearly involve, or that at least seem most nearly to involve, such communication by the poet—lyrics and elegies—are those that present the problem most squarely; but even descriptive poetry once occasioned a pertinent comment. Dryden's depiction of the London Fire in his *Annus Mirabilis*, Johnson claims,

> is painted by resolute meditation, out of a mind better formed to reason than to feel. The conflagration of a city, with all its tumults of concomitant distress, is one of the most dreadful spectacles which this world can offer to human eyes; yet it seems to raise little emotion in the breast of the poet: he watches the flame coolly from street to street, with now a reflection and now a simile, till at last he meets the king, for whom he makes a speech, rather tedious in a time so busy, and then follows again the progress of the fire. (*Lives*, 1:434)

It is not difficult, I believe, to agree with Johnson here, at least in principle; for what he is objecting to is a failure on Dryden's part to convey the kind of emotion required by the scene being described.

In other instances, however, Johnson goes beyond this failure, to introduce biographical issues. Just as with Aristotle's discussion of narrative (considered in chap. 2, above), Johnson seems to have no conception of a persona; the speaker or narrator and the author are for him exact equivalents, and questions of actual sincerity and actual experience arise. Johnson comments on Cowley's love lyrics:

> The man that sits down to suppose himself charged with treason or peculation, and heats his mind to an elaborate purgation of his character from crimes which he was never within the possibility of committing, differs only by the infrequency of his folly from him who praises beauty which he never saw, complains of jealousy which he never felt, supposes himself sometimes invited and sometimes forsaken, fatigues his fancy, and ransacks his memory, for images which may exhibit the gaiety of hope or the gloominess of despair, and dresses his imaginary Chloris or Phyllis sometimes in flowers fading as her beauty, and sometimes in gems lasting as her virtues. (*Lives*, 1:7-8)

Probably no one would disagree that actual experience is an asset to a writer, especially if he finds it necessary to resort to conventional expressions from lack of it, but surely Johnson is pushing his point too far.

Not that Johnson is wrong about the coldness or lack of sincerity in the poems he attacks; he errs rather by ascribing the failure to a biographical source. The poet has failed, but it was not necessarily owing to the biographical fact that the poet never experienced the emotions to be conveyed. Such a proposition limits too strictly the literary imagination. Johnson may have been influenced here by Horace, for at another place in the life of Cowley he echoes the *Ars Poetica* (lines 102-3): "When he wishes to make us weep he forgets to weep himself" (*Lives*, 1:37).

In the same fashion, Johnson may be correct in arraigning *Lycidas* on the point of coldness and insincerity; it has always seemed so to me, at least as far as the elegiac aspects of the poem go. He may even have been right that pastoral was largely a dead convention. Like Wordsworth, Johnson longed for a return to "true" pastoral—"just representations of rural manners and occupations" (*Lives*, 2:269). But the biographical fact that Milton and King "never drove a field, and . . . had no flocks to batten" (*Lives*, 1:164) is clearly beside the point. And when Johnson comments on another pastoral elegy that "where there is fiction, there is no passion"(*Lives*, 2:315), he just as clearly fails to recognize that the most artificial form can convey the most turbulent emotions.

iv

Inseparably linked with mimesis is the Aristotelian concept of the universality of literature. There is no trouble citing evidence of its presence in Johnson's theory. Everyone is familiar with the following passage in the preface to his edition of Shakespeare: "Nothing can please many, and please long, but just representations of general nature. Particular manners can be known to few, and therefore few only can judge how nearly they are copied" (Yale ed., 7:61). Shakespeare, Johnson comments later, "always makes nature predominate over accident" (Yale ed., 7:65). A writer must avoid "personal allusions, local customs, or temporary opinions" (Yale ed., 7:61) if his works are to survive.

The sources of Johnson's universality are variously described by scholars. Scott Elledge attributes it to the revival of Longinus and the sublime; W. K. Wimsatt, Jr., and René Wellek in their respective histories ascribe Johnson's universality to the Neoplatonic classical tradition, while Jean Hagstrum insists it is rather a Lockean concept; Arieh Sachs claims that Johnson was led to universality by his religious and moral views. While some of these suggested sources no doubt did have an influence on Johnson's thought, I believe that his concept of universality derives in the main from the Aristotelian tradition of literary theory.

There is, for one thing, the same constant references to its basis, the uniformity of nature, especially human nature:

There is such an uniformity in the state of man, considered apart from adventitious and separable decorations and disguises, that there is scarce any possibility of good or ill, but is common to human kind. A great part of the time of those who are placed at the greatest distance by fortune, or by temper, must unavoidably pass in the same manner; and though, when the claims of nature are satisfied, caprice, and vanity, and accident, begin to produce discriminations and peculiarities, yet the eye is not very heedful, or quick, which cannot discover the same causes still terminating their influence in the same effects, though sometimes accelerated, sometimes retarded, or perplexed by multiplied combinations. We are all prompted by the same motives, all deceived by the same fallacies, all animated by hope, obstructed by danger, entangled by desire, and seduced by pleasure.[5]

This passage might in fact stand as the ultimate expression within the tradition of the concept of uniformity.

Johnson's examples of successfully generalized literature also conform to the traditional concept. Shakespeare's works are one example; Homer's provide another—his "positions are general, and . . . representations natural, with very little dependence on local or temporary customs, on those changeable scenes of artificial life, which, by mingling original with accidental notions, and crowding the mind with images which time effaces, produce ambiguity in diction, and obscurity in books" (Lives, 3:114). Prime examples of works that suffer from too much dependence on the topical are the Dunciad and Hudibras. Of the latter, Johnson comments that the manners satirized, "being founded on opinions, are temporary and local, and therefore become every day less intelligible and less striking"(Lives, 1:213-14).

In spite of Johnson's traditional views on the universality of literature, at times he appears to have pushed the concept too far. The two most famous examples of such overextension are Imlac's pronouncements in chapter 10 of Rasselas and the general comments on Shakespeare's characterization in the preface to Johnson's edition.

Imlac, who apparently more or less represents Johnson, says:

> The business of a poet . . . is to examine, not the individual, but the species; to remark general properties and large appearances: he does not number the streaks of the tulip, or describe the different shades in the verdure of the forest. He is to exhibit in his portraits of nature such prominent and striking features, as recall the original to every mind; and must neglect the minuter discriminations, which one may have remarked, and another have neglected, for those characteristics which are alike obvious to vigilance and carelessness.[6]

The phrasing about "the streaks of the tulip" is probably the best-known in Johnson's criticism; it has perhaps assumed an exaggerated importance from the memorable figure used.

The first thing worth noting is that Imlac's remarks are confined to natural description, to "portraits of nature." Within that context, it can be argued that extreme particularity is at issue, not the mere presence of details. The poet should not present a hand count of how many streaks a particular tulip has, nor should he recount the many exact shades of green in a forest scene. These would constitute "the minuter discriminations." And the poet, Imlac mentions earlier, must store his mind with "inexhaustible variety," which hardly consorts with an idea of strict generalization.

Johnson, moreover, argues elsewhere against the opposite fault—too much generality. On the subject of epitaphs, for example, he first argues the difficulty of "particular and appropriate praise" and adds: "Whenever friendship or any other motive obliges a poet to write on such subjects, he must be forgiven if he sometimes wanders in generalities" (*Lives*, 3:264). And yet there is no denying that Johnson in *Rasselas* overstates his case.

Besides the description of nature, Johnson also has been arraigned for a similar statement on the universality involved in characterization. In the preface, he remarks of Shakespeare:

> His characters are not modified by the customs of particular places, unpractised by the rest of the world; by the peculiarities of studies or professions, which can operate but upon small numbers; or by the accidents of transient fashions or temporary opinions: they are the genuine progeny of common humanity, such as the world will always supply, and observation will always find. His persons act and speak by the influence of those general passions and principles by which all minds are agitated, and the whole system of life is continued in motion. In the writings of other poets a character is too often an individual; in those of Shakespeare it is commonly a species. (Yale ed., 7:62)

I believe few would be troubled by all but the final sentence, where Johnson uses the term *species,* just as he did in the passage quoted from *Rasselas* above. Whatever Johnson intends by this curious usage with respect to characterization, he apparently does not have in mind *types,* for he comments a few pages later: "Characters thus ample and general were not easily discriminated and preserved, yet perhaps no poet ever kept his personages more distinct from each other" (Yale ed., 7:64). Johnson, furthermore, rejects the criticisms of such Neoclassical Rationalists as John Dennis, Thomas Rymer, and Voltaire, who would limit Shakespeare to types (Yale ed., 7:65–66). Finally, what we know of Shakespeare's characters precludes our thinking that Johnson *could* have praised them as types.

v

Although Johnson is a kind of epitome of the Aristotelian tradition, as a great thinker in his own right he has raised problems as well. On the issue of mimesis, he at points seems to have confused life and literature, and he appears to have exaggerated in at least one place the extent to which literature is universalized. Johnson also epitomizes the tradition on the issue of the morality of literature, but only that part of the tradition from Horace to his own times that saw the moral workings of literature as direct.

And yet the case is not as simple as that. Even here a problem arises, for a number of scholars have claimed, albeit with very little evidence offered, that Johnson favored a view of the indirect working of literature, that in fact he saw literature as instructing the reader largely through the knowledge gained from mimesis/universality. Jean Hagstrum puts the case most clearly: "How, then, does art instruct? It instructs by performing its essential function, that is, by imitating nature in its two large aspects"—mimesis and universality. [7]

There is indeed some evidence to support this claim. In the preface to his edition of Shakespeare, just after pointing up Shakespeare's qualities of mimesis and universality, Johnson comments: "It is from this wide extension of design that so much instruction is derived" (Yale ed., 7:62). But, unfortunately, he follows this statement with another that appears from its parallel construction to be in apposition:

> It is this which fills the plays of Shakespeare with practical axioms and domestick wisdom. It was said of Euripides, that every verse was a precept; and it may be said of Shakespeare, that from his works may be collected a system of civil and oeconomical prudence.

Similarly, Johnson praises Shakespeare for presenting "scenes from which a hermit may estimate the transactions of the world, and a confessor predict the progress of the passions" (Yale ed., 7:65), but he makes no explicit connection between mimesis and moral purpose. Later, in an endnote to *Twelfth Night*, he comes perhaps closest to doing so when he criticizes an event for failing "to produce the proper instruction required in the drama, as it exhibits no just picture of life" (Yale ed., 7:326). Here, however, the connection seems to be limited to drama, and the statement may mean simply that mimesis is a necessary basis for instruction by example.

Several other passages should be cited. In the *Lives*, Johnson remarks:"From poetry the reader justly expects, and from good poetry always obtains, the enlargement of his comprehension and elevation of his fancy" (*Lives*, 1:292). In this instance, Johnson seems to make it a matter of evaluation: good poetry does, lesser poetry does not. In an early *Rambler* essay, literature seems to offer a kind of surrogate experience:

> The purpose of these writings is surely not only to show mankind, but to provide that they may be seen hereafter with less hazard; to teach the means of avoiding the snares which are laid by Treachery for Innocence, without infusing any wish for that superiority with which the betrayer flatters his vanity; to give the power of counteracting fraud, without the temptation to practise it; to initiate youth by mock encounters in the art of necessary defence, and to increase prudence without impairing virtue. (Yale ed., 3:22–23)

But even here the manner in which literature is presented as working could easily be construed as directly though examples.

Johnson, in any event, did sometimes attack writers for being overly moral. One work was criticized for having "morality too frequent" (*Lives*, 1:78) and another for being "tediously instuctive" (*Lives*, 1:169). *Paradise Lost* itself is arraigned on this point: "Its perusal is a duty rather than a pleasure. We read Milton for instruction" (*Lives*, 1:183).

The evidence that can be cited seems to me, nevertheless, to be short of overwhelming. Never is the indirect moral working of literature emphasized, and never is the evidence unequivocal. And for every one quotation that might be construed as supporting indirect morality, there are three or four that clearly come out for the direct.

The Horatian formula occurs a number of times, although Johnson seems to be less fond of it than is Dryden. The best-known instance can be found in the preface to Johnson's edition of Shakespeare: "The end of poetry is to instruct by pleasing" (Yale ed., 7:67), which shows the by now traditional ends and means relationship. For some reason, perhaps because of the more immediate influence of Horace, the formula is almost always given elsewhere by Johnson in its original Horatian phrasing, instruct *or* please, rather than the Renaissance rendition, instruct *and* please. But this change seems to have no significance.

The direct moral working takes several forms in Johnson's criticism. Teaching by example is the most prevalent and is phrased both positively and negatively. Good examples work because "we are improved only as we find something to be imitated" (*Lives*, 3:438); bad examples exert perhaps an even more powerful moral influence, especially on the young, who are "not informed by experience, and consequently open to every false suggestion and partial account" (Yale ed., 3:21). Johnson also draws morals for Shakespeare's plays, and complains that some of them have none and others not enough. Both of these latter charges are leveled at other writers as well. The presentation of vicious heroes, with dangerous mixtures of vice and virtue, was especially attacked by Johnson in *Rambler* number 4; the reviewers in the early nineteenth century were to inherit this particular moral objection and apply it to Byron and others.

Poetic justice, the most extreme form of morality by example, is argued but twice in Johnson's criticism. Unfortunately, one instance is found in the preface to his edition of Shakespeare and so has attained notoriety beyond its importance; if the preface had never been written many misleading clichés about Johnson might never have arisen.[8] In any event, Johnson accuses Shakespeare of making "no just distribution of good or evil" (Yale ed., 7:71). Earlier in the preface, however, Johnson praises Shakespeare for "exhibiting the real state of sublunary nature, which partakes of good and evil" (Yale ed., 7:66), and several other passages in Johnson's works show an awareness that poetic justice ill consorts with the principle of mimesis. The clearest instance occurs in a defense of Addison's *Cato* from the strictures of John Dennis, a Neoclassical Rationalist:

> Whatever pleasure there may be in seeing crimes punished and virtue rewarded, yet, since wickedness often prospers in real life, the poet is certainly at liberty to give it prosperity on the stage. For if poetry has an imitation of reality, how are its laws broken by exhibiting the world in its true form? The stage may sometimes gratify our wishes; but, if it be truly the *mirror of life*, it ought to shew us sometimes what we are to expect. (*Lives*, 2:135)

T.S. Eliot observed that Johnson never overrates a work on moral grounds, and I believe that Johnson did manage to keep his direct moral premises under control, in general. His critical career came at a point in the history of literary criticism at which the view of the direct moral workings of literature was sinking fast—and no one mourns its passing. The new view of a morality that works in literature by creating a growing moral awareness or understanding of life is evident in some of Johnson's ambiguous pronouncements. But the old view is still prominent and constitutes, I believe, the worst element of Johnson's critical theory.

vi

Johnson makes one statement about the purposefulness of literature that is both empirical and likely to gain easy assent today: "Compositions merely pretty have the fate of other pretty things, and are quitted in time for something useful" (*Lives*, 1:284). But his concept of direct morality, especially the extreme forms of instruction by example, is not based on experience, but is an a priori principle. In a mind as empirical as Johnson's, it doubtless derived from his moral and religious predisposition, so often the subject of Johnsonian scholars. Even so, once this source has been noted, one should insist that such departure from an empirical approach to literature is unusual for Johnson, and, as we have noted, he paid the price.

The deductive moral approach in any case was more than offset by Johnson's constant appeal to the principle that literature pleases. Assuming a basic uniformity in human nature, nothing constitutes a more empirical principle than pleasure: one is either pleased or not. As in the criticism of Longinus and Dryden, pleasure became the main criterion. It was so basic as to become a veritable touchstone of quality: "Since the end of poetry is pleasure, that cannot be unpoetical with which all are pleased" (*Lives,* 1:175), and "He who pleases many must have some species of merit" (*Lives,* 1:302).

Pleasure impinges upon moral considerations:

> Works of imagination excel by their allurement and delight; by their power of attracting and detaining the attention. That book is good in vain which the reader throws away. He only is the master who keeps the mind in pleasing captivity; whose pages are perused with eagerness, and in hope of new pleasure are perused again; and whose conclusion is perceived with an eye of sorrow, such as the traveller casts upon departing day. (*Lives* 1:454)

Even the adverse pronouncements of critics fall before the principle of pleasure: "Such is the censure of Dennis. . . . His arguments are strong. Yet as we love better to be pleased than to be taught, *Cato* is read, and the critick is neglected" (*Lives,* 2:144). And sometimes the lack of pleasure precludes criticism altogether:

> To examine such compositions singly cannot be required; they have doubtless brighter and darker parts: but when they are once found to be generally dull all further labour may be spared, for to what use can the work be criticised that will not be read. (*Lives,* 3:420)

If it were not for the notoriety of Johnson's moral bias, he could easily be considered as nearly a hedonist, so strong is his allegiance to literary pleasure.

Despite the simplicity of the pleasure principle, some slight problems arise. One is present in the following statement, which perhaps shows the influence of Longinus:

> Whatever professes to benefit by pleasing must please at once. The pleasures of the mind imply something sudden and unexpected; that which elevates must always surprise. What is perceived by slow degrees may gratify us with the consciousness of improvement, but will never strike with the sense of pleasure. (*Lives,* 1:59)

T.S. Eliot considers this statement an exaggeration, and I would agree. Another problem pertains to the application of the pleasure principle; Johnson tends at points toward the sentimental, seeks a "vibration to the heart" (Yale ed., 7:84) in literature. He is thus led to praise a domestic tragedy like Nicholas Rowe's *Tragedy of Jane Shore* (*Lives,* 2:69). Such is the subjective flaw in the pleasure principle.

Pleasure in any event provides an empirical basis for Johnson's criticism: "What is good only because it pleases cannot be pronounced good till it has been found to please" (*Lives,* 1:340). Johnson, in fact, has been accused of taking empiricalness too far, of being even skeptical of the critical function. Johnson, of course, was skeptical by temperament. It causes him to question constantly his biographical sources in the *Lives* and, more importantly, leads him to question received critical opinions and theories. But Johnson is a long way from the sort of skepticism that leads to anarchy.

For one thing, Johnson believed in the empirical method itself. He professed to have difficulty understanding enemies of the Royal Society, "since the philosophers professed not to advance doctrines but to produce facts; and the most zealous enemy of innovation must admit the gradual progress of experience, however he may oppose hypothetical temerity" (*Lives,* 1:208–09). Even the principles derived from experience must give way before further experience; Johnson attacks "the cant of those who judge by principles rather than perception" (*Lives,* 3:248).

The rejection of the Unities is the most famous instance of Johnson's empirical approach in action. In a *Rambler* essay, Johnson argues that since "some delusion must be admitted" in a spectator, it was difficult to limit the extent of the delusion (Yale ed., 5:68). By the time he wrote the preface to his edition of Shakespeare, Johnson seems to have rejected delusion and changed his attack to the mimetic argument discussed above—to the argument that "it is false . . . that any dramatick fable in its materiality was ever credible, or, for a single moment, was ever credited" (Yale ed., 7:76). In his endnotes to the plays, Johnson does mention several times how well or poorly Shakespeare has handled the Unities, presumably because his plays had been attacked on these grounds. Arthur Sherbo has claimed that Johnson was inconsistent, that in the endnotes, in contrast to the preface, "the nonobservance of the unities is to be deprecated."[9] And yet even in the case of *Othello,* where it is easiest to construe Johnson's remarks in that direction, Johnson seems to be defending Shakespeare rather than deprecating him: "Had the scene opened in Cyprus, and the preceding incidents been occasionally related, there had been little wanting to a drama of the most exact and scrupulous regularity" (Yale ed., 8:1048). Johnson could easily be showing how little fuss can be made even on an issue that does not really matter. In any case, Johnson's rejection of the Neoclassical Rationalist rule of the Unities remains the prime example of his empirical approach, and, even if his stand on the issue was not as original as once thought, it was final. Byron was the only notable literary figure after Johnson to defend the Unities.

vii

Johnson, with all his empirical bias, nonetheless never

succumbed to the anarchy of experience. For, as Johnson himself realized, before principles were discovered, "audiences
applauded by instinct; and poets perhaps often pleased by
chance" (*Lives*, 1:411). He also observed that "Confusion and
irregularity produce no beauty, though they cannot always
obstruct the brightness of genius and learning" (Yale ed., 5:78).
To allow for intelligent criticism and more productive creativity, principles are essential:

> It is . . . the task of criticism to establish principles; to im-
> prove opinion into knowledge; and to distinguish those
> means of pleasing which depend upon known causes and
> rational deduction, from the nameless and inexplicable
> elegancies which appeal wholly to the fancy, from which
> we feel delight, but know not how they produce it, and
> which may well be termed the enchantresses of the soul.
> (Yale ed., 4:122)

Johnson then goes on to add a remark very much in conso-
nance with his defense of the Royal Society and its empirical
method: "Criticism reduces those regions of literature under
the dominion of science, which have hitherto known only the
anarchy of ignorance, the caprices of fancy, and the tyranny
of prescription." Just like Dryden, only often more explicitly,
Johnson was determined to uncover literary principles at a
level just above the rock-bottom foundation of mimesis/
universality and moral purposiveness.

  The process whereby principles can be ascertained requires
the use of experience and reason, or, in Johnson's usual terms,
"nature and reason." The critic's reason must scrutinize raw
literary experience and attempt to arrive at principles to explain the phenomena. Vast material must be condensed and
simplified, "complications analised into principles, and
knowledge disentangled from opinion" (Yale ed., 5:66). Johnson, however, was no rationalist; the literary experience, as
we have seen, always took prcedence over abstract reason.

  But most literary principles will not be new. Once principles have become traditional, a process of distinction becomes necessary:

> Among the laws of which the desire of extending authority, or ardour of promoting knowledge has prompted the prescription, all which writers have received, had not the same original right to our regard. Some are to be considered as fundamental and indispensable, others only as useful and convenient; some as dictated by reason and necessity, others as enacted by despotick antiquity; some as invincibly supported by their conformity to the order of nature and operations of the intellect; others as formed by accident, or instituted by example, and therefore always liable to dispute and alteration. (Yale ed., 5:67)

The critic must "distinguish nature from custom, or that which is established because it is right, from that which is right only because it is established (Yale ed., 5:70); those principles not founded on experience and reason, "the arbitrary edicts of legislators, authorised only by themselves" (Yale ed., 5:76), must be rejected. Such processes, from the establishing of new principles to the distinguishing the valid from the invalid among the old, depend, of course, on an absolutist basis. Johnson leaves no doubt as to where he stands: "Truth indeed is always truth, and reason is always reason; they have an intrinsick and unalterable value, and constitute that intellectual gold which defies destruction" (*Lives*, 1:59).

Johnson was an absolutist, not a dogmatist. Even the principles that reason derives from experience must bow, as we have seen, to further experience, thus resulting in the ultimate of flexibility. Flexibility indeed is the direct result of Johnson's empirical bent: put most simply, "there is always an appeal open from criticism to nature" (Yale ed., 7:67), or, in other words, to experience. This quality of open-mindedness put Johnson clearly outside the Neoclassical Rationalist tradition; but to be fair to Dryden, who had strong tendencies toward that tradition, by the time Johnson wrote, that tradition was moribund, and rejection already was doubtless less difficult.

Johnson's basic flexibility is generally accepted today, as well it might in view of the numerous instances of its operation in his criticism. In spite of his considered dislike of blank verse, for example, Johnson concluded that he would not have had *Paradise Lost* in any other form (*Lives,* 1:194). Other examples abound; in fact, after reading a while in the *Lives,* one comes to expect adverse criticism to be followed by a *But* or *Yet.*

Johnson is also tolerant in the biographical portions of the *Lives.* In his life of Savage, Johnson recounts Savage's ridicule of Sir Richard Steele, his patron; instead of the anticipated moral indignation at the ingratitude, one is confronted by Johnson's forbearance:

> A little knowledge of the world is sufficient to discover that such weakness is very common, and that there are few who do not sometimes, in the wantonness of thoughtless mirth or the heat of transient resentment, speak of their friends and benefactors with levity and contempt, though in their cooler moments they want neither sense of their kindness nor reverence for their virtue. The fault therefore of Mr. Savage was rather negligence than ingratitude. (*Lives,* 2:333–34)

Then Johnson compounds the tolerance: "But Sir Richard must likewise be acquitted of severity, for who is there that can patiently bear contempt from one whom he has relieved and supported, whose establishment he has laboured, and whose interest he has promoted?"

But perhaps the best example of Johnson's open-mindedness occurs in the preface to his edition of Shakespeare. When he is in the process of rejecting the Unities of time and place, he gives the best possible case for the other side:

> The criticks hold it impossible, that an action of months or years can be possibly believed to pass in three hours; or that the spectator can suppose himself to sit in the theatre, while ambassadors go and return between distant kings, while armies are levied and towns besieged, while an exile

wanders and returns, or till he whom they saw courting his mistress, shall lament the untimely fall of his son. The mind revolts from evident falsehood, and fiction loses its force when it departs from the resemblance of reality. (Yale ed., 7:76)

It is doubtful whether Johnson in his own behalf could have offered a more forceful case, with its details reinforcing the argument and all of it capped off with a Johnsonian generalization in support. The Unity of place is likewise given a favorable rendition, and the false argument favoring delusion that follows is presented in such convincing rhetoric that it has often been taken as Johnson's own view. But after Johnson's four-page onslaught against the Unities, he provides the ultimate in open-mindedness:

Yet when I speak thus slightly of dramatick rules, I cannot but recollect how much wit and learning may be produced against me; before such authorities I am afraid to stand, not that I think the present question one of those that are to be decided by mere authority, but because it is to be suspected, that these precepts have not been so easily received but for better reasons than I have yet been able to find. (Yale ed., 7:80)

Johnson's only serious slip into dogmatism occurs in his pronouncement in the life of Pope that the heroic couplet is the ultimate in versification: " To attempt any further improvement of versification will be dangerous" (*Lives,* 3:251). Johnson himself offered the antidote to such a view earlier in one of the *Ramblers:* "The laws of every species of writing have been settled by the ideas of him who first raised it to reputation, without enquiry whether his performances were not yet susceptible of improvement" (Yale ed., 5:76).
Another observation might likewise have proved useful:

Definitions have been no less difficult or uncertain in criticism than in law. Imagination, a licentious and vagrant

faculty, unsusceptible of limitations, and impatient of restraint, has always endeavoured to baffle the logician, to
perplex the confines of distinction, and burst the inclosures
of regularity. There is therefore scarcely any species of
writing, of which we can tell what is its essence, and what
are its constituents; every new genius produces some
innovation, which, when invented and approved, subverts
the rules which the practice of foregoing authors had established. (Yale ed., 4:300)

But such statements as this seem to go beyond a warning about
the scope of principles almost to the point of despairing of
their practicability. Johnson indeed was aware of the problems
facing the critic, no matter how principled:

The beauties of writing have been observed to be often such
as cannot in the present state of human knowledge be
evinced by evidence, or drawn out into demonstrations;
they are therefore wholly subject to the imagination, and do
not force their effects upon a mind preoccupied by un-
favourable sentiments, nor overcome the counteraction of
a false principle or of stubborn partiality. (Yale ed., 4:130)

Such observations as these hardly leave one thinking of Johnson as a literary dictator.

viii

Armed with literary principles, Johnson became the first
great literary judge in the Aristotelian tradition, the first to
examine and evaluate many individual works for reasons
other than illustration of a point. Having already searched for
what gives intelligent pleasure in literature and how it does
so, Johnson turned to particular works, asked himself whether
they gave pleasure, and attempted to explain the answer either
by resorting to traditional principles or, as was sometimes
necessary, by establishing new ones.

One of his new principles was that pleasure is obtained by
variety (*Lives*, 1:212), by a mixture of the new with the familiar

or true—in other words, with the mimetic (*Lives*, 3:233). Invention and originality—sources of the new—became prime virtues in the writer; whatever had become stale and conventional—mythology, the pastoral, religious verse (as he saw it)—was inherently a handicap. He also saw that pleasure depended on certain formal considerations, especially on that unity of form demanded by all theorists in the Aristotelian tradition. The only time he departed from this highly empirical pleasure principle was on the issue of the direct moral working of literature.

But the pleasure involved was strictly his own when he approached immediately new literary works. Apparently partly to offset problems of subjectivity and partly from an innate humility, Johnson often turned to the *consensus gentium*. He constantly remarks in the *Lives* that the public judgment on various works appears to be right. As he explains, "About things on which the public thinks long it commonly attains to think right" (*Lives*, 2:132). But sometimes the public makes judgments too quickly; contemporary fame can be "a possession of very uncertain tenure; sometimes bestowed by a sudden caprice of the publick, and again transferred to a new favourite, for no other reason than that he is new" (*Lives*, 3:118). Time is a better judge, pleasure over the long run the real indicator of true worth:

> The books which have stood the test of time, and been admired through all the changes which the mind of man has suffered from the various revolutions of knowledge, and the prevalence of contrary customs, have a better claim to our regard than any modern can boast, because the long continuance of their reputation proves that they are adequate to our faculties, and agreeable to nature. (Yale ed., 4:122)

Johnson, of course, did not always give a final obeisance to traditional reputations, but he had a healthy respect for them.

As for his own judgments, Johnson did not view the task of criticism as existing for its own sake. There is a serious purpose: "If bad writers were to pass without reprehension, what should restrain them?" (*Lives,* 3:241). Johnson, indeed, tends to emphasize the negative side of criticism:

> He that writes may be considered as a kind of general challenger, whom every one has a right to attack; since he quits the common rank of life, steps forward beyond the lists, and offers his merit to the publick judgment. To commence author is to claim praise, and no man can justly aspire to honour, but at the hazard of disgrace. (Yale ed. 4:133–34)

And yet Johnson always points out the beauties as well as the defects, and, theoretically at least, he held that "the duty of criticism is neither to depreciate, nor dignify by partial representations, but to hold out the light of reason, whatever it may discover; and to promulgate the determinations of truth, whatever she shall dictate" (Yale ed., 4:134).

The result of such a proceeding Johnson clearly foresaw as well:

> It is common, says Bacon, to desire the end without enduring the means. Every member of society feels and acknowledges the necessity of detecting crimes, yet scarce any degree of virtue or reputation is able to secure an informer from publick hatred. The learned world has always admitted the usefulness of critical disquisitions, yet he that attempts to show, however modestly, the failures of a celebrated writer, shall surely irritate his admirers, and incur the imputation of envy, captiousness, and malignity. (Yale ed., 4:376)

Johnson, of course, has continued to irritate admirers of Shakespeare, Milton, and Donne.

It is not my business here to evaluate Johnson's evaluations; such a course would lead us inevitably away from Johnson to the writers in question. He is, nevertheless, generally considered successful in his criticism of Pope and Dryden, to whom he was most closely sympathetic, and of Shakespeare and Milton in a lesser degree. Contemporary poets Johnson tended to have little use for; he seems to have considered them more correct than powerful, and few would quarrel with this judgment.

His critical mistakes are not, in my opinion, his infamous judgments of *Lycidas* and of the Metaphysical poets, which have been convincingly defended in recent articles. What is difficult to take are incidental comments in which he dismisses such works as "Chevy Chase" ("chill and lifeless imbecility" [*Lives*, 2:148]) and Chaucer's "Nun's Priest's Tale" ("hardly worth revival" [*Lives*, 1:455]), although there are extenuations to be considered on the latter—Chaucer's versification was still not understood. And yet every critic, as Johnson would have himself insisted, is entitled to a few mistakes.

Johnson's evaluative approach is, on the whole, simple. He does not much affect the comparative method, as Dryden does, nor the historical, although there are enough instances of both to show that he was familiar with them. He does not really practice what could be called biographical criticism either; he seldom discusses the works merely in terms of the man, except in those instances of mimesis run wild, mentioned already. Usually Johnson makes general judgments, such as that Shakespeare was good at characterization or poor at moral instruction; or he presents a close reading of a text. Since most of his criticism is of poetry, diction and imagery are especially scrutinized for meaning and propriety. He is never willing to abandon himself to poetry and demands that it at least make sense.

T. S. Eliot claimed that Johnson had almost no influence after his own time. This was not altogether true, as we have seen; the reviewers in the early nineteenth century used the same approach and probably received their initial incentive from Johnson's example. It is even conceivable that that great heyday of literary reviewing might never have occurred had Johnson never written. But beyond that—and it alone evinced no small amount of influence—Johnson was part of the Aristotelian tradition and brought that tradition to its highest point, thus influencing inestimably, but certainly, all who came after, and, if we accept Eliot's view of tradition, changing all who came before as well.

NOTES

1. Harry H. Clark, ed., *Literary Criticism: Pope to Croce* (Detroit, Mich., 1962), p. 60.

2. Emerson Marks, *The Poetics of Reason* (New York, 1968), chap. 5.

3. Samuel Johnson, *Lives of the English Poets*, ed. G.B. Hill, 3 vols. (Oxford, 1905), 1:411. Subsequent references to this work appear in parentheses in the text.

4. Samuel Johnson, *Johnson on Shakespeare*, ed. Arthur Sherbo, 2 vols., Yale edition of *The Works of Samuel Johnson*, vols. 7 and 8 (New Haven, Conn., 1958-71), 7:62. Subsequent references to this work appear in parentheses in the text.

5. Samuel Johnson, *Rambler*, ed. Walter Jackson Bate and Albrecht Strauss, 3 vols., Yale edition of *The Works of Samuel Johnson*, vols. 3, 4, and 5 (New Haven, Conn., 1958-71), 3:320. Subsequent references to this work appear in parentheses in the text.

6. Samuel Johnson, *The History of Rasselas, Prince of Abissinia*, ed. R. W. Chapman (Oxford, 1927), p. 50.

7. Jean Hagstrum, *Samuel Johnson's Literary Criticism* (Minneapolis, Minn., 1952), p. 71.

8. The other ambiguous instance of poetic justice can be found in Johnson, *Johnson on Shakespeare*, 8:1011.

9. Arthur Sherbo, *Samuel Johnson, Editor of Shakespeare*, Illinois Studies in Language and Literature, vol. 42 (Urbana, Ill., 1956), p. 92.

8

Samuel Taylor Coleridge
and William Wordsworth

i

What was described in the opening chapter as the Romantic tradition seems to be a major tradition; it certainly has had its adherents from the eighteenth century to the present. And yet, in England at least, it has never held the allegiance of major figures in literary theory. The biggest names it can boast are Walter Pater and A. C. Bradley. More often one confronts names familiar mainly to the historian of ideas—John Keble, Sir William Jones, or B. W. Proctor. Just as the Neoclassical Rationalists were minor figures in the history of literary criticism, so were the Romantic literary theorists, at least in England.

M. H. Abrams, who in *The Mirror and the Lamp* has documented the Romantic tradition of literary theory as it evolved in the eighteenth and nineteenth centuries, has, however, included Wordsworth and Coleridge as members of the tradition. Abrams does indeed qualify that membership again and again, even to the point of seeming to place them as he does simply because he does not know what else to do with them.[1] And they were, of course, too famous to be ignored.

Abrams's view of the Romantic literary tradition itself is, nevertheless, valid as far as it goes. He sees Romantic theory as involving a change of metaphor that implies a radical change in the view of the nature of art. The traditional metaphor of the mirror (mimesis) changed to one of a lamp (expressionism), as well as to the metaphor of a heterocosm (art as a new universe in its own right). As far as I can determine, Abrams never makes a distinct connection between these two new and fundamentally distinct Romantic metaphors.

In any event, poetry (as lamp) is "the expression of feeling, or of the human spirit, or of an impassioned state of mind and imagination."[2] As one of these kinds of expression, poetry began to be equated with the lyric, the genre that would most easily lend itself to such a purpose; in aesthetic comparisons, painting began to be replaced by music, the art form most obviously free from nonexpressive or representational elements. It was but a small jump to seeing poetry as a revelation of the poet's personality. Poetry as heterocosm, on the other hand, considers each poem its own self-contained universe; probability loses its mimetic/universal significance and refers to the inner consistency of the work.

Both of these new views of poetry are nonmimetic at least by implication. Both, too, lead inevitably to art for art's sake. If poetry is *merely* expressive, it makes no assertions about the world. And, if poetry is a self-contained universe, it likewise makes no statements that are in any way verifiable. Poetry is therefore seen as nonpurposive; it is, at its most "useful," the object of aesthetic contemplation.

Abrams's documentation, however, suffers from some questionable methods. Lacking any distinction between an Aristotelian tradition and Neoclassical Rationalism, his representation of mimesis tends toward the extreme view of the latter tradition. All of his *unequivocal* quotations supporting Romantic expressionism and rejecting mimesis, on the other hand, come from distinctly minor figures in literary theory, such as Keble and Mill. Abrams furthermore sticks to explicit theory; he never, as far as I am aware, goes beneath the surface to ferret out underlying theories.

The largest problem, however, arises from the absence of a distinction between literary and creative theory. The minor figures Abrams quotes are the only ones explicitly to reject mimesis. What appears to be expressionistic in the criticism of Wordsworth and Coleridge, moreover, is not necessarily so: they were interested in creative theory, which is easily confused with expressionism, but, while expressionism and mimesis are by nature mutually exclusive, creative theory and mimesis are not. A minor eighteenth-century theorist, Bishop Lowth, saw that mimesis and the examination of the emotional or mental origins of poetry are compatible.[3] Why presume Wordsworth and Coleridge saw them otherwise?

Part of the difficulty proceeds from the contrast between theories of the origins of poetry—that is, whether poetry originates in feeling or in Aristotle's instinct for imitation. Regardless of the immediate psychological origin of poetry, feeling and imitation itself *are* compatible: the one is fundamental to creation, the other tells us about the nature of poetry, its relation to life. My contention is that Wordsworth and Coleridge are solidly in the Aristotelian tradition and that what makes them at times seem expressionistic is their interest, quite natural at the time, in creative theory.

ii

William Wordsworth's literary theory was published between 1798 (the Advertisement to the *Lyrical Ballads*) and 1815 (the Essay, Supplementary to the Preface). In between came the preface to the *Lyrical Ballads* (1800, 1802), the three-part *Essay upon Epitaphs* (1810), and the prefaces to *The Excursion* (1814) and to the *Poems* (1815). Other bits and pieces of literary theory can also be found scattered in various prose pieces and notes.[4]

The preface to the *Lyrical Ballads* is generally seen as the most important of Wordsworth's literary documents, especially the extended version of 1802, which contains almost three thousand words added to the approximately seven thousand words of the 1800 version. An appendix of about two thousand words was also added in 1802, making the complete second version well over half again as long. This is the document on which I intend to concentrate in my discussion of Wordsworth's literary theory.

One of the snags that immediately confronts the reader of

the preface is the question of the scope of Wordsworth's assertions. Does he mean his comments to refer to *all* of poetry or only to *part*? Near the beginning, Wordsworth mentions that if his views materialized, "a class of Poetry would be produced" (1:121); later, however, he mentions that his concern for what he is saying is "far less for the sake of these particular Poems than from the general importance of the subject" (1:129). As the preface proceeds, Wordsworth's vacillation continues, until in the second-to-last paragraph he seems to reaffirm the largest possible scope under cover of heavy irony: the contemporary reader enjoys the kind of composition opposite to that proposed in the preface, "composition to which he has peculiarly attached the endearing name of Poetry" (1:157). The confusion was enough to have been questioned by both the contemporary reviewers and Samuel Taylor Coleridge.[5]

This problem is, however, part of a much larger difficulty; for the preface, like most of the documents in the history of literary theory, is poorly organized. Wordsworth himself admits as much: early in the preface, he warns that he has "altogether declined to enter regularly upon [the] defense" of the theory underlying the *Lyrical Ballads* (1:121). Later he again adverts to the lack of system in his defense (1:149). The preface is indeed as poorly organized as Wordsworth admits; it is especially fuzzy in the connection between parts, but it is unusual for a theorist to be so honest.

iii

Samuel Taylor Coleridge, Wordsworth's friend and collaborator, produced his literary theory during approximately the same period. He is known to have been involved to some extent in the thinking behind Wordsworth's preface, and he gave five lecture series on poetry from 1808 to 1818. Almost all of his criticism is occasional: lectures, reviews, marginalia; even the *Biographia Literaria* (1817) is partly an answer to

Wordsworth's literary position as set forth in the prefaces to the *Lyrical Ballads* and to the *Poems* (1815). The large group of chapters in the *Biographia* on Wordsworth constitutes one segment of Coleridge's criticism. Another is the criticism of Shakespeare contained largely in reports of his lectures and in his notes and marginalia.[6] A final segment could be made of miscellaneous theory and evaluations of poetry, especially of the English seventeenth century, found in the *Biographia Literaria* and elsewhere (collected in two modern editions).[7]

A major difficulty a commentator on Coleridge's criticism must face is plagiarism. It is still not always squarely faced. R. H. Fogle, for example, not only denies the plagiarism in general, but offers the following defense of a particular instance: "First, the multiplicity of his possible sources is so great as to neutralize the effect of any one in particular."[8] Apparently, if there is more than one source available, one cannot plagiarize from any single one of them.

It should be clearly understood: it is not a matter of mere influence, and it is not just a stray passage here or there that is concerned. Coleridge took over with no acknowledgment and word for word whole essays and sections of works, usually from his German contemporaries. Among Coleridge's works so plagiarized are "The Theory of Life," "On Poesy or Art," "On the Principle of Genial Criticism," and substantial sections of *Biographia Literaria* and of the Shakespeare Lectures. Recently, Norman Fruman, in *Coleridge: The Damaged Archangel* (1971), has made even more extensive charges.

Coleridge himself once took occasion to defend his borrowings in a now-famous passage: "I regard truth as a divine ventriloquist: I care not from whose mouth the sounds are supposed to proceed, if only the words are audible and intelligible."[9] This defense would be acceptable as far as *influence* might be concerned, but it can hardly hold for verbatim unacknowledged "borrowings." One escape from moral indignation is, however, open: several scholars have suggested that Coleridge, when going over earlier passages in his notebooks, probably mistook for his own work translations he had made from the Germans. And to be fair to Coleridge, in many cases he does adapt and assimilate his borrowings.

Another problem presented by Coleridge's criticism is the uncertain form of the material. Much of the criticism, such as the notes and marginalia, was not intended for publication. The lectures, furthermore, have come down to us in the form of reports, and are therefore secondhand. The only critical book published in his lifetime was the *Biographia Literaria,* which is also undoubtedly his most famous work and which will therefore be emphasized in the following discussion.

The *Biographia Literaria* presents its own obstacles, for, like Wordsworth's preface and so many other documents of literary theory, the work is poorly organized. It is, in fact, a hodge-podge of autobiography, evaluation, creative theory, religious comments, self-defense, and so on. One recent scholar, George Whalley, has attempted to uncover a basic unity in the *Biographia,* but, despite a very ingenious argument, he is not convincing inasmuch as his view does not conform to one's experience of reading the work.[10] There is, however, a kind of system in the *Biographia:* the first volume is generally philosophical and the second generally an evaluation of Wordsworth's theories and poetry. This sequence displays Coleridge's usual efforts to base his literary principles on his philosophic, and yet no such connection is evident between the two sections.

iv

An examination of Wordsworth's and Coleridge's views of the double concept of mimesis/universality will establish whether these critics belong to the Aristotelian tradition or are Romantic expressionists, as Abrams claims. I intend to show now that they did indeed subscribe to a mimetic theory; later I will demonstrate that their creative theories were not inconsistent with mimesis.

Wordsworth is quite explicit a number of times. In the preface of 1802, for example, he sets forth mimesis as self-evident: "Poetry is the image of man and nature" (1:139). Except for the need to give pleasure, he adds a few lines later, "there is no object standing between the Poet and the image of things". But the "image," he makes clear, is not mere realism, but is tempered with universality. In the same passage, he even cites Aristotle: "Aristotle, I have been told, has said, that Poetry is the most philosophic of all writing: it is so: its object is truth, not individual and local, but general, and operative." And in a later passage occurs a phrase that might have been written by Dr. Johnson: "The Poet . . . converses with general nature" (1:140).

Wordsworth is especially concerned with the concept of universality as operative in his poetry. In the preface he confides: "I am sensible that my associations must have sometimes been particular instead of general, and that, consequently, giving to things a false importance, I may have sometimes written upon unworthy subjects" (1:153). Uniformity, the basis of universality, is plainly spelled out in his *Essay upon Epitaphs:* "Indeed, the favourite style of different ages is so different and wanders so far from propriety that if it were not that first rate writers in all nations and tongues are governed by common principles, we might suppose that truth and nature were things not to be looked for in books" (2:98). Uniformity and the test of time are both fundamental premises of the Essay, Supplementary to the Preface, his long explanation of his own contemporary lack of popularity. Unabashedly he assures the reader

that there never has been a period, and perhaps never will be, in which vicious poetry, of some kind or other, has not excited more zealous admiration, and been far more generally read, than good; but this advantage attends the good, that the *individual,* as well as the species, survives from age to age. (3:83)

So clear and constant are such explicit acceptances of mimesis/universality and references to "truth" and "nature" in relation to poetry, that most scholars have noted that Wordsworth ascribed to the concept at least at some time in his career as a literary theorist. W. J. B. Owen, who is heavily influenced by Abrams, sees a changeover in Wordsworth from mimesis to expressionism by 1802.[11] An easy refutation of such a claim, or at least an easy defense of the irrefutable presence of mimesis/universality after 1802, is that the quotations given in the last two paragraphs all appeared after that date.

Some commentators take another tack: Wordsworth is *too* mimetic; that is, he confuses literature and life—as we saw in the last chapter, such a charge was brought against Samuel Johnson. One of these commentators, Roger Sharrock, who made the charge in his article "Wordsworth's Revolt against Literature," has already been answered elsewhere.[12] As for the rest, it should suffice to refer to Wordsworth's explicit concept of universality, which works against simple and strict realism.

Wordsworth's epistemology also is inconsistent with photographic realism. Setting aside a more prolonged discussion of creative theory for later, one quotation will show that Wordsworth saw mimesis as something other than mere reporting, that he saw the poet as coming between life and the literature he is creating: "The appropriate business of poetry . . . , her appropriate employment, her privilege and her *duty*, is to treat of things not as they *are*, but as they *appear*; not as they exist in themselves, but as they *seem* to exist to the *senses,* and to the *passions*" (3:63). Mimesis was becoming a much more subtle concept.

As for Coleridge, most scholars note his traditional views on mimesis and universality; some even remark how "neo-classical" he seems in this regard. Coleridge indeed leaves little room for doubt; at the opening of chapter 14 of the *Biographia,* he sets forth one of the "cardinal points of poetry": "the power of exciting the sympathy of the reader by a faithful adherence to the truth of nature" (*BL,* 2:5). On the same page, he repeats the practical application of the mimetic theory mentioned in my first chapter, his objection to "moral miracles ": Coleridge was to contribute to the *Lyrical Ballads* poems at least partly on supernatural subjects "and the excellence aimed at was to consist in the interesting of the affections by the dramatic truth of such emotions, as would naturally accompany such situations, supposing them real." In works of fantasy, the characterization at least had to be mimetic.

The other "cardinal point of poetry" presented—"the power of giving the interest of novelty by the modifying colors of imagination" (ibid.)—introduces the epistemological and creative element also seen above in Wordsworth's theory. Even more clearly than his friend, Coleridge sees the poet as creatively manipulating the stuff of experience: he remarks upon the presence in poetry of "the apparent naturalness of the *representation,* as raised and qualified by an imperceptible infusion of the author's own knowledge and talent, which infusion does, indeed, constitute it an *imitation* as distinguished from a mere *copy*" (*BL,* 2:30).

Also like Wordsworth, Coleridge has been charged with too much insistence on mimesis, on psychological realism, in his criticism of Shakespeare. Coleridge has been accused of insisting on psychological truth of characterization in the teeth of Elizabethan dramatic conventions. This charge is very likely true; if it is, it is a mistake Coleridge shares with most Shakespearean critics, for it is immensely difficult to remember that Shakespeare was influenced by conventions.

Coleridge followed Wordsworth in his advocacy of universality as well, complete with his reference to Aristotle.

I adopt with full faith the principle of Aristotle, that poetry as poetry is essentially *ideal,* that it avoids and excludes all *accident*; that its apparent individualities of rank, character, or occupation must be *representative* of a class; and that the *persons* of poetry must be clothed with *generic* attributes, with the *common* attributes of a class: not with such as one gifted individual might *possibly* possess, but such as from his situation it is most probable before-hand that he *would* possess. (*BL,* 2:33-34)

The test of time, which relies on the uniformity of human nature, is likewise appealed to: "The philosophic critics of all ages coincide with the ultimate judgement of all countries" in rejecting certain kinds of verse (*BL,* 2:10).

Coleridge, of course, differed philosophically from Aristotle, but even at his most transcendental, Coleridge never ceases to expect that literature will reflect life in certain fundamental ways and that it will be universal as well. A recent study of Coleridge's literary theory sees it as firmly based in his transcendental philosophy; but even in this philosophical scheme, which posits the divinely given Reason as a reservoir of knowledge (also called the "Communicative Intelligence") tapped by the poetic imagination, that Reason is objective, the source of universals; and objective reality exists as well.

v

The question whether literature serves any purpose is also at issue in deciding whether Wordsworth and Coleridge are Aristotelians or expressionists. For how can the need for literary purpose be reconciled with expressionistic theory? If a poem merely expresses the emotions of the poet, then purpose is beside the point, just as it has always been seen in Romantic theory. The double concept of mimesis/universality, on the other hand, almost presupposes purpose by its very nature.

Wordsworth felt a deep moral concern with regard to both poetry and life. In a passage in his short "Reply to 'Mathetes' " (1809-10), he echoes Sidney's dicta "The ending end of all earthly learning [is] vertuous action" with his own pronouncement: "Knowledge efficacious for the production of virtue, is the ultimate end of all effort" (2:19). From this basis, Wordsworth makes his view of literary morality quite clear in the preface: from contemporary verse "the Poems in these volumes will be found distinguished at least by one mark of difference, that each of them has a worthy *purpose*" (1:125).

That this purpose is not limited to the *Lyrical Ballads,* Wordsworth goes on to indicate, and in the process gives the first clear rendition by any major theorist of the concept of an indirect moral working of literature: Poets

> shall describe objects, and utter sentiments, of such a nature, and in such connection with each other, that the understanding of the Reader must necessarily be in some degree enlightened, and his affections strengthened and purified. (1:127)

No longer is there a need for teaching by example or precept; a new concept has come into being, one that frees literary theory from a good deal of a priori argument.

There is no question what Wordsworth had in mind, for within a page he puts the same matter in a different, but equally clear, guise:

> The human mind is capable of being excited without the application of gross and violent stimulants; and . . . one being is elevated above another, in proportion as he possesses this capability. It has therefore appeared to me, that to endeavour to produce or enlarge this capability is one of the best services in which, at any period, a Writer can be engaged. (1:129)

In his *Letter to a Friend of Robert Burns* (1816), Wordsworth shows that he retained this concept. In defending Burns's poetry from charge of lack of moral purpose, he retorts that "though there was no moral purpose, there is a moral effect" (3:124). Speculation concerning the sympathetic imagination in the eighteenth century may have led to Wordsworth's view of the indirect moral working of literature, but he was the first major theorist to make it a cornerstone of his theory.

The Horatian formula, so much a part of the Aristotelian tradition before Wordsworth, did not appear as such in his theory before 1814, and thereafter only a few times. Pleasure, the other half of the formula, was, nevertheless, very much evident in Wordsworth's early theory. In the preface to the *Lyrical Ballads* (1802), he pronounces that "the Poet writes under one restriction only, namely, that of the necessity of giving immediate pleasure to a human Being" with human interests (1:139). He then goes on to expand upon what he calls "the grand elementary principle of pleasure" (1:140), which goes far beyond, but includes, literary concerns. Pleasure becomes a standard point of reference for much of the literary theory of the preface—it constitutes, for example, the main defense of meter; another generalization is worded so strongly that it needs the qualification of Wordsworth's moral observations if it is not to impute to him a strong hedonism: "The end of Poetry is to produce excitement in co-existence with an over-balance of pleasure" (1:147).

Coleridge, on the other hand, does not have a great deal of explicit theory about either the moral effects of literature or the pleasure to be derived from it. The central passage on the subject, however, shows a change in the traditional Horatian formula: a nonliterary composition may give pleasure, and

> pleasure, and that of the highest and most permanent kind, may *result* from the *attainment* of the end; but it is not itself the immediate end. In other works the communication of pleasure may be the immediate purpose; and . . . truth, either moral or intellectual, ought to be the *ultimate* end. . . .
> A poem is that species of composition, which is opposed to works of science, by proposing for its *immediate* object pleasure, not truth. (*BL,* 2:9–10)

No longer is pleasure seen as the means, and morality the end, of poetry. Both pleasure and morality are now the ends of poetry; but pleasure is the immediate end, morality the ultimate. It is, I suppose, a more organic way of looking at the

Horatian formula, and, as we shall see, Coleridge was an organicist.

vi

The rise of creative theory took place in the eighteenth century, and it flourished especially in England. The possible reasons for the rise at this time are highly speculative, but a few seem worthy of consideration. One with respect to Wordsworth at the end of the century suggests itself. With increased urbanization and industrialization, new forces of corruption were set loose, and poets perhaps felt the need to consider emotional and psychological states of creativity. Wordsworth at least claimed something like this in the preface to the *Lyrical Ballads*: "For a multitude of causes, unknown to former times, are now acting with a combined force to blunt the discriminating powers of the mind, and, unfitting it for all voluntary exertion, to reduce it to a state of almost savage torpor" (1:129). And later on he warns that the poet's "own feelings are his stay and support" (1:153). A concern for contemporary corruption runs through most of Wordsworth's theory; it, rather than the mere concern for poetic diction, might indeed be seen as the real motive for the preface. Another possible reason for the rise of creative theory is more general: the new empirical psychology stemming from Thomas Hobbes and John Locke naturally led literary theorists to a new interest in creativity.

The relatively new empirical epistemology, in any event, was part of the cause of Coleridge's interest in creative theory, at least in a negative way. For Coleridge objected to the mechanistic epistemology of Locke and the other empiricists, wherein the mind is seen as predominately, if not exclusively, passive. As Basil Willey has described it,

> The eighteenth century had reduced the universe to an assemblage of parts, the mind of man to an aggregate of

sense-impressions, and poetry to a judicious arrangement of ready-made images culled from the memory. [13]

The plight of poetry, according to another scholar, was especially desperate: "If Hobbes and Hartley were true then poetry was reduced to elegant trifling and the poet could, at best, only take over the truths of science and decorate them with the fanciful trappings of verse." [14]

Coleridge's own epistemology was itself a kind of compromise between such strict materialism and the idealism of his Neoplatonic and German influences. This compromise is contained in a paradox: objects exist, but we have to "create" them. [15] For Coleridge, at any rate, there is an underlying objective reality.

All knowledge, moreover, is in a sense "created." And the active, creative faculty that was involved, Coleridge called the imagination. In the famous passage in the *Biographia*, Coleridge distinguished three faculties:

> The IMAGINATION then, I consider either as primary, or secondary. The primary IMAGINATION I hold to be the living Power and prime Agent of all human Perception, and as a repetition in the finite mind of the eternal act of creation in the infinite I AM. The secondary Imagination I consider as an echo of the former, co-existing with the conscious will, yet still as identical with the primary in the *kind* of its agency, and differing only in *degree,* and in the *mode* of its operation. It dissolves, diffuses, dissipates, in order to recreate; or where this process is rendered impossible, yet still at all events it struggles to idealize and to unify. It is essentially *vital,* even as all objects (*as* objects) are essentially fixed and dead.
>
> FANCY, on the contrary, has no other counters to play with, but fixities and definites. The Fancy is indeed no other than a mode of Memory emancipated from the order of time and space; while it is blended with, and modified by that empirical phenomenon of the will, which we express by the word CHOICE. But equally with the ordinary memory the Fancy must receive all its materials ready made from the law of association. (*BL*, 1:202)

Coleridge's "primary Imagination" is usually interpreted as the mental faculty that orders ordinary, everyday perceptions and that constitutes consciousness. Other ways of describing its function are that it transforms "stimuli into mind-stuff," "externalizes the world of objects by opposing it to the self," and "imposes form upon [the] flux" of ordinary perception.[16] Imagine having been born at age twenty exposed to the chaos of sensory perception for the first time, and you have an idea of the role of the primary Imagination.

The term "secondary Imagination" is misleading inasmuch as it is not secondary because it is less valuable, but only because it depends upon the primary Imagination to function. But one advantage of the confusion is that by making the creative faculty dependent upon everyday perception, Coleridge draws literature closer to life, rather than establishing a separate aesthetic realm.

The secondary Imagination is the faculty used to create literature. By pressing the term *Imagination* (as well as the term denoting its fellow poetic faculty, *Fancy*) into the service of creative theory, Coleridge was moving them away from their usual meanings. The secondary Imagination breaks down the writer's past experience and then recreates it in the form of a work of literature. Imagination is described as *fusing* this material into unity: "the power by which one image or feeling is made to modify many others and by a sort of *fusion to force many into one*" (*SC*,1:188). It "reveals itself in the balance or reconcilliation of opposite or discordant qualities" (*BL*, 2:12). Coleridge also attempts to make the creative act voluntary, but partly unconscious as well—a kind of compromise between Romantic creative abandon and Neoclassical Rationalist insistence upon wholly conscious craftsmanship: the Imagination is "first put in action by the will and understanding, and retained under their irremissive, though gentle and unnoticed, controul" (*BL*, 2:12).

Coleridge contrasts the secondary Imagination to the Fancy, to which he assigns a much inferior role, that of connecting material in a mechanical, associative way. The distinction, however, is not always very lucid. While sometimes the Fancy has been seen as a kind of catchall for the creative functions Coleridge considered beneath the dignity of the Imagination to perform, some scholars have considered it to have been in Coleridge's view indispensable to creativity.

In any event, the Imagination is the faculty that fuses, unifies in a special way; for, while the Fancy is mechanical, the Imagination is organic in its function. The organic concept is often misunderstood; most usually it is seen as a simple metaphor that can be found in Aristotle and others in his tradition. Coleridge indeed uses organic metaphors constantly himself; some of his favorite esoteric terms, such as *coadunating* and *assimilative* were taken over from the biological sciences.

But the concept as Coleridge introduced it into England was of recent German origin. James Benziger has traced it from Leibnitz to Karl Phillip Moritz, from Moritz to A. W. Schlegel and thence to Coleridge.[17] In the traditional view, organicism is little more than a figure; a whole is made up of parts, but no part has value on its own. For Coleridge and his sources, however, organicism was not just a metaphor reflecting a harmony of parts as in a living body. As a recent commentary put it, "Organic form is not materially separable from its content, and is present in all parts of the whole."[18] Organic structural theory

> discovers a value in the parts as well as in the context formed by their interaction, so that the whole is *more than* the sum of its parts. . . . Each part thus contains the essence of the whole, or—to shift the metaphor—*is* the whole in germ.[19]

The organic concept was not a purely theoretical issue in Coleridge's criticism, but was used in his analysis and evaluation of literature. For example, R. H. Fogle, who makes the organic concept central to Coleridge's theory, points out that when analyzing a work, he first searches for the "germ" or "informing principle" and follows it through the work.[20] But organicism also threatens literary analysis by proposing an organic whole that cannot be dissected. Coleridge apparently recognized the problem, for at one point in the *Biographia* he observed: "The office of philosophical *disquisition* consists in just *distinction;* while it is the privilege of the philosopher to preserve himself constantly aware, that distinction is not division" (*BL,* 2:8).

Wordsworth's creative theory was, on the whole, quite similar to Coleridge's; in fact, Coleridge was probably the source of many of his ideas about literary creativity. In the early criticism, there is not all that much creative theory; the main passage occurs in the preface, where the famous "spontaneous overflow" passage is followed by a Hartleian explanation of the interworkings of the poet's mind and emotions. Later, however, Wordsworth speculates on the functions of the imagination and the fancy, both of which work "to modify, to create, and to associate" (3:26).

Wordsworth elaborates upon both faculties, but is not all that clear on either. He tends toward a mixture of incompatible epistemologies, the empiricist and the transcendental— "Hartley transcendentalized by Coleridge" in Ernest De Selincourt's formula. [21] Likewise, his view of the imagination was mixed; René Wellek observes:

> In many pronouncements imagination is substantially the 18th-century faculty of arbitrary recall and willful combination of images. In others it is the neo-Platonic intellectual vision. There is apparently no chronological progress from one conception to the other. [22]

What Coleridge in the *Biographia* objected to in Wordsworth's creative theory was the Empiricist-based, mechanistic elements ascribed to the imagination.

Both Wordsworth and Coleridge were extremely interested in creative theory; many of their poems, such as *The Prelude* and "Dejection: An Ode," are themselves concerned with the psychology of composition. It is clearly a central interest in

Coleridge's criticism, where, nevertheless, he attempted to meld the literary and the creative theory into one great critical system.

There is nothing inherent in the combination that prevented Coleridge from finally working his system out. There is nothing, that is, incompatible between mimetic theory, which explains the relationship of literature and life, and creative theory, which speculates on the immediate origins of literature in the mind of the writer. The shift in epistemology between the static world of the empiricists and the active mind of the transcendentalists should not be allowed to confuse the issue.

In the criticism of Wordsworth and Coleridge, literature is clearly mimetic. For Coleridge the literary imagination recreates, but what results is not a heterocosm. Rather, the stuff of experience is re-formed, and the work thus created can be judged by reference to experience. In view of his other statements about poetry in the preface to the *Lyrical Ballads*, when Wordsworth claims that "poetry is the spontaneous overflow of powerful feelings" (1:149), he must mean "is the final product of," and, even rephrased, the pronouncement is misleading in its expressionist overtones.[23] The preface, however, contains another passage that seems to me clearly antiexpressionistic: "The Poet might then be allowed to use a peculiar language when expressing his feelings for his own gratification, or that of men like himself. But Poets do not write for Poets alone, but for men" (1:142–43).

Much also has been made of Wordsworth's concern for sincerity as demonstrating expressionism; but if the passages in which he calls for sincerity are scrutinized, it is clearly not necessary that the poet *actually* should have felt what he writes, but only that he should *seem* to have: in epitaphs, "our sensations and judgment depend upon *our opinion or feeling* of the Author's state of mind" (2:97, italics added). "It is required that these truths should be instinctively ejaculated, or should rise irresistibly from circumstances; in a word that they should be uttered in such connection as shall *make it felt* that they are not adopted—not spoken by rote, but perceived in their whole compass with the freshness and clearness of an original intuition" (2:78, italics added). To this insistence on appearance of, rather than actual, sincerity and originality, add the clear concept of the use of the *persona* (3:125), and you have a theorist who can be called expressionistic only at the expense of the evidence.

vii

In what is surely unique in the history of literary criticism, Coleridge uses his creative theory for the evaluation of literature. As he mentions in the *Biographia:* "According to the faculty or source, from which the pleasure given by any poem or passage was derived, I estimated the merit of such poem or passage" (*BL,* 1:14). In practice it results in such qualitative statements as "Milton had a highly *imaginative,* Cowley a very *fanciful* mind" (*BL,* 1:62) and is evident in such evaluations as his discussion of Shakespeare's *Venus and Adonis* in chapter 15.

But such use of creative theory is limited, and even Coleridge's use of the derivative concepts of organicism and reconciliation of opposites could take him only so far in literary judgments. He turned to what he called "TRUTH, NATURE, LOGIC, and the LAWS of UNIVERSAL GRAMMAR" (*BL,* 1:14) for principles with which to judge literature, and he used traditional concepts, such as mimesis/universality and purposiveness, as his basic premises.

Compared to Dr. Johnson's, Coleridge's critical works do not contain much evaluation. George Watson, a historian of English criticism, has gone so far as to claim that Coleridge is even antagonistic to literary judging, citing as proof the following passage from his Shakespeare criticism: "Reviews are generally pernicious, because the writers determine without reference to fixed principles . . . , because they teach people rather to judge than to consider, to decide than to reflect" (*SC*, 2:33). [24] But if the quotation is continued, it is clear that Coleridge is merely objecting to superficial and unthinking judgments, not to judgments themselves: "Thus they encourage superficiality, and induce the thoughtless and the idle to adopt sentiments conveyed under the authoritative We, and not, by the working and subsequent clearing of their own minds, *to form just original opinions*" (italics added). Coleridge was very much in favor of making distinctions, literary and otherwise:

> The greater part of our success and comfort in life depends on distinguishing the similar from the same, that which is peculiar in each thing from that which it has in common with others, so as still to select the most probable, instead of the merely possible or positively unfit. (*BL*, 2:117)

Literary evaluation, of course, constitutes one kind of distinction, between the good, the not-so-good, and the bad.

When dealing with Shakespeare, Coleridge is often more appreciative than evaluative, when he is not downright bardolatrous ("My reluctance to think Shakespeare wrong, and yet—" [*SC*, 1:59]). Coleridge does concern himself a good deal with the psychological analysis of Shakespeare's characters, but Coleridge scholars have recently shown that he was at least as interested in the overall structure of the plays.

Coleridge's evaluation of the works of his friend Wordsworth is often considered Coleridge at his best. It is likewise sometimes noticed that in the sections of the *Biographia* on Wordsworth his approach seems especially traditional. Coleridge and his contemporary reviewers have much the same things to say about Wordsworth, and the theory and evaluation of both belong to the Aristotelian tradition. Coleridge's evaluative techniques—from his listing of the faults and excellencies of Wordsworth's poetry to the close analysis with which he supports his listing—could have been lifted from chapter 25 of the *Poetics* or from Longinus's remarks on Sappho's ode.

Wordsworth's own evaluation of other writers is mainly incidental, and what there is has not been very highly esteemed. He was, nevertheless, like Coleridge, in favor of literary judgment:

> Minute criticism is in its nature irksome; and, as commonly practised in books and conversation, is both irksome and injurious. Yet every mind must occasionally be exercised in this discipline, else it cannot learn the art of bringing words rigorously to the test of thoughts; and these again to a comparison with things, their archetypes; contemplated first in themselves, and secondly in relation to each other; in all which processes the mind must be skillful, otherwise it will be perpetually imposed upon. (2:77)

This quotation occurs in a passage in which Wordsworth shares Coleridge's technique of close analysis, quarreling in this case with (no less!) Pope's careless use of language.

An expressionist view of literature that is thoroughgoing cannot support an evaluative approach to a work of literature. The usual substitute is either a resort to impressionism or an evaluation, not of the work, but of the man who wrote it. Since Wordsworth and Coleridge did engage in literary evaluation, this fact should be added to the other arguments as presumptive evidence that they were Aristotelians, not Romantic expressionists.

viii

Walter Jackson Bate's *From Classic to Romantic* (1946) provides a much wider view of the phenomenon called Romanticism than does Abrams's *The Mirror and the Lamp*, which deals mainly with the new changes in artistic theory lumped together as "Expressionism." Essentially, Romanticism in the wider view consists in a rejection of seventeenth- and eighteenth-century Rationalism, itself a rejection of Humanism (a collective system of classical values). Rationalism attempted to explain life by the use of abstract reason (what

I have called Neoclassical Rationalism comprised its literary theory) and, as such, was considered inadequate by many who then rejected reason *in general* in favor of feeling. Without the ordering capabilities of Humanistic principles or of reason, Romanticism was left with empirical relativity; thus a shift occurred from the one to the many, the general to the particular; thence came an emphasis on the individual and the subjective. Romanticism had a metaphysic of sorts.

Without reason or unchanging principles, furthermore, the rejector of Rationalism and Humanism was left without an ethic, and so again he turned to feelings, accepting them as a trustworthy guide to conduct. Man in this view is said to be by nature good and, what is more, perfectible. Romantic primitivism held that it is man's institutions that corrupt him.

In aesthetics the same phenomena occurred: feeling or sensibility was taken as the basis for creativity and criticsm—the School of Sensibility was born. Direct outgrowths in literary theory are the Romantic concepts of spontaneity and originality, expressionism, and art for art's sake. In literature itself, Romantic manifestations include such secondary characteristics as sentimentality, melancholy, exoticism, gothicism, and fantasy. These characteristics are, I believe, all symptomatic of the emotional and insecure basis of Romantic literary theory.

Romanticism so defined consists of a world view, a "system," even though Romanticism is ironically a rejection of system. In England it evolved very slowly, and, as I suggested early in this chapter, it never really flourished in English literary theory. The so-called Romantic period—the early nineteenth century—was Romantic only in some of its minor critics and in some manifestations of secondary Romantic characteristics in its literature. The later nineteenth century in England—the Victorian period—has much more claim than the early part of the century to the title *Romantic.*

There have of course been many attempts to define *Romanticism,* and I do not intend to force on anyone Bates's definition nor my elaboration of it. But at least it makes sense and has a wide consistency and, most importantly, it is useful in describing what has occurred in the history of literary theory for the past three hundred years.

In any event, there are "Romantic" elements discernible (from this point of view) in the theory of Wordsworth, although they are not part of his basic theory. Wordsworth in the preface, for example, subscribes to a form of primitivism in claiming that rustics are closer to nature and better for it (1:125). He also emphasizes feeling in poetry beyond the balance with thought seen as desirable in the Aristotelian tradition. Indeed, Wordsworth maintains that feeling is the center of his poetry: "The feeling therein developed gives importance to the action and situation, and not the action and situation to the feeling" (1:129). Coleridge's theory, so far as I am aware, contains almost no specifically "Romantic" elements as described above. But even Wordsworth lashed out occasionally at manifestations of Romanticism. Wordsworth in the preface to the *Lyrical Ballads* attacked what can be called the new "Romantic" literature as a positive threat to the literary tradition:

A multitude of causes, unknown to former times, are now acting with a combined force to blunt the discriminating powers of the mind, and, unfitting it for all voluntary exertion, to reduce it to a state of almost savage torpor. The most effective of these causes are the great national events which are daily taking place, and the increasing accumulation of men in cities, where the uniformity of their occupations produces a craving for extraordinary incident, which the rapid communication of intelligence hourly gratifies. To this tendency of life and manners the literature and theatrical exhibitions of the country have conformed themselves. The invaluable works of our elder writers . . . are driven into neglect by frantic novels, sickly and stupid German Tragedies, and deluges of idle and extravagant stories in verse. (1:129)

Wordsworth wished to put the full weight of his influence behind stemming these new literary trends.

Wordsworth was of course unsuccessful. He and Coleridge are frequently considered notable literary influences, not so much on nineteenth-century, but rather on twentieth-century literature and criticism. Wordsworth's influence was largely confined to literature: he opened up the possibility of using undignified subject matter in serious poetry, as well as a less exclusive kind of poetic diction. Coleridge, on the other hand, influenced modern criticism, especially the theory and practice of the New Critics. Coleridge was the most direct transmitter of the concept of organic form, the identification of form and content, and his concept of the reconciliation of opposites led to the New Critical concept of inclusiveness.

But both Wordsworth and Coleridge were, in terms of fundamental literary theory, in the Aristotelian tradititon, and, as such, they were not so much innovative influences as they were torchbearers. One exception to this statement was Wordsworth's introduction of the concept of the indirect working of morality in literature, which he passed on to Matthew Arnold, the next major figure in the tradition, who elaborated upon the concept.

NOTES

1. M. H. Abrams, *The Mirror and the Lamp: Romantic Theory and the Critical Tradition* (New York, 1953), pp. 48, 56, 103-4, 107, 124, 225, 328. At his most inconsistent, Abrams claims: "Wordsworth remained within a well-defined tradition in the general pattern of his criticism, no less than in its details" (p. 104), and yet within a few pages he refers to Wordsworth's "expressive theory of poetry" (p. 108).

2. Ibid., pp. 70-71.

3. Ibid., p. 77.

4. All these pieces appear in William Wordsworth, *The Prose Works of William Wordsworth,* ed. W. J. B. Owen and J. W. Smyser, 3 vols. (Oxford, 1974). All quotations from Wordsworth are from this edition; subsequent references to his works appear in parentheses in the text.

5. John O. Hayden, "Coleridge, the Reviewers, and Wordsworth," *Studies in Philology* 68 (1971):106.

6. Coleridge's Shakespeare criticism has been collected in *Shakespearian Criticism*, ed. Thomas M. Raysor (London, 1960), 2 vols. Subsequent references to this work, cited as *SC*, appear in parentheses in the text.

7. Samuel Taylor Coleridge, *Coleridge's Miscellaneous Criticism*, ed. Thomas M. Raysor (London, 1936), and idem, *Coleridge on the Seventeenth Century*, ed. R. F. Brinkley (Durham, N. C., 1955).

8. R. H. Fogle, *The Idea of Coleridge's Criticism* (Berkeley, Calif., 1962), pp. x, 121.

9. Samuel Taylor Coleridge, *Biographia Literaria*, ed. John Shawcross, 2 vols. (London, 1965), 1:105. Subsequent references to this work, cited as *BL*, appear in parentheses in the text.

10. George Whalley, "The Integrity of *Biographia Literaria*," *Essays and Studies*, 6 n.s. (1953):87–101.

11. W. J. B. Owen, *Wordsworth as Critic* (Toronto, 1969), p. 112.

12. Roger Sharrock, "Wordsworth's Revolt against Literature," *Essays in Criticism* 3 (1953) :396–412; answered in Stephen M. Parrish, "Wordsworth and Coleridge on Meter," *Journal of English and Germanic Philology* 59 (1960):41–49.

13. Basil Willey, *Coleridge on Imagination and Fancy* (London, 1947), p. 11.

14. R. L. Brett, "Coleridge's Theory of the Imagination," *Essays and Studies*, 2 n.s. (1949):80.

15. Nicholas Brooke, "Coleridge's 'True and Original Realism,' " *Durham University Journal* 22 (1961):59.

16. Clarence Thorpe, "Coleridge as Aesthetician and Critic," *Journal of the History of Ideas* 5 (1944):399; John Shawcross, Introduction to *Biographia Literaria*, by Coleridge, 1:1xvii; Brett, "Coleridge's Theory," p. 77.

17. James Benziger, "Organic Unity: Leibnitz to Coleridge," *Publications of the Modern Language Association* 66 (1951):27.

18. G. N. G. Orsini, "Coleridge and Schlegel Reconsidered," *Comparative Literature* 16 (1964):113.

19. Emerson R. Marks, "Means and Ends in Coleridge's Critical Method," *Journal of English Literary History* 26 (1959):395.

20. Fogle, *Idea of Coleridge's Criticism*, pp. 12. 112.

21. William Wordsworth, *The Prelude*, ed. Ernest DeSelincourt 2d ed., rev. Helen Darbishire (Oxford, 1959), p. 1xix.

22. René Wellek, *A History of Modern Criticism; 1750-1950*, 4 vols. (London, 1966), 2:144.

23. George Watson, *The Literary Critics*, 2d ed. (New York, 1964), p. 106.

24. Ibid., pp. 104–5.

Matthew Arnold

i

Matthew Arnold is considered the most important literary critic, at least in England, of the second half of the nineteenth century. But, coming as he does after the splintering of criticism so often noted as following the modern trends set by Coleridge, Arnold's place in the history of literary criticism is not nearly so easily agreed upon. Often he is seen as a throwback to "classical values" held sometime in the past. Such, for example, is Walter Jackson Bate's view of Arnold.[1]

The reactionary side of his criticism is indeed prominent; Arnold does appear at first glance to represent little progress in literary theory. The creative theories of Wordsworth and Coleridge, especially their analyses of imagination and fancy, are largely missing. Arnold, furthermore, was at least partly against the then-current Romantic literary trends (as I have defined them in the last chapter). Thus he attacks Ruskin's "romanesque" sentimentality, although at least one scholar has argued at length that Arnold was himself a Romantic in his interest in feeling over ideas and in the personal life of poets. A look below the surface, nevertheless, will show that in elemental ways, Arnold belongs to the Aristotelian tradition of literary theory, that he held to traditional concepts of mimesis/universality and purposiveness. Often to be traditional is to *seem* stubbornly reactionary, especially when the current of ideas has changed directions radically.

Part of the difficulty of placing Arnold's literary criticism involves the writing itself. Arnold is frequently accused, and quite rightly, of being unsystematic in his thought, a charge that leads to the long lists of inconsistencies brought forward by many commentators. Vagueness and inability to define terms sharply, moreover, make dealing with Arnold's prose a hazardous business, even though one believes he has caught the drift of Arnold's argument.

Arnold's style and tone tend to put readers off, thus compounding existing obscurities. Arnold's repetitions of words and phrases can easily annoy, and annoyance lead to misunderstanding. More than one scholar has cautioned, nevertheless, that despite Arnold's stated antagonism to rhetoric, he was out to persuade his readers, and that if he used persuasive rhetorical devices such as repetition, he was very often effective in emphasizing his ideas by such use. Arnold's usual tone in his criticism has been described by H. W. Garrod as "High-Church ceremonial," even though he found that the final effect of the essays was not to overwhelm but to flatter the reader into submission "by the constant sense that he is acquiring sweetness and light and that he is one of a very few persons who are doing so."[2]

Another problem in trying to place Arnold's literary criticism is that it is often merged in very subtle ways with other kinds of criticism—political, social, religious. For Arnold in a very real sense was a literary critic "by accident," with most of his published work in other fields; to his contemporaries he probably seemed (with a little exaggeration) "a successful writer upon educational, political, and theological subjects—who had once written poetry which nobody read, and who from time to time wrote literary criticism which not very many people read."[3] In any case, Arnold was quite aware, as he put it, that "literature is a part of civilisation; it is not the whole."[4] He did, nonetheless, devote two of the three periods of his writing career mostly to literary criticism—the middle of his career was given over to religious, social, and political criticism. Even in the first and last parts of his career, however, the literary criticism is often diluted with other concerns; for, although much of his "criticism" (as a whole) was occasional—prefaces and reviews—Arnold's evangelical urge brought him again and again to one extraliterary concern or another.

His first prose piece, the preface to his *Poems* of 1853, contains, at least in embryo, most of what Arnold later said about literature. But immediately the position of his literary criticism, especially with relation to contemporary critics, is tangled in complexities. The antagonism to romantic literary trends ("individualism, subjectivism, and expressionism") appears eccentric and reactionary when contrasted to the views of a number of early Victorian literary theorists.[5] But compared to attitudes current in contemporary reviews, Arnold's views, according to one scholar, were "fairly widely shared by at least a substantial minority of critics and general readers."[6] And yet to complicate matters further, other positions taken in the reviews, especially the preference for modern subjects and the insistence on the responsibility of the poet as the help and comforter of his age, became the major targets of Arnold's preface.

"On the Modern Element in Literature" (1857), originally Arnold's inaugural lecture as Professor of Poetry at Oxford, continued one of the themes of the 1853 preface—that Greek literature should be a model for contemporary poets. It was never collected by Arnold. *On Translating Homer* (1861) was the first volume of criticism published by Arnold and sometimes is considered among his best. For almost the first time, Saintsbury points out, "we have ancient literature treated more or less like modern," that is, neither philologically nor pedantically.[7]

The next volume published, the *Essays in Criticism, First Series* (1865), represents the most important bulk of the literary criticism of his first period. Although published previously, the essays were probably intended when written to be published later as a unit; one scholar has argued persuasively that a unity of inspiration, theme, method, and aim reinforces Arnold's own claims of integrity for the volume. Most of the essays were, moreover, written or conceived during less than three months, from "about the end of November, 1862" to before the end of January, 1863."[8]

The first series is largely concerned with Continental subjects. Most essays deal with individual authors who are of minor importance—Joubert and the Guerins, for example. Various reasons are given for this choice, usually reflecting the overall attitude toward Arnold of the commentator who is speculating: snobbery, the desire to awaken curiosity, the exploratory nature of Arnold's criticism. Less than half the material in the volume, in any case, could strictly be called literary in its major concern.

The *Essays* have occasioned a number of accusations. The Continental bias probably is responsible for Walter Raleigh's charge that Arnold is blindly un-English in his critical approach.[9] Any number of later critics have accused Arnold of being unscholarly or, as John Eells put it, "quite unburdened by learning."[10] Unlike most, however, Eells is quick to point out that Arnold was nevertheless "an admirably educated, perfectly cultivated man." Another scholar has attempted to place him more specifically: "He was more learned than our journalists, and not so learned as our professors," somewhere, that is, between popularizer and specialist.[11]

The essays themselves show the influence of Sainte-Beuve, especially Arnold's appropriation of the portrait littéraire and the causerie from this contemporary French critic whom he so admired. With Sainte-Beuve as model, Arnold's essays become a mixture of "biography, liberal quotation, and psychological observation."[12] Four of the essays were even suggested by previous treatment by Sainte-Beuve; and the term *disinterested* apparently originated with the French critic.

"The Function of Criticism at the Present Time," which led off the volume, is the most important of the essays in the first series. The occasion of the essay, which has led to some misunderstanding, has only recently been uncovered. The purpose of the essay was to modify previous statements concerning the scope of criticism made initially in a theological controversy involving Bishop Colenso.

After almost twenty years of dealing with largely nonliterary concerns, Arnold returned to literary criticism about 1880. The fruits of this return were collected in the *Essays in Criticism, Second Series,* selected by Arnold but published posthumously in 1888. Now the subjects were predominantly British with special attention to Romantic writers; and, unlike the earlier collection, the emphasis was now on verse. The trend, too, was toward more evaluation.

This trend can be seen in the opening essay, again the most important, "The Study of Poetry." Originally the preface to a selected edition of English poetry produced by his nephew-in-law, this essay has frequently been praised for its ability to say so much in so little space. One of the methods making the conciseness possible is Arnold's use of the "touchstone" method, which will be dealt with later. The essay on Wordsworth is also important as containing Arnold's clearest treatment of the indirect moral workings of literature.

Other essays that treat literary subjects, at least in part, are scattered in various periodicals and volumes edited by Arnold and others; some were collected in 1910 into a volume entitled *Essays in Criticism, Third Series.* But the most important items have already been mentioned. I shall emphasize the two collections of *Essays in Criticism* edited by Arnold himself.

ii

Arnold was not much interested in creative theory. Some of the ramifications of previous theory are, however, evident in his criticism. The organic concept of poetry occurs here and there in Arnold's criticism, even if perhaps not in its purer forms. He comments on Byron's mode of improvisation: "Nor could Byron have produced his work in any other fashion; his poetic work could not have first grown and matured in his own mind, and then come forth as an organic whole."[13] Byron, he continues, could not produce "the instinctive artistic creation of poetic wholes."

Not even a thoroughgoing New Critic denies that form and

content are separable for the purpose of analyzing a poem; otherwise analysis would be at an end. But Arnold goes beyond just such "distinction . . . not division" (in Coleridge's phrase). Before his last phase, he did not really concern himself with the relationship of form and content, and, even during the last decade, he is not always consistently an organicist. In the 1853 preface, Arnold emphasized the subject matter of poetry as if it was distinct; in "The Study of Poetry" his touchstones are anything but organic, and yet in "Wordsworth" he attacked those who would distill Wordsworth's "philosophy" from his poetry. Later, Arnold seems to have adhered to a concept of form he termed *"architectonicé,"* which Vincent Buckley has called "built-form"—very closely connected with the character of the poet and, although distinct from organic form, nevertheless not mechanical in its process. [14]

Evaluation, rather than creative theory, was Arnold's major interest as a literary critic. Yet he did not produce all that much close analysis and judgment of texts. In this respect, he earned T. S. Eliot's stricture that he was "rather a propagandist for criticism than a critic." [15] In any event, he was extremely concerned about literary evaluation. In "The Function of Criticism," he remarks: "Judging is often spoken of as the critic's one business, and so in some sense it is." [16] Again, in *On Translating Homer* he comments that "it is the critic's first duty—prior even to his duty of stigmatizing the bad—*to welcome everything that is good.* " [17] Literary criticism was, however, seen by Arnold as only part of a wider "criticism" or scrutiny of political, social, and religious matters, and finally of life in general.

The greater part of the more strictly literary evaluations occur in the *Essays in Criticism, Second Series*—both in "The Study of Poetry," which attempts a revaluation of English literature, and in the essays on particular authors. Like the judgments of Johnson and Coleridge, his are not incidental to the essays. Arnold was concerned that distinctions be made:

> In poetry, which is thought and art in one, it is the glory, the eternal honour, that charlatanism shall find no entrance; that this noble sphere be kept inviolate and inviolable. Charlatanism is for confusing or obliterating the distinctions between excellent and inferior, sound and unsound or only half-sound, true and untrue or only half-true. It is charlatanism, conscious or unconscious, whenever we confuse or obliterate these. . . . In poetry . . . distinction . . . is of paramount importance because of the high destinies of poetry.[18]

In an even more general view, evaluation is important because "the world is forwarded by having its attention fixed on the best things."[19]

Arnold's concern for literature evidently arises from the same source as Wordsworth's earlier in the century, that is, from dismay at corrupt literary trends, and the concern led him to insist on evaluation. For evaluation is justified because "the benefit of being able clearly to feel and deeply to enjoy the best, the truly classic, in poetry—is an end . . . of supreme importance.[20] And, he continues in a passage reminiscent of Wordsworth's warning in the preface, "we are often told that an era is opening in which we are to see multitudes of a common sort of readers, and masses of a common sort of literature; that such readers do not want and could not relish anything better than such literature, and that to provide it is becoming a vast and profitable industry." Literature, Arnold insisted to the contrary, is not merely a high-class form of entertainment. Just as Wordsworth attacked the dilettantes, those "who talk of poetry as a matter of amusement and idle pleasure," so Arnold insists that "we should conceive of poetry worthily, and more highly than it has been the custom to conceive of it."[21] For such insistence, Arnold has often been accused of taking too serious a view toward literature.

He had a distaste for most of Victorian literature, and concerned himself with it very little. Instead, he spent most of his judgmental efforts revaluating the literature of the past. His estimation of Chaucer is very often dismissed; the most that is usually said in extenuation is that he probably had not read all of Chaucer's works. Arnold was not interested in the lyric, and thus slights Elizabethan and most of seventeenth-century English poetry. In fact, his knowledge of English literature before the eighteenth century seems to have been meager. Even what he says about the Augustans tends more to reflect the feelings of his own period than to present a fresh view of their work.

Arnold's evaluations of the English Romantic poets have been most influential; where his other judgments have been most often ignored, his judgments of Wordsworth and Byron, Shelley and Keats, have had more endurance. His choice of Wordsworth and Byron as the best of the Romantics still seems arguable, even if based on mostly the wrong reasons. This is especially true in the case of Byron, whose satires were ignored by Arnold.

It is generally conceded that Arnold missed at least part of Wordsworth's greatness, but the motives ulterior to Arnold's position are usually ignored. He was attempting to save Wordsworth from the Cambridge Wordsworthians, one of whom, Leslie Stephen, had published an essay on Wordsworth a few months before, stressing his "philosophy." This circumstance perhaps accounts for Arnold's totally ignoring Wordsworth's ideas. Another essay on Wordsworth, by Walter Pater (1879), was also published just before Arnold's; Pater's essay was probably responsible for Arnold's attack on an exaggerated concern for style and on indifference to morality in literature. Arnold's strictures on Gautier can even be attributed to Pater's praise of him.

iii

In *On Translating Homer*, Arnold parenthetically complains: "I dislike to meddle with general rules"; and there is in his criticism a general reluctance to deal with abstract theory. Some commentators have seen this as merely part of Arnold's inability to give clear definitions and as representative of his general lack of system, even as a sign of romantic tendencies. Arnold did distrust abstractions and had a healthy preference for concreteness, but he also ended the 1853 preface with a call for "boundaries and wholesome regulative laws" and with an attack on their opposite, the "eternal enemy [of poetry], caprice."[22] In any case, literary theory was present at least implicitly in Arnold's criticism whether he liked it or not.

The only basic element in the literary theory of the Aristotelian tradition still needing elaboration was the concept of the indirect moral working of literature. This concept, as we have seen, was first casually enunciated by William Wordsworth, Arnold's poetic mentor, who was surely a major influence on Arnold's theory in this regard. If Wordsworth had not provided him with such a concept, it is perhaps doubtful whether Arnold would have arrived at moral indirectness; for the age during which he was forming his literary principles was staunchly pragmatic and moralistic in its views of art. His contemporaries likewise rejected the Romantic concept of the strict autonomy of art; although D. G. James emphasizes Arnold's failure to maintain that concept, obviously Arnold deserves little credit for originality in this matter.[23]

In "The Study of Poetry" Arnold introduces the Horatian formula: "The best poetry will be found to have a power of forming, sustaining, and delighting us, as nothing else can."[24] But it is only the moral half of the formula that constitutes his importance for the tradition. The strongest case for the indirect moral working of literature, the classic phrasing for the concept in fact, occurs in his essay "Wordsworth." After claiming that poetry is the application of ideas to life, Arnold pauses:

> If it is said that to call these ideas *moral* ideas is to introduce a strong and injurious limitation, I answer that it is to do nothing of the kind, because moral ideas are really so main a part of human life. The question, *how to live,* is itself a moral

idea; and it is the question which most interests every man, and with which, in some way or other, he is perpetually occupied. A large sense is of course to be given to the term *moral*. Whatever bears upon the question "how to live," comes under it. [25]

Arnold has sometimes been attacked for vagueness in his expression "a large sense," but his meaning has always seemed clear enough to me.

Arnold nevertheless is still attacked for being moralistic, even by those who recognize that he had no use for didacticism in literature. Vincent Buckley, in *Poetry and Morality,* seems never to have conceived of an indirect moral process—that literature is moral in expanding the reader's understanding of life. Lacking such a concept, he is left with claiming that Arnold requires too immediate a moral effect, that he believes that literature teaches by example and insists in a sort of "didactic" manner on a literature that stimulates one directly to virtuous action. [26] An antidote to Buckley's view is that of David Perkins, who perhaps makes Arnold's position even clearer than it is:

To study poetry, then, is a vital way of deepening the experience of living. And by enlarging and deepening the content of one's experience, the material or subject-matter of poetry may be said to have a moral significance. For poetry, unless it is merely formalistic, necessarily occupies itself with human experiences and human reactions to experience. Its subject is "that great and inexhaustible word *life.*" Furthermore, . . . the best poetry brings out and emphasizes the actual value and worth of this experience. Thus by implication poetry treats the "question, *how to live,*"and therefore assumes an important moral significance. Moreover, poetry corresponds to human experience by presenting its moral evaluation not as an abstraction but as a vital process of reacting to concrete objects and situations. . . . In other words, poetry offers a unified rendition of things so that they constitute a significant experience. [27]

Literature, for Arnold, finally involves a kind of surrogate experience.

And yet there is something in Arnold's concept of the morality of literature that continues to bother readers. Admittedly he does not make nearly enough of a case for the pleasure side of the Horatian formula. In the 1853 preface he does contend of poets that "their business is not to praise their age, but to afford to the men who live in it the highest pleasure which they are capable of feeling." But such remarks are rare, especially when compared to those made by Dr. Johnson or Wordsworth. Perhaps the reason for the lopsided moral emphasis was that the contemporary aesthetic movement with its hedonistic bias was seen as a misguided threat by Arnold.

Ironically, Arnold has been accused of partial responsibility for Walter Pater and the whole aesthetic movement. The principal passage usually cited in the accusations occurs at the beginning of "The Study of Poetry":

> More and more mankind will discover that we have to turn to poetry to interpret life for us, to console us, to sustain us. Without poetry, our science will appear incomplete; and most of what now passes with us for religion and philosophy will be replaced by poetry.[28]

George Watson, zeroing in on the phrase "what now passes with us for," has claimed that Arnold is merely prophesying the replacement of "the sham religion of dogmatic assertion," not religion itself.[29] And yet the drift of Arnold's ideas about the role of literature is all too clear: it will supply the moral foundation and impetus traditionally supplied by religion. As H. W. Garrod has so succinctly put it: "Matthew Arnold's religion was poetry—those of us who are so happy as to have better ones are, I suppose, the better for it. In the collapse of the creeds, Matthew Arnold took what he could get."[30]

Arnold was doubtless asking of literature more than can be expected of it, thereby doing it an injustice. On the other hand, it is surely doing Arnold an injustice to trace Pater and the aesthetes to his door. Arnold is not the first critic to have the drift of his words distorted, for even if his words may have led circuitously to the religion of art, they are themselves based on his general view of the morality of literature. He was pushing that view too hard, not too little. The aesthetes held to the Romantic concept that art is autonomous and autotelic; Arnold abominated such theory.

On the other hand, Matthew Arnold was just as dead set against literary didacticism or the *direct* moral working of literature. Immediately before his classic passage on morality in "a large sense," Arnold comes out against "the composing moral and didactic poems," adding: "That brings us but a very little way in poetry."[31] So too, Arnold qualified his heavily moral commitment that "poetry is at bottom a criticism of life" with the phrase "under the conditions immutably fixed by the laws of poetic beauty and poetic truth."[32] The influence of Pater in this qualification is a distinct possibility.

iv

In the 1853 preface, Arnold contends that a modern poet may use past actions as his subject, for although "the externals of a past action, indeed, he cannot know with the precision of a contemporary," such a limitation is unimportant, since "his business is with its essentials."[33] The houses and ceremonies of characters from the past

he cannot accurately figure to himself; but neither do they essentially concern him. His business is with their inward man; with their feelings and behaviour in certain tragic situations, which engage their passions as men; these have in them nothing local and casual.

Several paragraphs preceding, Arnold also mentions that the best actions to select are those "which most powerfully appeal to the great primary human affections," echoing

Wordsworth's own appeal to universality in the preface to *Lyrical Ballads*. Arnold's appeal to the traditional concept of universality and his debt to previous theorists in the tradition is reinforced, furthermore, by a direct reference to Aristotle's *Poetics*, which he quotes in "The Study of Poetry" as a criterion of poetic worth: "a higher truth" or universality.[34]

Besides appearing as direct theory, the concept of universality appears in many guises. For one thing, historical realism is out of the question. In "Dante and Beatrice," for example, Arnold remarks: "Art requires a basis of fact, but it also desires to treat this basis of fact with the utmost freedom; and this desire for the freest handling of its object is even thwarted when its object is too near, and too real."[35] Arnold also uses the concept in his practical criticism, when, for instance, he remarks about the "intimations" of Wordsworth's Ode: "To say that universally this instinct is mighty in childhood, and tends to die afterwards, is to say what is extremely doubtful."[36]

Perhaps the clearest evidence of the concept in Arnold's criticism is his belief that there is something permanent in great literature, something that can even be refined to the essence of "touchstones." The use of lines as touchstones, set forth in "The Study of Poetry," is not confined to that essay; this comparative method is rather a characteristic of Arnold's criticism.

While it is often allowed that the touchstones Arnold presents in "The Study" demonstrate an impressive taste, they are nevertheless the subject of considerable criticism. In "The Study" Arnold claims that "short passages, even single lines, will serve our turn quite sufficiently." He later qualifies this in his evaluation of Chaucer: "A single line, however, is too little if we have not the strain of Chaucer's verse well in our memory."[37] And yet Arnold only expands his sample to a stanza.

It is this lack of representative quality, the tearing of the line or short passage out of context, that has elicited the most objections. His touchstones have been compared to the classic anecdote of the fellow who carried a brick to show what his house looked like, and to the incident in Aristophanes' *Frogs,* in which poetry is sold by the pound.

And if such objections were not damaging enough, John Eells in his study of the touchstones has shown that they do not really differ much, as Arnold had claimed they did, and that they thus point up a kind of personal bias rather than universal qualities.[38] That four of the eleven touchstones in "The Study" are misquoted likewise supports the evidence of the personal touch. And, as part of an evaluative approach, they beg the question of just who the greatest poets are.

Some of these objections can, I believe, be put aside by taking a closer look at what Arnold has in mind. He does not intend his touchstones to be compared unimaginatively with the lines of other poets. It is rather a matter of feeling: "If we are thoroughly penetrated by their power, we shall find that we have acquired a sense enabling us, whatever poetry may be laid before us, to feel the degree in which a high poetical quality is present or wanting there."[39] "The characters of a high quality of poetry," he continued, emphasizing the pervasive, emotional quality of the criterion, "are far better recognized by being felt in the verse of the master, than by being perused in the prose of the critic."

The sureness of Arnold's remarks, as well as the mistaken belief that the touchstones were to be applied mechanically, has led to frequent charges of dogmatism. Such charges are also no doubt partly owing to Arnold's absolutism, evident in his attack (in "The Literary Influence of Academies") on those who entertain "the baneful notion that there is no such thing as a high, correct standard in intellectual matters; that every one may as well take his own way; they are at variance with the severe discipline necessary for all real culture; they confirm us in habits of wilfulness and eccentricity."[40]

Arnold's absolutism forced him to question for the first time in the tradition that old standby, the test of time. The "real estimate" he contrasted to the personal and historical estimates (in my terms, relativism and historical relativism, respectively). With modern corruption of taste, no longer could one take as final the endurance of a work or its present popularity, although such evidence could of course be indicative. Eighteenth-century literature was a case in point: "An historic estimate of that poetry has established itself; and the question is, whether it will be found to coincide with the real estimate.[41]

"Real estimates" presuppose enduring, supranatural values, and despite all his insistence on them, Arnold was in trouble. For Arnold was a naturalist, and such absolute values are incompatible with naturalism. As E. B. Greenwood has observed, they were for Arnold "a kind of fiction" that he found necessary.[42] Arnold was in many respects the first modern literary theorist.

v

To discuss universality before mimesis is to put the cart before the horse, even if the concepts work together as a single element, but it testifies to Arnold's strong reputation for insisting on the close relationship of literature and life that evidence of his mimetic beliefs could be postponed.

In the 1853 preface Arnold links his views with those of the founder of the tradition: "We all naturally take pleasure, says Aristotle, in any imitation or representation whatever: this is the basis of our love of poetry. . . . Any accurate representation may therefore be expected to be interesting."[43] In his last volume, Arnold reiterates the concept: "It is by a large, free, sound representation of things, that poetry, this high criticism of life, has truth of substance."[44] The same volume contains his famous dictum that "poetry is at bottom a criticism of life," which makes the connection between literature and life so strongly that many have been annoyed. In the phrase, Arnold was also pointing up the interworkings of

30. Garrod, *Poetry and the Criticism of Life,* p. 70.

31. Arnold, *Essays in Criticism,* p. 301.

32. Ibid., pp. 301–2.

33. Arnold, *Prose Works,* 1:5.

34. Arnold, *Essays in Criticism,* p. 244.

35. Matthew Arnold, *Essays in Criticism: Third Series* (Boston, 1910), p. 93.

36. Arnold, *Essays in Criticism,: First and Second Series,* p. 306.

37. Ibid., pp. 242, 248; W. K. Wimsatt, Jr., and Cleanth Brooks, *Literary Criticism: A Short History* (New York, 1965), p. 445.

38. Eells, *Touchstones of Arnold,* p. 208.

39. Arnold, *Essays in Criticism, First and Second Series,* pp. 243, 244.

40. Ibid., p. 45.

41. Ibid., p. 250.

42. E. B. Greenwood, "Matthew Arnold: Thoughts on a Centenary," *Twentieth Century* 162 (1957):475.

43. Arnold, *Prose Works,* 1:1–2.

44. Arnold, *Essays in Criticism, First and second Series,* p. 247.

45. Lionel Trilling, *Matthew Arnold* (New York, 1955), p. 179.

46. Arnold, *Prose Works,* 136–39.

47. Arnold, *Essays in Criticism, First and Second Series,* p. 244; Eells, pp. 222–24.

48. Arnold, *Essays in Criticism, First and Second Series,* p. 254.

49. William A. Madden, *Matthew Arnold: A Study of the Aesthetic Temperament in Victorian England* (Bloomington, Ind., 1967), p. 194.

Select Bibliography

The following lists, divided by chapters, contain those secondary sources which seem to me useful for understanding the individual critics involved, as well as the history of literary theory.

Abbreviations used:

AJP	American Journal of Philology
CJ	Classical Journal
CL	Comparative Literature
CP	Classical Philology
CQ	Classical Quarterly
ECS	Eighteenth Century Studies
EIC	Essays in Criticism
ELH	Journal of English Literary History
HSCP	Harvard Studies in Classical Philology
JEGP	Journal of English and Germanic Philology
MLN	Modern Language Notes
MLR	Modern Language Review
MP	Modern Philology
N&Q	Notes and Queries
PMLA	Publications of the Modern Language Association
PQ	Philological Quarterly
REL	Review of English Literature
RES	Review of English Studies
SEL	Studies in English Literature
SP	Studies in Philology
TAPA	Transactions of the American Philological Association
UTQ	University of Toronto Quarterly

CHAPTER 1: GENERAL

Abrams, Meyer H. *The Mirror and the Lamp.* New York, 1953.

Bate, Walter Jackson. *From Classic to Romantic.* Cambridge, Mass., 1946.

————, ed. *Criticism: The Major Texts.* New York, 1952.

Hall, Vernon. *Literary Criticism: Plato through Johnson.* New York, 1970.

Johnson, W. P. *Greek Literary Criticism.* Oxford, 1907.

Roberts, William Rhys. *Greek Rhetorical and Literary Theory.* New York, 1928.

Saintsbury, George. *A History of Criticism.* 3 vols. New York, 1950.

Watson, George. *The Literary Critics.* 2d ed. New York, 1964.

Weinberg, Bernard. *A History of Literary Criticism in the Italian Renaissance.* 2 vols. Chicago, 1963.

Wellek, René. *A History of Modern Criticism: 1750–1950.* 5 vols. to date New Haven, Conn., 1955–

Wellek, René, and Warren, Austin. *Theory of Literature.* 3d ed. New York, 1956.

Wimsatt, William K., Jr., and Brooks, Cleanth. *Literary Criticism: A Short History.* New York, 1965.

CHAPTER 2: PLATO AND ARISTOTLE

Abercrombie, Lascelles. *Principles of Literary Criticism.* London, 1932.

Armstrong, Angus. "Aristotle's Theory of Poetry." *Greece and Rome* 10 (1941):120–25.

Atkins, J. W. H. *Literary Criticism in Antiquity.* Vol. 1. Gloucester, Mass., 1961.

Baldwin, Charles Sears. *Ancient Rhetoric and Poetic.* Gloucester, Mass., 1959.

Boyd, James Dixon. *The Function of Mimesis and Its Decline.* Cambridge, Mass., 1968.

Brownson, Carleton L. *Plato's Studies and Criticisms of Poets.* Boston, 1920.

Collingwood, R. G. "Plato's Philosophy of Art." *Mind* 34 (1925): 154–72.

Cooper, Lane. *The "Poetics" of Aristotle: Its Meaning and Influence.* Boston, 1923.

Crane, Ronald S. "Poetic Structure in the Language of Aristotle." *The Languages of Criticism and the Structure of Poetry.* Toronto, 1953.

Else, Gerald. *Aristotle's "Poetics": The Argument.* Cambridge, Mass., 1957.

_____."'Imitation' in the Fifth Century." *CP* 53 (1958):72–90.

French, W. F. "The Function of Poetry according to Aristotle." *Studies* 19 (1930):549–63.

Gilbert, Allan H. "Did Plato Banish the Poets or the Critics? *SP* 36 (1939):1–19.

Gilbert, Katherine E. "Aesthetic Imitation and Imitators in Aristotle." *Philosophical Review* 45 (1936):558–73.

Golden, Leon. "Catharsis." *TAPA* 93 (1962):51–60.

_____."*Mimesis* and *Katharsis*," *CP* 64 (1969):145–53.

Golden, Leon, and Hardison, O. B., Jr. *Aristotle's "Poetics."* Englewood Cliffs, N.J., 1968.

Gomme, Arnold Wycombe. *The Greek Attitude to Poetry and History.* Berkeley, Calif., 1954.

Greene, William Chase. "The Greek Criticism of Poetry: A Reconsideration." *Perspectives of Criticism.* Edited by Harry Levin. Cambridge, Mass., 1950.

_____."Plato's View of Poetry." *HSCP* 29 (1918):1–76.

Gresseth, G. K. "The System of Aristotle's *Poetics*." *TAPA* 89 (1958): 312–35.

Grube, G. M. A. *The Greek and Roman Critics.* London, 1965.

_____. "Three Greek Critics." *UTQ* 21 (1952):345–61.

Hack, R. K. "The Doctrine of Literary Forms." *HSCP* 27 (1916): 1–65.

Hardie. R. R. "The Poetics of Aristotle." *Mind,* n.s. 4 (1895):350–64.

Herrick, Marvin Theodore. "The Early History of Aristotle's *Rhetoric* in England." *PQ* 5 (1926):242–57.

Hogan, James C. "Aristotle's Criticism of Homer in the *Poetics, CP* 68 (1973):95–108.

House, Humphrey. *Aristotle's "Poetics": A Course of Eight Lectures.* London, 1956.

Jones, John. *On Aristotle and Greek Tragedy.* New York, 1962.

Lodge, Rupert Clendon. *Plato's Theory of Art.* London, 1953.

Lucas, Frank L. *Tragedy in Relation to Aristotle's "Poetics."* London, 1928.

McKeon, Richard. "Literary Criticism and the Concept of Imitation in Antiquity." *Critics and Criticism.* Edited by Ronald S. Crane. Chicago, 1952.

Moss, Leonard, "Plato and the *Poetics,"PQ* 50 (1971):533-42.

Olson, Elder. "The Poetic Method of Aristotle." *English Institute Essays,* 1951. New York, 1951.

———, ed. *Aristotle's "Poetics" and English Literature: A Collection of Critical Essays.* Chicago, 1965.

Ostwald, Martin. "Aristotle on *Hamartia* and Sophocles' *Oedipus Tyrannus.*" In *Festschrift Ernst Kapp.* Hamburg, 1958.

Pitcher, Seymour M. "Aristotle on Poetic Art." *Journal of General Education* 7 (1952):56-76.

Post, Levi Arnold. "Aristotle and the Philosophy of Fiction." *From Homer to Menander.* Berkeley, Calif., 1951.

Potts, L. J. *Aristotle on the Art of Fiction.* Cambridge, 1953.

Preston, Raymond. "Aristotle and the Modern Literary Critic." *Journal of Aesthetics and Art Criticism* 21 (1962-63):57-71.

Prickard, A. O. *Aristotle on the Art of Poetry.* London, 1891.

Randall, J. H., Jr. *Aristotle.* New York, 1960.

Ransom, John Crowe. "The Literary Criticism of Aristotle." In *Lectures in Criticism,* edited by R. P. Blackmur. New York, 1961.

Ross, William David. *Aristotle.* London, 1923.

Sikes, Edward Ernest. *The Greek View of Poetry.* London, 1931.

Skulsky, Harold. "Aristotle's *Poetics* Revisited." *Journal of the History of Ideas* 19 (1958):147-60.

Solmsen, F. "The Origins and Methods of Aristotle's *Poetics.*" *CQ* 29 (1935):192-201.

Tate, J. "Imitation in Plato's *Republic.*" *CQ* 22 (1928):16-23.

———. "Plato and Imitation." *CQ* 26 (1932): 161-69.

Tracy, H. L. "Aristotle on Aesthetic Pleasure." *CP* 41 (1946):43-46.

Trench, W. F. "Mimesis in Aristotle's *Poetics.*" *Hermathena* 47 (1933): 1-24.

Verdenius, Willem Jacob. *Mimesis: Plato's Doctrine of Artistic Imitation and Its Meaning to Us.* Leiden, 1949.

Webster, T. B. L. "Fourth Century Tragedy and the *Poetics.*" *Hermes* 82 (1954):294-308.

———. "Plato and Aristotle as Critics of Greek Art." *Symbolae Osloenses* 29 (1951):8-23.

Worsfold, W. B. *The Principles of Criticism.* London, 1897.

CHAPTER 3: HORACE

Atkins, J. W. H. *Literary Criticism in Antiquity*. Vol. 2. Gloucester, Mass., 1961.

Beare, W. "Horace, Donatus and the Five-Act Law." *Hermathena* 67 (1946):53–59.

Brink, Charles O. *Horace on Poetry*. 2 vols. Cambridge, 1963-71.

Campbell, Archibald Y. *Horace: A New Interpretation*. London, 1924.

D'Alton, John F. *Roman Literary Theory and Criticism*. New York, 1962.

Fiske, George C. "Cicero's *De Oratore* and Horace's *Ars Poetica.*" *University of Wisconsin Studies* 27 (1929):446–68.

―――. "Lucilius, the *Ars Poetica* of Horace, and Persius." *HSCP* 24 (1913):1–36.

Frank, Tenney. "Horace on Contemporary Poetry." *CJ* 13 (1917–18): 550–64.

―――. "Horace's Definition of Poetry." *CJ* 31 (1935–36):167–74.

Goad, Caroline. *Horace in the English Literature of the Eighteenth Century*. New Haven, Conn., 1918.

Griffith, Helen. "The Horatian Strain in Literary Criticism." *Horace: Three Phases of His Influence*. Chicago, 1936.

Grimal, Pierre. *Horace: Art Poetique; Commentaire et Etude*. Paris, 1964.

Grube, G. M. A. *The Greek and Roman Critics*. London, 1965.

Gruening, L. "Horace et la Poesie." *Etudes Classiques* 4 (1935):52–73.

Haight, Elizabeth H. "The Lyre and the Whetstone: Horace Redivisius." *CP* 41 (1946):135–42.

Kenny, Margaret. "The Critic Looks at Horace." *CJ* 31 (1935–36): 183–88.

La Driere, Craig. "Horace and the Theory of Imitation." *AJP* 60 (1939):288–300.

Nettleship, Henry. "Horace, (2) The De Arte Poetica." *AJP* 12 (1883):43–61.

―――. *Lectures and Essays*. 2d ser. Edited by F. Haverfield. Oxford, 1895.

Ogle, M. B. "Horace an Atticist." *CP* 11 (1916):156–68.

Otis, Brooks. "Horace and the Elegists." *TAPA* 76 (1945):177–90.

Sellar, William Young. *Horace and the Elegiac Poets*. Oxford, 1899.

Sikes, Edward Ernest. *Roman Poetry*. London, 1923.

Smith, W. K. "Horace's Debt to Greek Literature." *Classical Review* 49 (1935):109–16.

Tate, J. "Horace and the Moral Function of Poetry." *CQ* 22 (1928): 65–72.

Tracy, H. L. "Horace's *Ars Poetica:* A Systematic Argument." *Greece and Rome* 17 (1948):104–15.

CHAPTER 4: LONGINUS

Allen, Walter, Jr. "The Terentinus of the Peri Hupsous." *AJP* 62 (1941):51–64.

Apfel, H. V. *Literary Quotations in Demetrius and Longinus.* New York, 1935.

Atkins, J. W. H. *Literary Criticism in Antiquity.* Vol. 2. Gloucester, Mass., 1961.

Baldwin, Charles S. *Ancient Rhetoric and Poetic.* Gloucester, Mass., 1959.

Boyd, M. J. "Longinus, the Philological Discourses and the Essay on the Sublime." *CQ,* n. s. 7 (1957):39–46.

Brody, Jules. *Boileau and Longinus.* Geneva, 1958.

Clark, Alexander F. *Boileau and the French Classical Critics in England.* Paris, 1928.

Collins, Churton. *Studies in Poetry and Criticism.* London, 1905.

Davidson, Hugh M. "The Literary Arts of Longinus and Boileau." *Studies in Seventeeth-Century French Literature Presented to Morris Bishop.* Edited by J. J. Demorest. Ithaca, N.Y., 1962.

Godolphin, F. R. B. "The Author of the *Peri Hupsous.*"*AJP* 63 (1942): 83–86.

_____ . "The Basic Critical Doctrine of Longinus' *On the Sublime.*" *TAPA* 68 (1937):172–83.

Greene, William C. "The Greek Criticism of Poetry: A Reconsideration." In *Perspectives of Criticism,* edited by H. Levin. Cambridge, Mass., 1950.

Grube, G. M. A. *The Greek and Roman Critics.* London, 1965.

_____ . "Notes on the *Peri Hupsous.*" *AJP* 78 (1957):355–74.

_____ . "Three Greek Critics." *UTQ* 21 (1952):345–61.

Henn, Thomas R. *Longinus and English Criticism.* Cambridge, 1934.

Menuez, C. F. "Longinus on the Equivalence of the Arts." *CJ* 36 (1940–41):346–53.

Monk, Samuel Holt. *The Sublime: A Study of Critical Theories in Eighteenth-Century England.* Ann Arbor, Mich., 1960.

Olson, Elder. "The Argument of Longinus' *On the Sublime.*" In *Critics and Criticism,* edited by Ronald S. Crane. Chicago, 1952.

Quiller-Couch, Arthur. *Studies in Literature.* 3d ser. New York, 1930.

Roberts, William Rhys. *Greek Rhetoric and Literary Theory.* London, 1928.

————."Longinus on the Sublime." *PQ* 7 (1928):209–19.

Russell, D. A. *Longinus on the Sublime.* Oxford, 1964.

Segal, Charles, P. "*Hupsous* and the Problem of Cultural Decline in *De Sublimitate.*"*HSCP* 64 (1959):121–46.

Sikes, Edward Ernest. *The Greek View of Poetry.* London, 1931.

Tate, Allen. "Longinus and the 'New Criticism.' " *Collected Essays.* Denver, Colo., 1959.

CHAPTER 5: SIR PHILIP SIDNEY

Atkins, J. W. H. *English Literary Criticism: The Renascence.* London, 1947.

Baldwin, Charles S. *Renaissance Literary Theory and Practice.* New York, 1939.

Bronowski, Jacob. *The Poet's Defence.* Cleveland, 1966.

Ditlevsen, Torben, " 'Truth's Journey to Word': On the Concept of 'Imitation' in Sidney's *Apology for Poetry.*" *Language and Literature* 2 (1972):54–70.

Dowlin, Cornell M. "Sidney's and Other Men's Thoughts." *RES* 20 (1944):257–71.

————. "Sidney's Two Definitions of Poetry." *Modern Language Quarterly* 3 (1942):573–81.

Friedland, Louis S. "The Dramatic Unities in England." *JEGP* 10 (1911):56–89, 280–99, 453–67.

Hall Vernon, Jr. *Renaissance Literary Criticism: A Study of Its Social Content.* New York, 1945.

Hallam, G. W. "Sidney's Supposed Ramism." *Renaissance Papers 1963.* Chapel Hill, N.C., 1963.

Hardison, O. B., Jr., ed. *English Literary Criticism: The Renaissance.* New York, 1963.

Hathaway, Baxter. *The Age of Criticism: the Late Renaissance in Italy.* Ithaca, N.Y., 1962.

————. *Marvels and Commonplaces: Renaissance Literary Criticism.* New York, 1968.

Hearsey, Marguerite. "Sidney's *Defence of Poesy* and Amyot's *Preface* in North's *Plutarch: A Relationship.*" *SP* 30 (1933):535–50.

Herrick, Marvin T. *The Fusion of Horatian and Aristotelian Literary Criticism.* Urbana, Ill., 1946.

Hyman, Virginia R. "Sidney's Definition of Poetry." *SEL* 10 (1970): 49–62.

Isler, A. D. "Heroic Poetry and Sidney's Two *Arcadias.*" *PMLA* 83 (1968):368–79.

Kishler, Thomas C. "Aristotle and Sidney on Imitation." *CJ* 59 (1963):63–64.

Krouse, F. Michael. "Plato and Sidney's *Defence of Poesy.*" *CL* 6 (1954): 138–47.

Lewis, C. S. *English Literature in the Sixteenth Century.* Oxford, 1954.

McIntyre, John P. "Sidney's Golden World." *CL* 14 (1962):356–65.

Miller, G. M. *The Historical Point of View in English Literary Criticism from 1570–1770.* Heidelberg, 1913.

Myrick, Kenneth O. *Sir Philip Sidney as a Literary Craftsman.* Cambridge, Mass., 1935.

Notte, F. O. "Imitation as an Aesthetic Norm." *Studies in Honor of Frederick W. Shipley.* St. Louis, Mo., 1942.

Quossek, C. "Sidney's *Defence of Poesy* and Die Poetik des Aristotels." Crefeld, Kuehler, 1880.

Roberts, Mark. "The Pill and the Cherries: Sidney and the Neoclassical Tradition." *EIC* 16 (1966):22–31.

Robertson, D. W. "Sidney's Metaphor of the Ulcer." *MLN* 56 (1941): 56–61

Robinson, Forest G. *The Shape of Things Known: Sidney's Apology in Its Philosophical Tradition.* Cambridge, Mass., 1972.

Samuel, Irene. "The Influence of Plato on Sir Philip Sidney's *Defence of Poetry.*" *Modern Language Quarterly* 1 (1940):383–91.

Schelling, F. E. *Poetic and Verse Criticism of the Reign of Elizabeth.* Philadelphia, 1891.

Shepherd, Geoffrey, ed. *An Apology for Poetry.* London, 1965.

"Sir Philip Sidney's *Defence of Poesy.*" *Retrospective Review* 10 (1824): 43–59.

Smith, G. G., ed. *Elizabethan Critical Essays.* 2 vols. Oxford, 1937.

Sowton, Ian. "Hidden Persuaders as a Means of Literary Grace: Sixteenth-Century Poetics and Rhetoric in England." *UTQ* 32 (1962–63):55–69.

Spingarn, Joel E. *A History of Literary Criticism in the Renaissance.* New York, 1963.

Sweeting, Elizabeth J. *Early Tudor Criticism.* New York, 1964.

Thompson, Guy Andrew. *Elizabethan Criticism of Poetry.* Menasha, Wis., 1914.

Thorne, J. P. "A Ramistical Commentary on Sidney's *An Apology for Poesy.*" *MP* 54 (1957):158–64.

Willey, Basil. *Tendencies in Renaissance Literary Theory.* Cambridge, 1922.

CHAPTER 6: JOHN DRYDEN

Aden, John M. *Critical Opinions of John Dryden: A Dictionary.* Nashville, 1963.

_____ . "Dryden and Boileau: The Question of Critical Influence." *SP* 50 (1953):491–509.

Archer, Stanley. "Persons in *An Essay of Dramatic Poesy.*" *Papers on Language and Literature* 2 (1966):305–14.

Atkins, J. W. H. *English Literary Criticism: Seventeenth and Eighteenth Centuries.* New York, 1961.

Bohn, W. E. "The Development of Dryden's Literary Criticism." *PMLA* 22 (1907):56–139.

Bredvold, Louis, I. *The Intellectual Milieu of John Dryden.* Ann Arbor, Mich., 1934.

Collins, G. S. *Dryden's Dramatic Theory and Praxis.* Leipsig, 1902.

Dryden, John. *Essays of John Dryden.* Edited by W. P. Ker. 2 vols. Oxford, 1900.

_____ . *The Works of John Dryden,* vol. 17, *Prose, 1668–1691: "An Essay of Dramatic Poesie" and Shorter Works.* Edited by Samuel Holt Monk, A. E. Wallace Maurer, and Vinton Dearing. Berkeley, Calif., 1971.

Ellis, Amanda M. "Horace's Influence on Dryden." *PQ* 4 (1925): 39–60.

Eliot, T. S. *John Dryden.* New York, 1932.

Falle, G. "Dryden: Professional Man of Letters." *UTQ* 26 (1956):443–55.

Freedman, Morris. "Milton and Dryden on Rhyme." *Huntington Library Quarterly* 24 (1960–61):337–44.

Friedland, L. S. "The Dramatic Unities in England." *JEGP* 10 (1911):56–89, 280–99, 453–67.

Frye, Prosser Hall. "Dryden and the Critical Canons of the 18th Century." *Nebraska University Studies* 7 (1907):1–39.

Hanzo, T. A. *Latitude and Restoration Criticism.* Copenhagen, 1961.

Hathaway, Baxter. "Dryden and the Function of Tragedy." *PMLA* 58 (1943):665–73.

Houston, Percy H. "The Inconsistency of John Dryden." *Sewanee Review* 22 (1914):469–82.

Hume, Robert D. *Dryden's Criticism.* Ithaca N.Y., 1970.

———. "Dryden's 'Heads of an Answer to Rymer': Notes toward a Hypothetical Revolution." *RES* n.s. 19 (1968):373–86.

Huntley, Frank L. "Dryden's Discovery of Boileau." *MP* 6 (1947–48), 112–17.

———. *On Dryden's "Essay of Dramatic Poesy."* Ann Arbor, Mich., 1951.

Kirsch, Arthur C. "Dryden's Theory and Practice of the Rhymed Heroic Play." *Dissertation Abstracts* 22 (1961), no. 1979.

———. "An Essay on *Dramatick Poetry.*" *Huntington Library Quarterly* 28 (1964):89–91.

Legouis, Pierre. "Corneille and Dryden as Dramatic Critics." *Seventeenth Century Studies Presented to Sir Herbert Grierson.* Oxford, 1938.

Mace, Dean. "Dryden's Dialogue on Drama." *Journal of the Warburg and Courtauld Institutes* 25 (1962):87–112.

Marks, Emerson R. *Relativist and Absolutist; the Early Neoclassical Debate in England.* New Brunswick, N.J., 1955.

Miller, G. M. *The Historical Point of View in English Literary Criticism from 1570–1770.* Heidelberg. 1913.

Miner, Earl. "Renaissance Contexts of Dryden's Criticism," *Michigan Quarterly Review* 12 (1973):97–115.

Monk, Smauel Holt. "Dryden and the Beginnings of Shakespeare Criticism in the Augustan Age." In *The Persistence of Shakespeare*

Idolatry: Essays in Honor of Robert W. Babcock, edited by H. M. Schueller. Detroit, Mich., 1964.

Moore, F. H. *The Nobler Pleasure: Dryden's Comedy in Theory and Practice.* Chapel Hill, N.C., 1963.

Pechter, Edward. *Dryden's Classical Theory of Literature.* Cambridge, 1975.

Sherwood, John C. "Dryden and the Rules: The Preface to the *Fables." JEGP* 52 (1953):13–26.

————. "Dryden and the Rules: The Preface to *Troilus and Cressida." CL* 2 (1950):73–83.

Sherwood, Margaret. *Dryden's Dramatic Theory and Practice.* Boston, 1898.

Simon, Irene. "Dryden's Revision of the *Essay of Dramatic Poesy." RES* 14 (1963):132–41.

Singh, Sarup. "Dryden and the Unities." *Indian Journal of English Studies* 2 (1961):78–90.

Smith, David Nichol. *John Dryden.* Cambridge, 1950.

Smith, John H. "Dryden's Critical Temper." *Washington University Studies, Humanistic Series* 12 (1925):201–20.

Strang, B. "Dryden's Innovation in Critical Vocabulary." *Durham University Journal* 51 (1959):114–23.

Thale, Mary. "Dryden's Critical Vocabulary: The Imitation of Nature." *Papers on Language and Literature* 2 (1966):315–26.

————. "Dryden's Dramatic Criticism." *CL* 18 (1966):36–54.

Tillyard, E. M. W. "A Note on Dryden's Criticism." In *The Seventeenth Century,* edited by R. F. Jones et al. Stanford, Calif., 1951.

Trowbridge, Hoyt. "Dryden's 'Essay of the Dramatic Poetry of the Last Age.'" *PQ* 22 (1943):240–50.

————. "The Place of Rules in Dryden." *MP* 44 (1946–47):84–96.

Verrall, A. W. *Lectures on Dryden.* Cambridge, 1914.

Walcott, Fred G. "Dryden's Answer to Thomas Rymer's *The Tragedies of the Last Age." PQ* 15 (1936):194–214.

Wasserman, G. R. *John Dryden.* New York, 1964.

Watson, George. "Dryden's First Answer to Rymer." *RES* 14 (1963):17–23.

Williamson, G. "The Occasion of *An Essay of Dramatic Poesy." MP* 44 (1946):1–9.

Wylie, Laura J. *Studies in the Evolution of English Criticism.* Boston, 1894.

CHAPTER 7: SAMUEL JOHNSON

Alder, Jacob H. "Johnson's 'He That Imagines This.'" *Shakespeare Quarterly* 11 (1960):225–28.

Basney, Lionel. "'Lucidus Ordo': Johnson and Generality." *ECS* 5 (1971):39–57.

Bate, Walter Jackson. *The Achievement of Samuel Johnson.* New York, 1955.

—————. *From Classic to Romantic.* New York, 1961.

Bosker, A. *Literary Criticism in the Age of Johnson.* 2d. ed. New York, 1953.

Boyce, Benjamin. "Samuel Johnson's Criticism of Pope in the *Life of Pope.*" *RES,* n.s. 5 (1954):37–46.

Bronson, Bertrand H. "The Double Tradition of Dr. Johnson." *ELH* 18 (1951):90–106.

Damrosch, Leopold. *The Uses of Johnson's Criticism.* Charlottesville, Va., 1976.

Daniel, R. W. "Johnson on Literary Texture." In *Studies in Honor of J. C. Hodges and A. Thaler,* edited by R. B. Davis and J. L. Lievsay. Knoxville, Tenn., 1961.

Downes, Rackstraw. "Johnson's Theory of Language." *REL* 3 (1962): 29–41.

Eliot, T. S. "Johnson as Critic and Poet." *On Poetry and Poets.* London, 1957.

Elledge, Scott. "The Background and Development in English Criticism of the Theories of Generality and Particularity." *PMLA* 62 (1947):147–82.

Fleischauer, Warren. "Johnson, *Lycidas,* and the Forms of Criticism." In *Johnsonian Studies,* edited by Magdi Wahba. Cairo, 1962.

Fleischmann, W. B. "Shakespeare, Johnson, and the Dramatic Unities of Time and Place." *SP* 64 (1967):128–34.

Fussell, Paul. *Samuel Johnson and the Life of Writing.* New York, 1971.

Gardner, H. "Johnson on Shakespeare." *New Rambler* 17 (1965):2–12.

Hagstrum, Jean. *Samuel Johnson's Literary Criticism.* Minneapolis, Minn., 1952.

Hamilton, Harlan W. "Samuel Johnson's Appeal to Nature." *Western Humanities Review* 21 (1969):339–45.

Hardy, John. "The 'Poet of Nature' and Self-knowledge: One Aspect of Johnson's Moral Reading of Shakespeare." *UTQ* 36 (1969): 143–60.

Havens, R. D. "Johnson's Distrust of the Imagination." *ELH* 10 (1939):243–55.

Johnson, Samuel. *The Critical Opinions of Samuel Johnson.* Edited by Joseph E. Brown. Princeton, N.J., 1926.

Kallich, M. "Samuel Johnson's Principles of Criticism and Imlac's 'Dissertation on Poetry.' " *Journal of Aesthetics and Art Criticism* 25 (1966):71–82.

Kaul, R. K. "Dr. Johnson on the Emotional Effect of Tragedy." *Cairo Studies in English* (1963–66), pp. 203–11.

————."The Unities Again: Dr. Johnson and Delusion." *N&Q* 207 (1962):261–64.

Keast, W. R. "Johnson's Criticism of the Metaphysical Poets." *ELH* 17 (1950):59–70.

————. "The Theoretical Foundations of Johnson's Criticism." In *Critics and Criticism,* edited by R. S. Crane. Chicago, 1952.

Krieger, Murray. "Fiction, Nature, and Literary Kinds in Johnson's Criticism of Shakespeare." *ECS* 4 (1971):184–98.

Leavis, F. R. "Johnson and Augustanism." *The Common Pursuit.* New York, 1952.

————. "Johnson as Critic." *Scrutiny* 12 (1944):187–204.

Marks, Emerson. *The Poetics of Reason.* New York, 1968.

Misenheimer, James B., Jr. "Dr. Johnson's Concept of Literary Fiction." *MLR* 62 (1967):598–605.

Mowat, J. "Samuel Johnson and the Critical Heritage of T. S. Eliot." *Studia Germanica Gandensia* 6 (1964):231–47.

Perkins, David. "Johnson on Wit and Metaphysical Poetry." *ELH* 20 (1953):200–17.

Raleigh, Walter. *Six Essays on Johnson.* Oxford, 1910.

Sachs, Arieh. *Passionate Intelligence: Imagination and Reason in the Work of Samuel Johnson.* Baltimore, Md., 1967.

Sen, S. K. *English Literary Criticism of the Second Half of the Eighteenth Century.* Calcutta, 1965.

Sherbo, Arthur. *Samuel Johnson, Editor of Shakespeare.* Illinois Studies in Language and Literature, vol. 42. Urbana, Ill., 1956.

Sigworth, Oliver. "Johnson's *Lycidas*: The End of Renaissance Criticism." *ECS* 1 (1967):159–68.

Spittal, J. K. *Contemporary Criticisms of Dr. Johnson.* London, 1923.

Stock, R. D. *Samuel Johnson and Neoclassical Dramatic Theory.* Lincoln, Nebr., 1973.

Tate, Allen. "Johnson on the Metaphysical Poets." *Kenyon Review* 11 (1949):379–94.

Tutt, Ralph. "Samuel Johnson on Pastoral Poetry." *Serif* 4 (1967): 12–16.

Watkins, W. B. C. *Johnson and English Poetry before 1660.* Princeton, N.J., 1936.

Weinbrot, Howard D. "The Reader, the General, and the Particular: Johnson and Imlac in Chapter Ten of *Rasselas.*" *ECS* 5 (1971): 80–96.

Wesling, D. "An Ideal of Greatness: Ethical Implication in Johnson's Critical Vocabulary." *UTQ* 34 (1965):133–45.

Young, K. "Samuel Johnson on Shakespeare." *Wisconsin University Studies* 18 (1923):146–226.

CHAPTER 8: SAMUEL TAYLOR COLERIDGE AND WILLIAM WORDSWORTH

Abrams, M. H. *The Mirror and the Lamp: Romantic Theory and the Critical Tradition.* New York, 1953.

Appleyard, J. A. *Coleridge's Philosophy of Literature: The Development of a Concept of Poetry, 1791–1819.* Cambridge, Mass., 1965.

Babbitt, Irving. "Coleridge and Imagination." *Nineteenth Century and After* 106 (1929):383–98.

Badawi, M. M. *Coleridge, Critic of Shakespeare.* Cambridge, 1973.

————. "Coleridge's Formal Criticism of Shakespeare's Plays." *EIC* 10 (1960):148–62.

Baker, James V. *The Sacred River.* Baton Rouge, La. 1957.

Ball, P. M. "Sincerity: The Rise and Fall of a Critical Term." *MLR* 59 (1964):1–11.

Banerjee, Srikumar. *Critical Theories and Poetic Practice in the "Lyrical Ballads."* London, 1931.

Barnet, Sylvan. "Coleridge on Puns: A Note on His Shakespeare Criticism." *JEGP* 56 (1957):602–9.

————. "Coleridge on Shakespeare's Villains." *Shakespeare Quarterly* 7 (1956):9–20.

Bate, Walter Jackson. "Coleridge on the Function of Art." In *Perspectives in Criticism,* edited by H. Levin. Cambridge, Mass., 1950.

Beach, J. W. "Coleridge's Borrowings from the German." *ELH* 9 (1942):36–58.

Benziger, James. "Organic Unity: Leibnitz to Coleridge." *PMLA* 66 (1951):24–48.

Blount, Paul G. "Matthew Arnold on Wordsworth." *Studies in the Literary Imagination* 1 (1968):3–11.

Brede, Alexander. "Theories of Poetic Diction in Wordsworth and Others and in Contemporary Poetry." *Papers of the Michigan Academy of Science, Arts, and Letters* 14 (1930):537–65.

Brett, R. L. "Coleridge's Theory of the Imagination." *Essays and Studies,* 2 n.s. (1949):75–90.

Bronson, Bertrand H. "The Willing Suspension of Disbelief." *EIC* 4 n.s. (1934):129–51.

Brooke, Nicholas. "Coleridge's 'True and Original Realism.' " *Durham University Journal* 22 (1961):58–69.

Bullitt, John, and Bate, Walter Jackson. "Distinctions Between Fancy and Imagination in Eighteenth-Century English Criticism." *MLN* 60 (1945):8–15.

Burgum, Edwin B. "Wordsworth's Reform in Poetic Diction." *College English* 2 (1940):207–16.

Campbell, O. J. "Wordsworth's Aesthetic Development, 1795–1802." *University of Michigan Essays and Studies* 10 (1933):1–57.

Coleridge, Samuel Taylor. *Biographia Literaria.* Edited by John Shawcross. 2 vols. London, 1965.

Collins, H. P. "The Criticism of Coleridge." *New Criterion* 5 (1927): 45–56.

Creed, H. H. "Coleridge on 'Taste.' " *ELH* 13 (1946):143–55.

––––––– . "Coleridge's Metacriticism." *PMLA* 69 (1954):1160–80.

Fogle, R. H. *The Idea of Coleridge's Criticism.* Berkeley, Calif., 1962.

Fruman, Norman. *Coleridge, The Damaged Archangel.* New York, 1971.

Greenbie, Marjorie L. B. *Wordsworth's Theory of Poetic Diction: A Study of the Historical and Personal Background of the Lyrical Ballads.* New York, 1966.

Griggs, E. L. "Wordsworth through Coleridge's Eyes." In *Wordsworth: Centenary Studies,* edited by G. T. Dunklin. Princeton, N.J., 1951.

Hardy, Barbara. "Distinction without Difference: Coleridge's Fancy and Imagination." *EIC* 1 (1951):336-44.

_____. " 'I Have a Smack of Hamlet': Coleridge and Shakespeare's Characters." *EIC* 8 (1958):238-55.

Hayden, John O. "Coleridge, the Reviewers, and Wordsworth." *SP* 68 (1971):105-19.

Heffernan, James A. W. *Wordsworth's Theory of Poetry: The Transforming Imagination.* Ithaca, N.Y., 1969.

Jackson, J. R. de J. "Coleridge on Dramatic Illusion and Spectacle in the Performance of Shakespeare's Plays." *MP* 62 (1964):13-21.

_____. "Coleridge on Shakespeare's Preparation." *REL* 7 (1966): 53-62.

_____. *"Method and Imagination in Coleridge's Criticism.* Cambridge, Mass., 1969.

Kaul, R. K. "Wordsworth's 'Preface' Reconsidered." *Literary Criterion* 4 (1961):17-22.

Klimenko, E. L. "The Language Reforms in the Poetry of the English Romanticist Wordsworth and Coleridge." *Transactions First Leningrad Pedagogical Institute of Foreign Language* 1 (1940):227-41.

Leavis, F. R. "Coleridge in Criticism." *Scrutiny* 9 (1940):57-69.

Lucas, F. L. *The Decline and Fall of the Romantic Ideal.* New York, 1937.

McKenzie, Gordon. "Organic Unity in Coleridge." *University of California Publications in English* 7 (1939):1-107.

Mahoney, John L. "Imitation and the Quest for Objectivity in English Romantic Theory." *Proceedings of the Fourth Congress of the International Comparative Literature Association.* The Hague, 1966.

Marks, Emerson R. "Means and Ends in Coleridge's Critical Method. *ELH* 26 (1959):387-401.

Metzger, Lore. "Imitation and Illusion in Coleridge's Criticism." *Proceedings of the Fourth Congress of the International Comparative Literature Association.* The Hague, 1966.

Morgan, R. "The Philosophical Basis of Coleridge's *Hamlet* Criticism." *ELH* 6 (1939):256-70.

Murry, John Middleton. "Coleridge's Criticism." In *Aspects of Literature.* New York, 1970.

Netherly, Wallace. "Coleridge's Use of *Judgment* in Shakespearean Criticism." *Personalist* 33 (1952):411-15.

Orsini, G. N. G. "Coleridge and Schlegel Reconsidered." *CL* 16 (1964):97–118.

Owen, W. J. B. *Wordsworth as Critic.* Toronto, 1969.

————. *Wordsworth's Preface to "Lyrical Ballads."* Copenhagen, 1957.

————. "Wordsworth, the Problem of Communication, and John Dennis." In *Wordsworth's Mind and Art,* edited by A. W. Thomson. Edinburgh, 1969.

Parrish, Stephen M. *The Art of the "Lyrical Ballads."* Cambridge, Mass., 1973.

————. "Wordsworth and Coleridge on Meter." *JEGP* 59 (1960): 41–49.

————. "The Wordsworth-Coleridge Controversy." *PMLA* 63 (1958):367–74.

Patterson, C. I. "Coleridge's Conception of Dramatic Illusion in the Novel." *ELH* 18 (1951):123–37.

Peacock, M. L., Jr. *The Critical Opinions of William Wordsworth.* Baltimore, Md., 1950.

Raysor, T. M. "Coleridge's Criticism of Wordsworth." *PMLA* 54 (1939):496–510.

Read, Herbert. "Coleridge as a Critic." In *Lectures in Criticism,* edited by R. P. Blackmur. New York, 1949.

————. *The True Voice of Feeling.* London, 1953.

Schulz, Max F. "Coleridge's 'Apologetic Prefaces.' " *Tulane Studies in English* 11 (1961):53–64.

————. "Coleridge's 'Debt' to Dryden and Johnson." *N&Q* 10 n. s. (1963):189–91.

————. "Coleridge, Wordsworth, and the 1800 Preface to *Lyrical Ballads.*" *SEL* 5 (1965):619–39.

Sharrock, Roger. "Speech and Prose in Wordsworth's Preface." *EIC* (1957):108–11.

————. "Wordsworth on Science and Poetry." *REL* 3 (1962):42–50.

————. "Wordsworth's Revolt against Literature." *EIC* 3 (1953): 396–412.

Snyder, Alice D. *The Critical Principle of the Reconciliation of Opposites As Employed by Coleridge.* Ann Arbor, Mich., 1918.

————. "A Note on Coleridge's Shakespeare Criticism." *MLN* 38 (1923):23–31.

Thorpe, Clarence. "Coleridge as Aesthetician and Critic." *Journal of the History of Ideas* 5 (1944):387–414.

_____. "The Imagination: Coleridge *vs.* Wordsworth." *PQ* 18 (1939):1–19.

Trilling, Lionel. "The Fate of Pleasure: Wordsworth to Dostoevsky." *Literary Views: Critical and Historical.* Chicago, 1964.

Warren, Alba, Jr. *English Poetic Theory, 1825–1865.* Princeton, N.J., 1950.

Watson, George. "Contributions to a Dictionary of Critical Terms: *Imagination* and *Fancy.*" *EIC* 3 (1953):201–14.

Whalley, George. "The Integrity of *Biographia Literaria.*" *Essays and Studies,* 6 n.s. (1953):87–101.

_____. "Preface to *Lyrical Ballads:* A Portent." *UTQ* 25 (1956): 467–83.

Wilkie, Brian. "Wordsworth and the Tradition of Avant-Garde." *JEGP* 72 (1973):194–222.

Willey, Basil. *Coleridge on Imagination and Fancy.* London, 1947.

Wordsworth, William. *Literary Criticism of William Wordsworth.* Edited by Paul M. Zall (Lincoln, Nebr., 1966).

Wylie, L. J. *Studies in the Evolution of English Criticism.* Boston, 1894.

CHAPTER 9: MATTHEW ARNOLD

Brown, E. K. "The Critic as Xenophobe: Matthew Arnold and the International Mind." *Sewanee Review* 38 (1930):301–9.

Buckley, Vincent. *Poetry and Morality: Studies on the Criticism of Matthew Arnold, T. S. Eliot, and F. R. Leavis.* London, 1961.

Carnall, Geoffrey. "Matthew Arnold's 'Great Critical Effort.' " *EIC* 8 (1958):256–68.

Connolly, Terrence L. "Matthew Arnold: Critic." *Thought* 9 (1934): 193–205.

Cooper, Lane. "Matthew Arnold's Essay on Wordsworth." *Bookman,* 69 (1929):479–84.

Corner, Martin. "Arnold, Lessing, and the Preface of 1853." *JEGP* 72 (1973): 223–35.

_____. "Text and context in Arnold's Essays in Criticism." *Neo-Philologus* 57 (1973):188–97.

Coulling, Sidney M. B. "The Background of 'The Function of Criticism at the Present Time' " *PQ* 42 (1963):36–54.

————. "Matthew Arnold's 1853 Preface: Its Origin and Aftermath." *Victorian Studies* 7 (1964):233–63.

Cox, R. G. "Victorian Criticism of Poetry: The Minority Tradition." *Scrutiny* 18 (1951):2–17.

De Laura, David J. "The 'Wordsworth' of Pater and Arnold: 'The Supreme, Artistic View of Life.' " *SEL* 6 (1966):651–67.

Donovan, Robert A. "The Method of Arnold's *Essays in Criticism*." *PMLA* 71 (1956):922–31.

Eells, John S. *The Touchstones of Matthew Arnold.* New York, 1955.

Eliot, T. S. *Selected Essays.* 2d ed. New York, 1950.

————. *The Use of Poetry.* 2d. ed. London, 1964.

Furer, Paul. *Der Einfluss Sainte-Beuve's auf die Kritik Matthew Arnold's.* Wetzikon, Switzerland, 1920.

Garrod, H. W. *Poetry and the Criticism of Life.* Cambridge, Mass., 1931.

Gottfried, Leon. *Matthew Arnold and the Romantics.* London, 1963.

Greenwood, E. B. "Matthew Arnold: Thoughts on a Centenary." *Twentieth Century* 162 (1957):469–79.

Hamilton, G. R. "Matthew Arnold as Critic." *Listener,* 5 September 1946, p. 317.

Harding, F. J. W. *Matthew Arnold the Critic and France.* Geneva, 1964.

Harvey, C. H. *Matthew Arnold: A Critic of the Victorian Period.* London, 1931.

Holloway, John. "Matthew Arnold and the Modern Dilemma." *EIC* 1 (1951): 1–16.

Hunt, Everett L. "Matthew Arnold: The Critic as Rhetorician." *Quarterly Journal of Speech* 20 (1924):481–507.

James, D. G. *Matthew Arnold and the Decline of English Romanticism.* Oxford, 1961.

Jamison, W. A. *Arnold and the Romantics.* Copenhagen, 1958.

Kelso, A. P. *Matthew Arnold on Continental Life and Literature.* Oxford, 1914.

Knickerbocker, W. S. "Matthew Arnold's Theory of Poetry." *Sewanee Review* 33 (1925):439–50.

Leavis, F. R. "Arnold as Critic." *Scrutiny* 7 (1939):319–32.

Madden, William A. "The Divided Tradition of English Criticism." *PMLA* 73 (1958):69–80.

_____ . *Matthew Arnold: A Study of the Aesthetic Temperament in Victorian England.* Bloomington, Ind., 1967.

More, Paul Elmer. *Shelburne Essays.* New York and London, 1910.

Osmond, T. S. "Arnold & Homer." *Essays and Studies English Association* 3 (1912):71–91.

Perkins, David. "Arnold and the Function of Literature." *ELH* 18 (1951):287–309.

Raleigh, Walter. *Some Authors.* Oxford, 1923.

Saintsbury, George. *Matthew Arnold.* New York, 1899.

Sherman, Stuart. *Matthew Arnold: How to Know Him.* Indianapolis, Ind., 1917.

Shumaker, Wayne. "Matthew Arnold's Humanism: Literature as a Criticism of Life." *SEL* 2 (1962):385–402.

Starchey, G. L. "A Victorian Critic." *New Statesman* 1 (1914):529–30.

Tillotson, Geoffrey. *Criticism and the Nineteenth Century.* London, 1951.

Trilling, Lionel. *Matthew Arnold.* New York, 1955.

Warren, Alba H., Jr. *English Poetic Theory, 1825–1865.* Princeton, N.J., 1950.

Wickelgrens, N. L. "Arnold's Literary Relations with France." *MLR* 33 (1938):200–14.

Williams, Stanely T. "Matthew Arnold as a Critic of Literature." *University of California Chronicle* 26 (1924):183–208.

Wilson, Dover. *Leslie Stephen and Matthew Arnold as Critics of Wordsworth.* Cambridge, 1939.

Index